THE WORLD AS IT IS

BOOKS BY CHRIS HEDGES

War Is a Force That Gives Us Meaning

What Every Person Should Know About War

Losing Moses on the Freeway

American Fascists

I Don't Believe In Atheists

Empire of Illusion

Death of the Liberal Class

THE
WORLD
AS IT IS

*Dispatches on the
Myth of Human Progress*

CHRIS HEDGES

NATION
BOOKS
New York

truthdig

Published by Nation Books,
A Member of the Perseus Books Group
116 East 16th Street, 8th Floor
New York, NY 10003

Nation Books is a co-publishing venture of the Nation Institute and the
Perseus Books Group.

Books published by Nation Books are available at special discounts for bulk
purchases in the United States by corporations, institutions, and other
organizations. For more information, please contact the Special Markets
Department at the Perseus Books Group, 2300 Chestnut Street, Suite 200,
Philadelphia, PA 19103, or call (800) 810-4145, ext. 5000, or e-mail
special.markets@perseusbooks.com.

Designed by Brent Wilcox

Library of Congress Cataloging-in-Publication Data
Hedges, Chris.
   The world as it is: Dispatches on the myth of human progress /
Chris Hedges.
      p.   cm.
   Includes bibliographical references and index.
   ISBN 978-1-56858-640-3 (hardcover : alk. paper)
   ISBN 978-1-568-58661-8 (e-book)
   1. United States—Politics and government—2009–   2. World politics—
2005–2015. I. Title.
   E907.H43 2009
   327.09'05—dc22
                                                        2010054397

10 9 8 7 6 5 4 3 2 1

For my children,
Thomas, Noëlle, Konrad, and Marina,
whose joy and laughter save me from despair and
for whom I must always hope

Contents

ISRAEL AND PALESTINE

THE MIDDLE EAST

THE DECAY OF EMPIRE

The essays in this book appeared in
Truthdig between 2006 and 2010.

Introduction

My good friend, the author and journalist Stephen Kinzer, once said to me, half in jest: "You're not a journalist. You're a minister pretending to be a journalist." He was not far off the mark. I have always been more concerned with truth and justice than with news. News and truth are not the same things. News, at least as it is configured in the faux objectivity of American journalism, can be used quite effectively to mask and obscure the truth. "Balance," in which you give as much space, for example, to the victimizer as to the victim, may be objective and impartial, but it is usually not honest. And when you are "objective," it means that, in your reasonableness, you ultimately embrace and defend the status quo. There is a deep current of cynicism that runs through much of American journalism, especially on commercial electronic media. It is safe and painless to produce "balanced" news. It is very unsafe, as the best journalists will tell you, to produce truth. The great journalists, like the great preachers, care deeply about truth, which they seek to impart to their reader, listener or viewer, often at the cost of their careers.

"When I sit down to write a book, I do not say to myself, 'I am going to produce a work of art.'" George Orwell wrote. "I write because there is some lie that I want to expose, some fact to which I want to draw attention, and my initial concern is to get a hearing."[1]

My former employer, the *New York Times*, with some of the most able and talented journalists and editors in the country, not only propagated the lies used to justify the war in Iraq, but also never saw the financial meltdown coming. These journalists and editors are besotted with their access to the powerful. They look at themselves as players, part of the inside elite. They went to the same elite colleges. They eat at the same restaurants. They go to the same parties and dinners. They live in the same exclusive neighborhoods. Their children go to the same schools. They are, if one concedes that propaganda is a vital tool for the power elite, important to the system. Journalists who should have been exposing the lies used to justify the Iraq war or reporting from low-income neighborhoods—where mortgage brokers and banks were filing fraudulent loan applications to hand money to people they knew could never pay it back—were instead "doing" lunch with the power brokers in the White House or on Wall Street. All that talent, all that money, all that expertise, all those resources proved useless when it came time to examine the two major cataclysmic events of our age. And all that news, however objective and balanced, turned out to be a lie.

I have never sought to be objective. How can you be objective about death squads in El Salvador, massacres in Iraq, or Serbian sniper fire that gunned down unarmed civilians, including children, in Sarajevo? How can you be neutral about the masters and profiteers of war who lie and dissemble to hide the crimes they commit and the profits they make? How can you be objective about human pain? And, finally, how can you be objective about those responsible for this suffering? I am not neutral about rape, torture, or murder. I am not neutral about rapists, torturers, or murderers. I am not neutral about George W. Bush or Barack Obama, who under international law are war criminals. And if you had to see the butchery of war up close, as I did for nearly two decades, you would not be neutral either.

But in the game of American journalism it is forbidden to feel. Journalists are told they must be clinical observers who interpret human reality through their eyes, not their hearts—and certainly not through their consciences. This is the deadly disease of American journalism. And it is the reason journalism in the United States has lost its moral core and its influence. It is the reason that in a time of crisis the traditional media have so little to say. It is why the traditional media are distrusted. The gross moral and professional failings of the traditional media opened the door for the hate-mongers on Fox News and the news celebrities on commercial networks who fill our heads with trivia and celebrity gossip.

As the centers of American power were seized and hijacked by corporations, the media continued to pay deference to systems of power that could no longer be considered honest or democratic. The media treat criminals on Wall Street as responsible members of the ruling class. They treat the criminals in the White House and the Pentagon as statesmen. The media never responded to the radical reconfiguration of American politics, the slow-motion coup d'etat that has turned phrases like *the consent of the governed* into a cruel joke. And because the media are not concerned with distinguishing truth from news, because they lack a moral compass, they have become nothing more than courtiers to the elite, shameless hedonists of power, and absurd court propagandists. At a moment when the country desperately needs vigorous media, it gets celebrities such as Katie Couric masquerading as journalists, who night after night "feel your pain." The few journalists who do not, as Couric does, function as entertainers and celebrities are so timid and removed from the suffering of our dispossessed working classes that they are rightly despised. The media are hated for a reason. They deserve to be hated. They sided with the corporate forces, like most liberal institutions, as these corporate forces decimated the working class, bankrupted the economy, corrupted the legislative, executive, and judicial systems of government, and unleashed endless war and the destruction of the ecosystem on which human life depends.

I keep my distance from the powerful. I distrust all sources of power regardless of their ideological orientation. I do not want to be their friend. I do not want to advise them or be part of their inner circle. The only benefit one gets from being a White House correspondent, as far as I can tell, is that the president knows your name. I made a conscious choice to report from the developing world and war zones during most of my career. What I witnessed rarely matched the version of events spun out for the media courtiers in Washington by the power elite. As a foreign correspondent I often fought my own Washington bureau, where reporters in suits were being fed a partial version of reality and had a vested interest in reporting it as fact. The longer reporters spent in Washington, the more they looked, sounded, and acted like the power brokers they covered. At a certain point, as any Sunday morning television talk show illustrates, these courtiers in the media became indistinguishable from the power elite.

Kinzer was right. Once unleashed from the restrictions and confines of American journalism, I began to write what are, in essence, sermons.

And when I read the columns collected in this book, that is how I would describe them. Sermons, when they are good, do not please a congregation. They do not make people happy. They are not a form of entertainment. They disturb many, if not most, of the listeners. They resonate with only a minority. Truth, at least as far as it can be discerned, is not comfortable or enjoyable to listen to, nor is the emotion and anger that accompanies all passionate assaults on lies and injustice. Sermons force those who hear them to be self-critical. They expose our inadequacies and failures. They demand that we become emotionally engaged. There are speakers and writers on the left and the right, including many preachers in pulpits, whose goal is to be admired and applauded. This is not my aim. It is not pleasant to be disliked—and I have faced crowds that deeply dislike me and my message—but it is necessary if your commitment is to truth and the harnessing of emotional energy and passion against those who carry out injustice. I write not with the anticipation of approval but often of hostility. And I write finally from the gut, not the head.

"The energy that actually shapes the world springs from emotions—racial pride, leader-worship, religious belief, love of war—which liberal intellectuals mechanically write off as anachronisms, and which they have usually destroyed so completely in themselves as to have lost all power of action," Orwell noted.[2]

The role of a preacher is not to provide self-help manuals for the future. It is to elucidate reality and get people to act on this reality. It is impossible to speak about hope if we substitute illusion for reality. If we believe that reality is not an impediment to our desires, that we can have everything we want by tapping into our inner strength or believing in Jesus, if we believe that the fate of the human species is never-ending advancement and progress, then we are crippled as agents for change. We are left responding to illusion. This makes everything we do or believe, such as our faith in the Democratic Party or electoral politics, futile and useless. The bleakness of what we face, economically and environmentally, is not a call to despair but a call to new forms of resistance and civil disobedience.

I am not religious in a traditional sense. There is no Christian denomination that would consider me a believer. I am as alienated from religious institutions as I am from secular institutions. But I was raised in the church, graduated from seminary at Harvard Divinity School, and cannot escape my intellectual and moral formation. I remain a preacher, although an unorthodox one. I believe that the truth is the only force that will set us free. I have hope, not in the tangible or in what I can personally accomplish, but in the faith that battling evil, cruelty, and injustice allows us to retain our identity, a sense of meaning and ultimately our freedom. Perhaps in our lifetimes we will not succeed. Perhaps things will only get worse. But this does not invalidate our efforts. Rebellion—which is different from revolution because it is perpetual alienation from power rather than the replacement of one power system with another—should be our natural state. And faith, for me, is a belief that rebellion is always worth it, even if all outward signs point to our lives and struggles as penultimate failures. We are saved not by what we can do or accomplish but by our fealty to revolt, our steadfastness to the weak, the poor, the marginalized, and those who endure oppression. We must stand with them against the powerful. If we remain true to these moral imperatives, we win. And I am enough of an idealist to believe that the struggle to live the moral life is worth it.

During the first Persian Gulf War, when I defied the media restrictions and was in the Saudi and later Kuwait desert to cover the fighting, I was accosted one afternoon by R.W. Apple, who was overseeing the coverage for the *New York Times*.

"What is it about you and authority?" he asked.

"I have no problem with authority, Johnny, as long as authority doesn't try and tell me what to do," I answered.

"You dumb fuck," he said. "That is what authority does."

POLITICS

It's Not Going to Be OK

FEBRUARY 2, 2009

The daily bleeding of thousands of jobs will soon turn our economic crisis into a political crisis. The street protests, strikes, and riots that have rattled France, Turkey, Greece, Ukraine, Russia, Latvia, Lithuania, Bulgaria, and Iceland will descend on us. It is only a matter of time. And not much time. When things start to go sour, when Barack Obama is exposed as a mortal waving a sword at a tidal wave, the United States could plunge into a long period of precarious social instability.

At no period in American history has our democracy been in such peril or has the possibility of totalitarianism been as real. Our way of life is over. Our profligate consumption is finished. Our children will never have the standard of living we had. And poverty and despair will sweep across the landscape like a plague. This is the bleak future. There is nothing President Obama can do to stop it. It has been decades in the making. It cannot be undone with a trillion or two trillion dollars in bailout money. Our empire is dying. Our economy has collapsed.

How will we cope with our decline? Will we cling to the absurd dreams of a superpower and a glorious tomorrow, or will we responsibly face our stark new limitations? Will we heed those who are sober and rational, those who speak of a new simplicity and humility, or will we follow the demagogues and charlatans who rise up out of the slime in moments of crisis to offer fantastic visions? Will we radically transform our system into one that protects the ordinary citizen and fosters the common good, that defies the corporate state, or will we employ the brutality and technology of our internal security and surveillance apparatus to crush all dissent? We won't have to wait long to find out.

There are a few isolated individuals who saw it coming. The political philosophers Sheldon S. Wolin, John Ralston Saul, and Andrew Bacevich, as well as writers such as Noam Chomsky, Chalmers Johnson, David Korten, and Naomi Klein, along with activists such as Bill McKibben, and Ralph Nader, rang the alarm bells. They were largely ignored or ridiculed. Our corporate media and corporate universities proved, when we needed them most, intellectually and morally useless.

In his book *Democracy Incorporated,* Wolin, who taught political philosophy at the University of California at Berkeley and at Princeton, uses the phrase *inverted totalitarianism* to describe our system of power. Inverted totalitarianism, unlike classical totalitarianism, does not revolve around a demagogue or charismatic leader. It finds its expression in the anonymity of the corporate state. It purports to cherish democracy, patriotism, and the Constitution while cynically manipulating internal levers to subvert and thwart democratic institutions. Citizens do elect political candidates, but those candidates must raise staggering amounts of corporate funds to compete. They are beholden to armies of corporate lobbyists in Washington or state capitals who write the legislation. Corporate media control nearly everything we read, watch or hear and impose a bland uniformity of opinion or divert us with trivia and celebrity gossip. In classical totalitarian regimes, such as Nazi fascism or Soviet communism, economics was subordinate to politics. "Under inverted totalitarianism the reverse is true," Wolin writes. "Economics dominates politics—and with that domination comes different forms of ruthlessness."[1]

I reached Wolin, 86, by phone at his home about twenty-five miles north of San Francisco. He was a bombardier in the South Pacific during World War II and went to Harvard after the war to get his doctorate. Wolin has written classics such as *Politics and Vision* and *Tocqueville Between Two Worlds*. His newest, *Democracy Incorporated*, is one of the most important and prescient critiques to date of the American political system. He is also the author of a series of remarkable essays on Augustine of Hippo, Richard Hooker, David Hume, Martin Luther, John Calvin, Max Weber, Friedrich Nietzsche, Karl Marx, and John

Dewey. His voice, however, has faded from public awareness because, as he told me, "it is harder and harder for people like me to get a public hearing." He said that publications, such as the *New York Review of Books*, that had often published his work a couple of decades ago, lost interest in his critiques of American capitalism, his warnings about the subversion of democratic institutions and the emergence of the corporate state. He does not hold out much hope for Obama.

"The basic systems are going to stay in place; they are too powerful to be challenged," Wolin told me when I asked him about the then-new Obama administration:

> This is shown by the financial bailout. It does not bother with the structure at all. I don't think Obama can take on the kind of military establishment we have developed. This is not to say that I do not admire him. He is probably the most intelligent president we have had in decades. I think he is well-meaning, but he inherits a system of constraints that makes it very difficult to take on these major power configurations. I do not think he has the appetite for it in any ideological sense. The corporate structure is not going to be challenged. There has not been a word from him that would suggest an attempt to rethink the American imperium.

Wolin argues that a failure to dismantle our vast and overextended imperial projects, coupled with the economic collapse, is likely to result in inverted totalitarianism. He said that without "radical and drastic remedies" the response to mounting discontent and social unrest will probably lead to greater state control and repression. There will be, he warned, a huge "expansion of government power."

"Our political culture has remained unhelpful in fostering a democratic consciousness," he said. "The political system and its operatives will not be constrained by popular discontent or uprisings."

Wolin writes that in inverted totalitarianism consumer goods and a comfortable standard of living, along with a vast entertainment industry that provides spectacles and diversions, keep the citizenry politically passive. I asked if the economic collapse and the steady decline in our standard of living might not, in fact, trigger classical totalitarianism. Could widespread frustration and poverty lead the working and middle classes to place their faith in demagogues, especially those from the Christian Right?

"I think that's perfectly possible," he answered:

That was the experience of the 1930s. There wasn't just FDR. There was Huey Long and Father Coughlin. There were even more extreme movements including the Klan. The extent to which those forces can be fed by the downturn and bleakness is a very real danger. It could become classical totalitarianism.

He said the current widespread political passivity is dangerous. It is often exploited by demagogues who pose as saviors and offer dreams of glory and salvation. He warned that

the apoliticalness, even anti-politicalness, will be very powerful elements in taking us towards a radically dictatorial direction. It testifies to how thin the commitment to democracy is in the present circumstances. Democracy is not ascendant. It is not dominant. It is beleaguered. The extent to which young people have been drawn away from public concerns and given this extraordinary range of diversions makes it very likely they could then rally to a demagogue.

Wolin lamented that the corporate state has successfully blocked any real debate about alternative forms of power. Corporations determine who gets heard and who does not, he said. And those who critique corporate power are given no place in the national dialogue.

"In the 1930s there were all kinds of alternative understandings, from socialism to more extensive governmental involvement," he said:

There was a range of different approaches. But what I am struck by now is the narrow range within which palliatives are being modeled. We are supposed to work with the financial system. So the people who helped create this system are put in charge of the solution. There has to be some major effort to think outside the box.

"The puzzle to me is the lack of social unrest," Wolin said when I asked why we have not yet seen rioting or protests. He said he worried that popular protests will be dismissed and ignored by the corporate media. This, he said, is what happened when tens of thousands protested the war in Iraq. This will permit the state to suppress local protests ruthlessly, as happened during past Democratic and Republican national conventions during election years. Antiwar protests in the 1960s gained momentum from their ability to spread across the country, he noted. Such dynamics, he said, may not happen this time. "The ways they can isolate protests and prevent it from [becoming] a contagion are formidable," he said.

"My greatest fear is that the Obama administration will achieve relatively little in terms of structural change," he added:

They may at best keep the system going. But there is a growing pessimism. Every day we hear how much longer the recession will continue. They are already talking about beyond next year. The economic difficulties are more profound than we had guessed and because of globalization more difficult to deal with. I wish the political establishment, the parties and leadership, would become more aware of the depths of the problem. They can't keep throwing money at this. They have to begin structural changes that involve a very different approach from a market economy. I don't think this will happen.

"I keep asking why and how and when this country became so conservative," he went on. "This country once prided itself on its experimentation and flexibility. It has become rigid. It is probably the most conservative of all the advanced countries."

The American Left, he said, has crumbled. It sold out to a bankrupt Democratic Party, abandoned the working class, and has no ability to organize. Unions are a spent force. The universities are mills for corporate employees. The media churn out info-entertainment or fatuous pundits. The Left, he said, no longer has the capacity to be a counter-weight to the corporate state. He said that if an extreme Right gains momentum there will probably be very little organized resistance.

"The Left is amorphous," he said. "I despair over the Left. Left parties may be small in number in Europe, but they are a coherent organization that keeps going. Here, except for Nader's efforts, we don't have that. We have a few voices here, a magazine there, and that's about it. It goes nowhere."

The False Idol of
Unfettered Capitalism

MARCH 15, 2009

When I returned to New York City after nearly two decades as a foreign correspondent in Latin America, Africa, the Middle East, and the Balkans, I was unsure where I was headed. I lacked the emotional and physical resilience that had allowed me to cope as a war correspondent. I was plagued by memories I wanted to forget, waking suddenly in the middle of the night, my sleep shattered by visions of gunfire and death. I was alienated from those around me, unaccustomed to the common language and images imposed by consumer culture, unable to communicate the pain and suffering I had witnessed, not much interested in building a career.

It was at this time that the Brooklyn Academy of Music began showing a ten-part film series called *The Decalogue*. *Deka*, in Greek, means "ten," and *logos* means "saying" or "speech." The Decalogue is the classical name of the Ten Commandments. The director was the Polish filmmaker Krzysztof Kieślowski, who had made the trilogy *Three Colors*, consisting of the films *White*, *Blue*, and *Red*. The ten films of *The Decalogue*, each about an hour long and based on one of the commandments, were to be shown two at a time over five consecutive weeks. I saw them on Sunday nights, taking the subway to Brooklyn, its cars rocking and screeching along the tracks in the darkened tunnels. The theater was rarely more than half full.

The films were quiet, subtle, and often opaque. It was sometimes hard to tell which commandment was being addressed. The characters never spoke about the commandments directly. They were too busy, as we all are, coping with life. The stories presented the lives of ordinary people confronted by extraordinary events. All lived in a Warsaw housing complex, many of them neighbors. They were on a common voyage, yet also out of touch with the pain and dislocation of those around them. The commandments, Kieślowski understood, were not dusty relics of another age, but rather a powerful compass with vital contemporary resonance.

In film after film he dealt with the core violation raised by each of the commandments. He freed the commandments from the clutter of piety and narrow definitions imposed upon them by religious leaders and institutions. Magda, the promiscuous woman portrayed in *Decalogue VI*, the film about adultery, was not married. She had a series of empty, carnal relationships. For Kieślowski, adultery, at its deepest level, was sex without love. Michał, the father in *Decalogue IV*, the film about honoring our parents, was not the biological father of his daughter, Anka. The biological mother was absent in the daughter's life. Parenting, Kieślowski knew, is not defined by blood or birth or gender. It is defined by commitment, fidelity and love. In *Decalogue* V, the film about killing, Jacek, an unemployed drifter, robs and brutally murders a cab driver. He is caught, sentenced and executed by the state. Kieślowski forces us to confront the barbarity of murder, whether committed by a deranged individual or sanctioned by society.

I knew the commandments. I had learned them at Sunday school, listened to sermons based on the commandments from my father's pulpit, and studied them as a seminarian at Harvard Divinity School. But Kieślowski turned them into living, breathing entities.

"For six thousand years these rules have been unquestionably right," Kieślowski said of the commandments:

And yet we break them every day. We know what we should do, and yet we fail to live as we should. People feel that something is wrong in life. There is some kind of atmosphere that makes people turn now to other values. They want to contemplate the basic questions of life, and that is probably the real reason for wanting to tell these stories.[2]

In eight of the films there was a brief appearance by a young man, solemn and silent. Kieślowski said he did not know who the character was. Perhaps he was an angel or Christ. Perhaps he represented the divine presence who observed with profound sadness the tragedy and folly we humans commit against others and against ourselves.

"He's not very pleased with us," was all the director said.

The commandments are a list of religious edicts, according to passages in Exodus and Deuteronomy, given to Moses by God on Mount Sinai. The first four are designed to guide the believer toward a proper relationship with God. The remaining six deal with our relations with others. It is these final six commands that are given the negative form of *You Shall Not*. Only two of the commandments, the prohibitions against stealing and murder, are incorporated into our legal code. Protestants, Catholics, and Jews have compiled slightly different lists, but the essence of the commandments remains the same. Muslims, while they do not list the commandments in the Koran, honor the laws of Moses, whom they see as a prophet.

The commandments are not defined, however, by the three monotheistic faiths. They are one of the earliest attempts to lay down moral rules and guidelines to sustain a human community. Nearly every religion has set down an ethical and moral code that is strikingly similar to the Ten Commandments. The Eightfold Path, known within Buddhism as the Wheel of Law, forbids murder, unchastity, theft, falsehood, and, especially, covetous desire. *Om*, the Hindus' Sacred Syllable, said or sung before and after prayers, ends with a fourth sound beyond the range of human hearing. This sound is called the "sound of silence." It is also called "the sound of the universe." Hindus, in the repetition of the Sacred Syllable, try to go beyond thought, to reach the stillness and silence that constitutes God. Five of the Ten Commandments delivered from Mount Sinai are lifted directly from the Egyptian *Book of the Dead*. No human being, no nation, no religion, has been chosen to be the sole interpreter of mystery. All cultures struggle to give words to the experience of the transcendent. It is a reminder that all of us find God not in what we know, but in what we cannot comprehend.

The commandments include the most severe violations and moral dilemmas in human life, although these violations often lie beyond the scope of the law. They were for the ancients, and are for us, the core rules that, when honored, hold us together, and when dishonored lead to alienation, discord, and violence. When our lives are shattered by tragedy, suffering, and pain, or when we express or feel the ethereal and overwhelming power of love, we confront the mystery of good and evil. Voices across time and cultures have struggled to transmit and pay homage to this mystery, what it means for our lives and our place in the cosmos. These voices, whether in the teachings of the Buddha, the writings of the Latin poets, or the pages of the Koran, are part of our common struggle as human beings to acknowledge the eternal and the sacred, to create an ethical system to sustain life.

The commandments retain their power because they express something fundamental about the human condition. This is why they are important. The commandments choose us. We are rarely able to choose them. We do not, however hard we work to insulate ourselves, ultimately control our fate. We cannot save ourselves from betrayal, theft, envy, greed, deception, and murder, nor always from the impulses that propel us to commit these acts. These violations, which can strike us or be committed without warning, can leave deep, often lifelong wounds. There are few of us who do not wrestle deeply with at least one of these violations.

We all stray. We all violate some commandments and do not adequately honor others. We are human. But moral laws bind us and make it possible to build a society based on the common good. They keep us from honoring the false covenants of greed, celebrity, and power that destroy us. These false covenants have a powerful appeal. They offer feelings of strength, status, and a false sense of belonging. They tempt us to be God. They tell us the things we want to hear and believe. They appear to make us the center of the universe. But these false covenants, covenants built around exclusive communities of race, gender, class, religion, and nation, inevitably carry within them the denigration and abuse of others. These false covenants divide us. A moral covenant recognizes that all life is sacred and love alone is the force that makes life possible.

It is the unmentioned fear of death, the one that rattles with the wind through the heavy branches of the trees outside, which frightens us the most, even as we do not name this fear. It is death we are trying to flee. The smallness of our lives, the transitory nature of existence, the inevitable road to old age, are what the idols of power, celebrity, and wealth tell us we can escape. They are tempting and seductive. They assure us that we need not endure the pain and suffering of being human. We follow the idol and barter away our freedom. We place our identity and our hopes in the hands of the idol. We need the idol to define ourselves, to determine our status and place. We invest in the idol. We sell ourselves into bondage.

The consumer goods we amass, the status we seek in titles and positions, the ruthlessness we employ to advance our careers, the personal causes we champion, the money we covet, and the houses we build and the cars we drive become our pathetic statements of being. They are squalid little monuments to our selves. The more we strive to amass power and possessions, the more intolerant and anxious we become. Impulses and emotions, not thoughts but mass feelings, propel us forward. These impulses, carefully manipulated by a consumer society, see us intoxicated with patriotic fervor and a lust for war, a desire to vote for candidates who appeal to us emotionally or to buy this car or that brand. Politicians, advertisers, social scientists, television evangelists, the news media, and the entertainment industry have learned what makes us respond. It works. None of us are immune. But when we act in their interests, we are rarely acting in our own. The moral philosophies we have ignored, once a staple of a liberal arts education, are a check on the deluge. They call us toward mutual respect and self-sacrifice. They force us to confront the broad, disturbing questions about meaning and existence. And our callous refusal to heed these questions as a society allowed us to believe that unfettered capitalism and the free market were forces of nature, decrees passed down from the divine, the only routes to prosperity and power. They turned out to be idols, and like all idols they have now demanded their human sacrifice.

Moral laws were not written so they could be practiced by some and not by others. They call on all of us to curb our worst instincts so we can live together, to refrain from committing acts of egregious exploitation that spread suffering. Moral teachings are guideposts. They keep us, even when we stray, as we all do, on the right path.

The strange, disjointed fragments of our lives can be comprehended only when we acknowledge our insecurities and uncertainties, when we accept that we will never know what life is about or what it is supposed to mean. We must do the best we can, not for ourselves, the great moralists remind us, but for those around us. Trust is the compound that unites us. The only lasting happiness in life comes with giving life to others. The quality of our life, of all life, is determined by what we give and how much we sacrifice. We live not by exalting our own life but by being willing to lose it.

The moral life, in the end, will not protect us from evil. The moral life protects us, however, from committing evil. It is designed to check our darker impulses, warning us that pandering to impulses can have terrible consequences. It seeks to hold community together. It is community that gives our lives, even in pain and grief, a healing solidarity. It is fealty to community that frees us from the dictates of our idols, idols that promise us fulfillment through self-gratification. These moral laws are about freedom. They call us to reject and defy powerful forces that rule our lives and to live instead for others, even if this costs us status and prestige and wealth.

Turn away from the moral life and you end in disaster. You sink into a morass of self-absorption and greed. You breed a society that celebrates fraud, theft, and violence, you turn neighbor against neighbor, you confuse presentation and image with your soul. Moral rules are as imperative to sustaining a community as law. And all cultures have sought to remind us of these basic moral restraints, ones that invariably tell us that successful communities do not permit their members to exploit one another but rather ensure that they sacrifice for the common good. The economic and social collapse we face was presaged by a moral collapse. And our response must include a renewed reverence for moral and social imperatives that acknowledge the sanctity of the common good.

The German philosopher Ludwig Wittgenstein said, "Tell me *how* you seek and I will tell you *what* you are seeking."[3] We all are seekers, even if we do not always know what we are looking to find. We are all seekers, even if we do not always know how to frame the questions. In those questions, even more than the answers, we find hope in the strange and contradictory fragments of our lives. And it is by recovering these moral questions, too often dismissed or ignored in universities and boardrooms across the country, laughed at on the stock exchange, ridiculed on reality television as an impediment to money and celebrity, that we will again find it possible to be whole.

Resist or Become Serfs

APRIL 6, 2009

America is devolving into a Third-World nation. And if we do not immediately halt our elite's rapacious looting of the public treasury, we will be left with trillions in debt that can never be repaid, and widespread human misery that we will be helpless to ameliorate. Our anemic democracy will be replaced with a robust national police state. The elite will withdraw into heavily guarded gated communities where they will have access to security, goods, and services that cannot be afforded by the rest of us. Tens of millions of people, brutally controlled, will live in perpetual poverty. This is the inevitable result of unchecked corporate capitalism. The stimulus and bailout plans are not about saving us. They are about saving them. We can resist—which means street protests, disruptions of the system, and demonstrations—or become serfs.

We have been in a steady economic decline for decades. The Canadian political philosopher John Ralston Saul detailed this decline in his 1992 book *Voltaire's Bastards: The Dictatorship of Reason in the West*. David Cay Johnston exposed the mirage and rot of American capitalism in *Free Lunch: How the Wealthiest Americans Enrich Themselves at Government Expense (and Stick You With the Bill)*, and David C. Korten, in *When Corporations Rule the World* and *Agenda for a New Economy*, laid out corporate malfeasance and abuse. But our universities and mass media, entranced by power and naively believing that global capitalism was an unstoppable force of nature, rarely asked the right questions or gave a prominent voice to those who did. Our elites hid their incompetence and loss of control behind an arrogant facade of specialized jargon and obscure economic theories.

The lies employed to camouflage the economic decline are legion. President Ronald Reagan included 1.5 million U.S. Army, Navy, Air Force, and Marine service personnel with the civilian work force to magically reduce the nation's unemployment rate by two percent. President Bill Clinton decided that those who had given up looking for work, or those who wanted full-time jobs but could find only part-time employment, were no longer to be counted as unemployed. This trick disappeared some five million unemployed from the official unemployment rolls. If you work more than twenty-one hours a week—most low-wage workers at places like Wal-Mart average twenty-eight hours a week—you are counted as employed, although your real wages put you below the poverty line. Our actual unemployment rate, when you include those who have stopped looking for work and those who can find only part-time jobs, is not 8.5 percent but 15 percent. A sixth of the country is now effectively unemployed. And we are shedding jobs at a faster rate than in the months after the 1929 crash.

The consumer price index (CPI), used by the government to measure inflation, is meaningless. To keep the official inflation figures low, the government has been substituting basic products it once measured to check for inflation with ones that do not rise very much in price. This sleight of hand has kept the cost-of-living increases tied to the CPI artificially low. *New York Times* consumer reporter W.P. Dunleavy, wrote that her groceries now cost $587 a month, up from $400 a year earlier. This is a forty percent increase. California economist John Williams, who runs an organization called Shadow Statistics, contends that if Washington still used the CPI measurements applied back in the 1970s, inflation would be at ten percent.

The corporate state, and the political and intellectual class that served the corporate state, constructed a financial and political system based on illusions. Corporations engaged in pyramid lending that created fictitious assets. These fictitious assets became collateral for more bank lending. The elite skimmed off hundreds of millions in bonuses, commissions, and salaries from this fictitious wealth. Politicians, who dutifully served corporate interests rather than those of citizens, were showered with campaign contributions and given lucrative jobs when they left office. Universities, knowing it was not good business to challenge corporatism, muted any voices of conscience while they went begging for corporate donations and grants. Deceptive loans and credit card debt fueled the binges of a consumer society and hid falling wages and the loss of manufacturing jobs.

The Obama administration, rather than chart a new course, is intent on re-inflating the bubble. The trillions of dollars of government funds being spent to sustain these corrupt corporations could have renovated our economy. We could have saved tens of millions of Americans from poverty. The government could have, as consumer activist Ralph Nader has pointed out, started ten new banks with $35 billion each and a ten-to-one leverage to open credit markets. Vast, unimaginable sums are being placed into these dirty, corporate hands without oversight. And they will use this money as they always have—to enrich themselves at our expense.

"You are going to see the biggest waste, fraud, and abuse in American history," Nader warned when I asked about the bailouts:

> Not only is it wrongly directed, not only does it deal with the perpetrators instead of the people who were victimized, but they don't have a delivery system of any honesty and efficiency. The Justice Department is overwhelmed. It doesn't have a tenth of the prosecutors, the investigators, the auditors, the attorneys needed to deal with the previous corporate crime wave before the bailout started last September. It is especially unable to deal with the rapacious ravaging of this new money by these corporate recipients. You can see it already. The corporations haven't lent it. They have used some of it for acquisitions or to preserve their bonuses or their dividends. As long as they know they are not going to jail, and they don't see many newspaper reports about their colleagues going to jail, they don't care. It is total impunity. If they quit, they quit with a golden parachute. Even [General Motors CEO Rick] Wagoner is taking away $21 million.

A handful of former executives have conceded that the bailouts are a waste. Maurice Greenberg, former chairman of American Interna-

tional Group Inc. (AIG), told the House Oversight and Government
Reform Committee on April 2, 2009, that the effort to prop up the firm
with $170 billion had "failed." He said the company should be re-
structured. AIG, he said, would have been better off filing for Chapter
11 bankruptcy protection instead of seeking government help.

"These are signs of hyper-decay," Nader said from his office in
Washington. "You spend this kind of money and do not know if it
will work."

"Bankrupt corporate capitalism is on its way to bankrupting the socialism that is trying to save it," Nader added. "That is the end stage.
If they no longer have socialism to save them then we are into feudalism. We are into private police, gated communities and serfs with a
twenty-first-century nomenclature."

We will not be able to raise another three or four trillion dollars, especially with commitments totaling some $12 trillion, to fix the mess.
Not long ago, such profligate government spending was unthinkable. A
year before the bailouts began, the entire Federal Reserve was evalu-
ated at only $800 billion. The economic stimulus and the bailouts will
not bring back our casino capitalism. And as the meltdown shows no
signs of abating, and the bailouts show no sign of working, the reck-
lessness and desperation of our capitalist overlords have increased. The
cost, to the working and middle classes, is becoming unsustainable. The
Fed reported in March 2009 that households lost $5.1 trillion, or nine
percent, of their wealth in the last three months of 2008, the most ever
in a single quarter in the fifty-seven-year history of record-keeping by
the central bank. For the full year, household wealth dropped $11.1
trillion, or about eighteen percent. These figures did not include the decline of investments in the stock market, which has probably erased
trillions more in the country's collective net worth.

The bullet to our heads, inevitable if we do not radically alter
course, will be sudden. We have been borrowing at the rate of more
than $2 billion a day over the last ten years, and at some point it has
to stop. The moment China, the oil-rich states, and other international
investors stop buying U.S. Treasury Bonds, the dollar will become junk.
Inflation will rocket upward. We will become Weimar Germany. A furious and sustained backlash by a betrayed and angry populace, one

unprepared intellectually and psychologically for collapse, will sweep aside the Democrats and most of the Republicans. A cabal of protofascist misfits, from Christian demagogues to simpletons like Sarah Palin to loudmouth talk-show hosts, whom their opponents naively dismiss as buffoons, will find a following with promises of revenge and moral renewal. The elites, the ones with their Harvard Business School degrees and expensive vocabularies, will retreat into their sheltered enclaves of privilege and comfort. We will be left bereft and abandoned outside the gates.

Buying Brand Obama

MAY 3, 2009

Barack Obama is a brand. And Brand Obama is designed to make us feel good about our government while corporate overlords loot the Treasury, our elected officials continue to have their palms greased by armies of corporate lobbyists, our corporate media divert us with gossip and trivia, and our imperial wars expand in the Middle East. Brand Obama is about being happy consumers. We are entertained. We feel hopeful. We like our president. We believe he is like us. But as is the case with all branded products spun out from the manipulative world of corporate advertising, we are being duped into doing and supporting a lot of things that are not in our interest.

What, for all our faith and hope, has Brand Obama given us? His administration has spent, lent or guaranteed $12.8 trillion in taxpayer dollars to Wall Street and insolvent banks in a doomed effort to reinflate the bubble economy, a tactic that at best forestalls catastrophe and will leave us broke in a time of profound crisis. Brand Obama has allocated nearly $1 trillion to defense-related spending and the continuation of our doomed imperial projects in Iraq, where military planners now estimate that seventy thousand troops will remain for the next fifteen to twenty years. Brand Obama has expanded the war in Afghanistan, including the use of drones sent on cross-border bombing runs into Pakistan that have doubled the number of civilians killed over the past three months. Brand Obama has refused to ease restrictions so workers can organize and will not consider single-payer, not-for-profit health care for all Americans. And Brand Obama will not prosecute the Bush administration for war crimes, including the use of torture, and has refused to dismantle Bush's secrecy laws or restore habeas corpus.

Brand Obama offers us an image that appears radically individualistic and new. It inoculates us from seeing that the old engines of corporate power and the vast military-industrial complex continue to plunder the country. Corporations, which control our politics, no longer produce products that are essentially different; what they produce are brands that are different. Brand Obama does not threaten the core of the corporate state any more than did Brand George W. Bush. The Bush brand collapsed. We became immune to its studied folksiness. We saw through its artifice. This is a common deflation in the world of advertising. So we have been given a new Obama brand with an exciting and faintly erotic appeal. Benetton and Calvin Klein were the precursors to Brand Obama, using ads to associate themselves with risqué art and progressive politics. It gave their products an edge. But the goal, as with all brands, was to make passive consumers mistake a brand for an experience.

"The abandonment of the radical economic foundations of the women's and civil-rights movements by the conflation of causes that came to be called political correctness successfully trained a generation of activists in the politics of image, not action," Naomi Klein wrote in her book *No Space, No Choice, No Jobs, No Logo*.[4]

Obama, who has become a global celebrity, was molded easily into a brand. He had almost no experience other than two years in the Senate, lacked any moral core, and could be painted as all things to all people. His brief Senate voting record was a miserable surrender to corporate interests. He was happy to promote nuclear power as "green" energy. He voted to continue the wars in Iraq and Afghanistan. He reauthorized the Patriot Act. He would not back a bill designed to cap predatory credit card interest rates. He opposed a bill that would have reformed the notorious General Mining Act of 1872. He refused to support the single-payer health-care bill House Resolution 676, sponsored by U.S. Representatives Dennis Kucinich and John Conyers. He supported the death penalty. And he backed a class-action "reform" bill that was part of a large lobbying effort by financial firms. The law, known as the Class Action Fairness Act, would effectively shut down state courts as venues in which to hear most class-action lawsuits and deny redress in many of the courts where these cases have a chance of defying powerful corporate challenges.

While Gaza was being bombarded and hit with air strikes in the weeks before Obama took office, "the Obama team let it be known that it would not object to the planned resupply of 'smart bombs' and other hi-tech ordnance that was already flowing to Israel," according to Seymour Hersh. Even his one vaunted antiwar speech as a state senator, perhaps his single real act of defiance, was swiftly reversed. He told the *Chicago Tribune* on July 27, 2004, that "there's not that much difference between my position and George Bush's position at this stage. The difference, in my mind, is who's in a position to execute." And unlike antiwar stalwarts like Kucinich, who gave hundreds of speeches against the war, Obama then dutifully stood silent until the Iraq war became unpopular.

Obama's campaign won the vote of hundreds of marketers, agency heads, and marketing-services vendors gathered at the Association of National Advertisers' annual conference in October. The Obama campaign was named *Advertising Age*'s marketer of the year for 2008, edging out runners-up Apple and Zappos.com. Take it from the professionals: Brand Obama is a marketer's dream. President Obama does one thing and Brand Obama gets you to believe another. This is the essence of successful advertising. You buy or do what the advertiser wants because of how he or she can make you feel.

Celebrity culture has leeched into every aspect of our culture, including politics, to bequeath us what Benjamin DeMott called "junk politics." Junk politics does not demand justice or the reparation of rights. Junk politics personalizes and moralizes issues rather than clarifying them. "It's impatient with articulated conflict, enthusiastic about America's optimism and moral character, and heavily dependent on feel-your-pain language and gesture," DeMott noted.[5] The result of junk politics is that nothing changes—"meaning zero interruption in the processes and practices that strengthen existing, interlocking systems of socioeconomic advantage." It redefines traditional values, tilting "courage toward braggadocio, sympathy toward mawkishness, humility toward self-disrespect, identification with ordinary citizens toward distrust of brains." Junk politics "miniaturizes large, complex problems at home while maximizing threats from abroad. It's also given to abrupt unexplained reversals of its own public stances, often spectacularly bloating problems previously miniaturized." And finally, it "seeks at every turn to obliterate voters' consciousness of socioeconomic and other differences in their midst."

An image-based culture, one dominated by junk politics, communicates through narratives, pictures, and carefully orchestrated spectacle and manufactured pseudo-drama. Scandalous affairs, hurricanes, earthquakes, untimely deaths, lethal new viruses, train wrecks—these events play well on computer screens and television. International diplomacy, labor union negotiations, and convoluted bailout packages do not yield exciting personal narratives or stimulating images. A governor who patronizes call girls becomes a huge news story. A politician who proposes serious regulatory reform or universal health care, or who advocates curbing wasteful spending is boring. Kings, queens, and emperors once used their court conspiracies to divert their subjects. Today cinematic, political, and journalistic celebrities distract us with their personal foibles and scandals. They create our public mythology. Acting, politics, and sports have become, as they were during the reign of Nero, interchangeable.

In an age of images and entertainment, in an age of instant emotional gratification, we do not seek reality. Reality is complicated. Reality is boring. We are incapable of handling or unwilling to handle its confusion. We ask to be indulged and comforted by clichés, stereotypes, and inspirational messages that tell us we can be whoever we seek to be, that we live in the greatest country on Earth, that we are endowed with superior moral and physical qualities, and that our future will always be glorious and prosperous, because of our own attributes, our national character, or because we are blessed by God. Reality is not accepted as an impediment to our desires. Reality does not make us feel good.

In his book *Public Opinion*, Walter Lippmann distinguished between "the world outside and the pictures in our heads."[6] He defined a "stereotype" as an oversimplified pattern that helps us find meaning in the world. Lippmann cited examples of the crude "stereotypes we carry about in our heads" of whole groups of people such as "Germans," "South Europeans," "Negroes," "Harvard men," "agitators," and others. These stereotypes, Lippmann noted, give a reassuring and false consistency to the chaos of existence. They offer easily grasped explanations of reality and are closer to propaganda because they simplify rather than complicate.

Pseudo-events—dramatic productions orchestrated by publicists, political machines, television, Hollywood, or advertisers—however, are very different. They have, as Daniel Boorstin wrote in his book *The Image: A Guide to Pseudo-Events in America*, the capacity to appear real even though we know they are staged. They are capable, because they can evoke a powerful emotional response, of overwhelming reality and replacing it with a fictional narrative that often becomes accepted truth. The unmasking of a stereotype damages and often destroys its credibility. But pseudo-events, whether they show the president in an auto plant or a soup kitchen or addressing troops in Iraq, are immune to this deflation. The exposure of the elaborate mechanisms behind the pseudo-event only adds to its fascination and its power. This is the basis of the convoluted television reporting on how effectively political campaigns and politicians have been stage-managed. Reporters, especially those on television, no longer ask whether the message is true but whether the pseudo-event worked or did not work as political theater. Pseudo-events are judged on how effectively we have been manipulated by illusion. Those events that appear real are relished and lauded. Those that fail to create a believable illusion are deemed failures. Truth is irrelevant. Those who succeed in politics, as in most of the culture, are those who create the brands and pseudo-events that offer the most convincing fantasies. And this is the art Obama has mastered.

A public that can no longer distinguish between truth and fiction is left to interpret reality through illusion. Random facts or obscure bits of data and trivia are used to bolster illusion and give it credibility or are discarded if they interfere with the message. The worse reality becomes—the more, for example, foreclosures and unemployment skyrocket—the more people seek refuge and comfort in illusions. When opinions cannot be distinguished from facts, when there is no universal standard to determine truth in law, in science, in scholarship, or in reporting the events of the day, when the most valued skill is the ability to entertain, the world becomes a place where lies become true, where people can believe what they want to believe. This is the real danger of pseudo-events and why pseudo-events are far more pernicious than stereotypes. They do not explain reality, as stereotypes attempt to, but replace reality. Pseudo-events redefine reality by the parameters set by their creators. These creators, who make massive profits peddling these illusions, have a vested interest in maintaining the power structures they control.

The old production-oriented culture demanded what the historian Warren Susman termed "character." The new consumption-oriented culture demands what he called personality. The shift in values is a shift from a fixed morality to the artifice of presentation. The old cultural values of thrift and moderation honored hard work, integrity and courage. The consumption-oriented culture honors charm, fascination, and likeability. "The social role demanded of all in the new culture of personality was that of a performer," Susman wrote. "Every American was to become a performing self."[7]

The junk politics practiced by Obama is a consumer fraud. It is about performance. It is about lies. It is about keeping us in a perpetual state of childishness. But the longer we live in illusion, the worse reality will be when it finally shatters our fantasies. Those who do not understand what is happening around them and who are overwhelmed by a brutal reality they did not expect or foresee search desperately for saviors. They beg demagogues to come to their rescue. This is the ultimate danger of the Obama brand. It effectively masks the wanton internal destruction and theft being carried out by our corporate state. These corporations, once they have stolen trillions in taxpayer wealth, will leave tens of millions of Americans bereft, bewildered, and yearning for even more potent and deadly illusions, ones that could swiftly snuff out what is left of our diminished open society.

Hold Your Applause

JUNE 8, 2009

Did they play Barack Obama's speech to the Muslim world in the prison corridors of Abu Ghraib, Bagram Airfield, Guantánamo, or the dozens of secret sites where we hold thousands of Muslims around the world? Did it echo off the walls of the crowded morgues filled with the mutilated bodies of the Muslim dead in Baghdad or Kabul? Was it broadcast from the tops of minarets in the villages and towns decimated by U.S. iron fragmentation bombs? Was it heard in the squalid refugee camps of Gaza, where 1.5 million Palestinians live in the world's largest ghetto?

What do words of peace and cooperation mean from us when we torture—yes, we still torture—only Muslims? What do these words mean when we sanction Israel's brutal air assaults on Lebanon and Gaza, assaults that demolished thousands of homes and left hundreds dead and injured? How does it look for Obama to call for democracy and human rights from Egypt, where we lavishly fund and support the despotic regime of Hosni Mubarak, one of the longest-reigning dictators in the Middle East?

We may thrill to Obama's rhetoric, but few of the 1.3 billion Muslims in the world are as deluded. They grasp that nothing so far has changed for Muslims in the Middle East under the Obama administration. The wars of occupation go on or have been expanded. Israel continues to flout international law, gobbling up more Palestinian land and carrying out egregious war crimes in Gaza. Calcified, repressive regimes in countries such as Egypt and Saudi Arabia are feted in Washington as allies.

The speech at Cairo University, which usually has trucks filled with riot police outside the university gates and a heavy security presence on campus to control the student body, is an example of the facade. Student political groups, as everyone who joined in the standing ovation for the president knew, are prohibited. Faculty deans are chosen by the administration, rather than elected by professors, "as a way to combat Islamist influence on campus," according to the U.S. State Department's latest human-rights report. And, as the *Washington Post* pointed out, students who use the Internet "as an outlet for their political or social views are on notice: One Cairo University student blogger was jailed for two months last summer for 'public agitation,' and another was kicked out of university housing for criticizing the government."[8]

The expanding imperial projects and tightening screws of repression lurch forward under Obama. We are not trying to end terror or promote democracy. We are ensuring that our corporate state has a steady supply of the cheap oil to which it is addicted. And the scarcer oil becomes, the more aggressive we become. This is the game playing out in the Muslim world.

The Bush White House openly tortured. The Obama White House tortures and pretends not to. Obama may have banned waterboarding, but as Luke Mitchell points out in the July 2009 edition of *Harper's* magazine, torture, including isolation, sleep and sensory deprivation, and force-feeding, continues to be used to break detainees. The president has promised to close Guantánamo, where only one percent of the prisoners held offshore by the United States are kept. And the Obama administration has sought to obscure the fate and condition of thousands of Muslims held in black holes around the globe. As Mitchell notes, the Obama White House "has sought to prevent detainees at Bagram prison in Afghanistan from gaining access to courts where they may reveal the circumstances of their imprisonment. It has sought to continue the practice of rendering prisoners to unknown and unknowable locations outside the United States, and sought to keep secret many (though not all) of the records regarding our treatment of those detainees."[9]

Muslim rage is stoked because we station tens of thousands of American troops on Muslim soil, occupy two Muslim nations, make possible the illegal Israeli occupation of Palestine, support repressive Arab regimes, and torture thousands of Muslims in offshore penal colonies where prisoners are stripped of their rights. We now have twenty-two times as many military personnel in the Muslim world as were deployed during the Crusades of the twelfth century. The rage comes because we have constructed massive military bases, some the size of small cities, in Iraq, Afghanistan, Saudi Arabia, Turkey, and Kuwait, and established basing rights in the Gulf States of Bahrain, Qatar, Oman, and the United Arab Emirates. The rage comes because we have expanded our military empire into neighboring Uzbekistan, Pakistan, Kyrgyzstan, and Tajikistan. It comes because we station troops and special forces in Egypt, Algeria, and Yemen. And this vast network of bases and military outposts looks suspiciously permanent.

The Muslim world fears, correctly, that we intend to dominate Middle East oil supplies and any Caspian Sea oil infrastructure. And it is interested not in our protestations of good will but in the elemental right of justice and freedom from foreign occupation. We would react, should the situation be reversed, no differently.

The brutal reality of expanding foreign occupation and harsher and harsher forms of control are the tinder of Islamic fundamentalism, insurgences, and terrorism. We can blame the violence on a clash of civilizations. We can naively tell ourselves we are envied for our freedoms. We can point to the Koran. But these are fantasies that divert us from facing the central dispute between us and the Muslim world, from facing our own responsibility for the virus of chaos and violence spreading throughout the Middle East. We can have peace when we shut down our bases, stay the hand of the Israelis to create a Palestinian state, and go home, or we can have long, costly, and ultimately futile regional war. We cannot have both.

Obama, whose embrace of American imperialism is as naïve and destructive as that of George W. Bush, is the newest brand used to peddle the poison of permanent war. We may not see it. But those who bury the dead do.

The Truth Alone Will Not Set You Free

JUNE 29, 2009

The ability of the corporate state to pacify the country by extending credit and providing cheap manufactured goods to the masses is gone. The pernicious idea that democracy lies in the choice between competing brands and the freedom to accumulate vast sums of personal wealth at the expense of others has collapsed. The conflation of freedom with the free market has been exposed as a sham. The travails of the poor are rapidly becoming the travails of the middle class, especially as unemployment insurance runs out and people get a taste of Bill Clinton's draconian welfare reform. And class warfare, once buried under the happy illusion that we were all going to enter an age of prosperity with unfettered capitalism, is returning with a vengeance.

Our economic crisis—despite the corporate media circus around the death of Michael Jackson, or South Carolina governor Mark Sanford's marital infidelity, or the outfits of Sacha Baron Cohen's latest incarnation, Brüno—barrels forward. And this crisis will lead to a period of profound political turmoil and change. Those who care about the plight of the working class and the poor must begin to mobilize quickly, or we will lose our last opportunity to save our embattled democracy. The most important struggle will be to wrest the organs of communication from corporations that use mass media to demonize movements of social change and empower protofascist movements such as the Christian Right.

American culture—or cultures, for we once had distinct regional cultures—was systematically destroyed in the twentieth century by corporations. These corporations used mass communication, as well as an understanding of the human subconscious, to turn consumption into an inner compulsion. Old values—thrift; regional identity that had its own iconography; aesthetic expression and history; diverse immigrant traditions; self-sufficiency; and media that were decentralized to provide citizens with a voice in their communities—were all destroyed to create mass corporate culture. New desires and habits were implanted by corporate advertisers to replace the old. Individual frustrations and discontents could be solved, corporate culture assured us, through the wonders of consumerism and cultural homogenization. American culture—or cultures—was or were replaced with junk culture and junk politics. And now, standing on the ash heap, we survey the ruins. The very slogans of advertising and mass culture have become the idiom of common expression, robbing us of the language to make sense of the destruction. We confuse this manufactured commodity culture with American culture.

How do we recover what was lost? How do we reclaim the culture(s) destroyed by corporations? How do we fight back now that the consumer culture has fallen into a state of decay? What can we do to reverse the cannibalization of government and the national economy by the corporations?

All periods of profound change occur in a crisis. It was a crisis that brought us the New Deal, now largely dismantled by the corporate state. It was also a crisis that gave the world Adolf Hitler and Slobodan Milošević. We can go in either direction. Events move at the speed of light when societies and cultural assumptions break down. There are powerful forces, which have no commitment to the open society, ready to seize the moment to snuff out the last vestiges of democratic egalitarianism. Our bankrupt liberalism, which naively believes Barack Obama is the antidote to our permanent war economy and Wall Street fraud, will either rise from its coma or be rolled over by an organized corporate elite and their right-wing lapdogs. The corporate domination of the airwaves, of most print publications, and an increasing number of Internet sites means we will have to search, and search quickly, for alternative forms of communication to thwart the rise of totalitarian capitalism.

Stuart Ewen, whose books *Captains of Consciousness: Advertising and the Social Roots of the Consumer Culture* and *PR!—A Social History of Spin* chronicle how corporate propaganda deformed American culture and pushed populism to the margins of American society, argues that we have a fleeting chance to save the country. I fervently hope he is right. He attacks the ideology of "objectivity and balance" that has corrupted news, saying that it falsely evokes the scales of justice. He describes the curriculum at most journalism schools as "poison."

" 'Balance and objectivity' creates an idea where both sides are balanced," he said when I spoke to him by phone:

> In certain ways it mirrors the two-party system, the notion that if you are going to have a Democrat speak you need to have a Republican speak. It offers the phantom of objectivity. It creates the notion that the universe of discourse is limited to two positions. Issues become black or white. They are not seen as complex with a multitude of factors.

Ewen argues that the forces for social change—look at any lengthy and turgid human-rights report—have forgotten that rhetoric is as important as fact. Corporate and government propaganda, aimed to sway emotions, rarely uses facts to sell its positions. And because progressives have lost the gift of rhetoric, once a staple of a university education, because they naively believe in the Enlightenment ideal that facts alone can move people toward justice, they are largely helpless.

"Effective communication requires not simply an understanding of the facts, but how those facts will take place in the public mind," Ewen said. "When Gustave Le Bon says it is not the facts in and of themselves which make a point but the way in which the facts take place, the way in which they come to attention, he is right."

The emergence of corporate and government public relations, which drew on the studies of mass psychology by Sigmund Freud and others after World War I, found its bible in Walter Lippmann's book *Public Opinion*, a manual for the power elite's shaping of popular sentiments. Lippmann argued that the key to leadership in the modern age would depend on the ability to manipulate "symbols which assemble emotions after they have been detached from their ideas." The public mind could be mastered, he wrote, through an "intensification of feeling and a degradation of significance."[10]

These corporate forces, schooled by Woodrow Wilson's vast Committee for Public Information, which sold World War I to the public, learned how to skillfully mobilize and manipulate the emotional responses of the public. The control of the airwaves and domination through corporate advertising of most publications restricted news to reporting facts, to "objectivity and balance," while the real power to persuade and dominate a public remained under corporate and governmental control.

Ewen argues that pamphleteering, which played a major role in the seventeenth and eighteenth centuries in shaping the public mind, recognized that "the human mind is not left-brain or right-brain, that it is not divided by reason which is good and emotion which is bad."

He argues that the forces of social reform, those organs that support a search for truth and self-criticism, have mistakenly shunned emotion and rhetoric because they have been used so powerfully within modern society to disseminate lies and manipulate public opinion. But this refusal to appeal to emotion means "we gave up the ghost and accepted the idea that human beings are these divided selves, binary systems between emotion and reason, and that emotion gets you into trouble and reason is what leads you forward. This is not true."

The public is bombarded with carefully crafted images meant to confuse propaganda with ideology and knowledge with how we feel. Human-rights and labor groups, investigative journalists, consumer watchdog organizations, and advocacy agencies have, in the face of this manipulation, inundated the public sphere with reports and facts. But facts alone, Ewen says, make little difference. And as we search for alternative ways to communicate in a time of crisis, we must also communicate in new forms. We must appeal to emotion as well as to reason. The power of this appeal to emotion is evidenced in the photographs of Jacob Riis, a New York journalist, who, with a team of assistants at the end of the nineteenth century, initiated urban-reform photography. His stark portraits of the filth and squalor of urban slums awakened the conscience of a nation. The photographer Lewis Hine at the turn of the twentieth century and Walker Evans during the Great Depression did the same thing for the working classes, along with writers such as Upton Sinclair and James Agee. It is a recovery of this style, one that turns the abstraction of fact into a human flesh, one that is not afraid of emotion and passion, which will permit us to counter the force of corporate propaganda.

We may know that fossil fuels are destroying our ecosystem. We may be able to cite the statistics. But the oil and natural gas industry continues its flagrant rape of the planet. It is able to do this because of the money it uses to control legislation and a massive advertising campaign that paints the oil and natural gas industry as part of the solution. A group called Energy Tomorrow, for example—an advocacy arm of the American Petroleum Institute—has been running a series of television ads. One ad features an attractive, middle-aged woman—an actor named Brooke Alexander, who once worked as the host of *WorldBeat* on CNN and for Fox News. Dressed in a black pantsuit, Alexander walks around a blue-screen studio that surrounds her with digital renditions of American life. She argues, before each image, that oil and natural gas are critical to providing not only energy needs but also health care and jobs.

"It is almost like they are taking the most optimistic visions of what the stimulus package could do and saying, 'This is what the development of oil and natural gas will bring about,'" Ewen said:

> If you go to the Web site, there is a lot of sophisticated stuff you can play around with. As each ad closes you see in the lower right-hand corner, in very small letters, *API*, the American Petroleum Institute, the lobbying group for ExxonMobil and all the other big oil companies. For the average viewer there is nothing in the ad to indicate this is being produced by the oil industry.

The modern world, as Kafka predicted, has become a world where the irrational has become rational, where lies become true. And facts alone will be powerless to thwart the mendacity spun out through billions of dollars in corporate advertising, lobbying, and control of traditional sources of information. We will have to descend into the world of the forgotten, to write, photograph, paint, sing, act, blog, video, and film with anger and honesty that have been blunted by the parameters of traditional journalism. The distinctions among artists, social activists, and journalists have to be erased. These distinctions diminish the power of reform, justice, and an understanding of the truth. And it is for this purpose that these distinctions are there.

"As a writer, part of what you are aiming for is to present things in ways that will resonate with people, which will give voice to feelings and concerns, feelings that may not be fully verbalized," Ewen said. "You can't do that simply by providing them with data. One of the major problems of the present is that those structures designed to promote a progressive agenda are antediluvian."

Corporate ideology, embodied in neoconservatism, has seeped into the attitudes of most self-described liberals. It champions unfettered capitalism and globalization as eternal. This is the classic tactic power elites use to maintain themselves. The loss of historical memory, which "balanced and objective" journalism promotes, has only contributed to this fantasy. But the fantasy, despite the desperate raiding of taxpayer funds to keep the corporate system alive, is now coming undone. The lie is being exposed. And the corporate state is running scared.

"It is very important for people like us to think about ways to present the issues, whether we are talking about the banking crisis, health care, or housing and homelessness," Ewen said:

We have to think about presenting these issues in ways that are two steps ahead of the media rather than two steps behind. That is not something we should view as an impossible task. It is a very possible task. There is evidence of how possible that task is, especially if you look at the development of the underground press in the 1960s. The underground press, which started cropping up all over the country, was not a marginal phenomenon. It leeched into the society. It developed an approach to news and communication that was ten steps ahead of the mainstream media. The proof is that even as it declined, so many structures that were innovated by the underground press, things like the *Whole Earth Catalog*, began to affect and inform the stylistic presentation of mainstream media.

"I am not a prophet," Ewen said. "All I can do is look at historical precedence and figure out the extent we can learn from it":

This is not about looking backwards. If you can't see the past you can't see the future. If you can't see the relationship between the present and the past, you can't understand where the present might go. Who controls the past controls the present, who controls the present controls the future, as George Orwell said. This is a succinct explanation of the ways in which power functions.

"Read The Gettysburg Address," Ewen said:

Read Frederick Douglass's autobiography or his newspaper. Read *The Communist Manifesto*. Read Darwin's *Descent of Man*. All of these things are filled with an understanding that communicating ideas and producing forms of public communication that empower people, rather than disempowering people, relies on an integrated understanding of who the public is and what it might be. We have a lot to learn from the history of rhetoric. We need to think about where we are going. We need to think about what twenty-first-century pamphleteering might be. We need to think about the ways in which the rediscovery of rhetoric—not lying, but rhetoric in its more conventional sense—can affect what we do. We need to look at those historical antecedents where interventions happened that stepped ahead of the news. And to some extent this is happening. We have the freest and most open public sphere since the village square.

The battle ahead will be fought outside the journalistic mainstream, he said. The old forms of journalism are dying or have sold their souls to corporate manipulation and celebrity culture. We must now wed fact to rhetoric. We must appeal to reason and emotion. We must not be afraid to openly take sides, to speak, photograph, or write on behalf of the disempowered. And, Ewen believes, we have a chance in the coming crisis to succeed.

"Pessimism is never useful," he said. "Realism is useful, understanding the forces that are at play. To quote Antonio Gramsci, 'pessimism of the intellect, optimism of the will.'"

The Crooks Get the Cash While the Poor Get Screwed

JULY 6, 2009

Tearyan Brown became a father when he was sixteen. He did what a lot of inner-city kids desperate to make money do. He sold drugs. He was arrested and sent to jail three years later for dealing marijuana and PCP on the streets of Trenton, New Jersey, mostly to white kids driving in from the suburbs. It was a job that saw him robbed at gunpoint and stabbed in the chest. But it made him about $1,400 a week.

Brown, when he got out after three and a half years, was done with street life. He got a job as a security guard and then as a fork lift operator. He eventually made about $30,000 a year. He shepherded his son through high school, then college and a master's degree. His boy, now twenty-four, is a high school teacher in Texas. Brown would not leave the streets of Trenton but his son would. It made him proud. It gave him hope.

And then one morning in 2005, when he was visiting his mother's house, the cops showed up. He saw the cruiser and the officers standing on his mother's porch. He hurried down the block toward the home to see what was wrong. What was wrong was him. On the basis of a police photograph, he had been identified by an eighty-two-year-old woman as the man who had robbed her of nine dollars at gunpoint a few hours earlier. The only other witness to the crime insisted the elderly victim was confused. That witness told the police Brown was innocent. Brown's friends said Brown was with them when the robbery took place.

"Why would I rob a woman for nine dollars?," he asks me. "I had been paid the day before. I had not committed a crime in twenty years. It didn't make any sense."

He was again sent to jail. But this time he was charged with armed robbery. If convicted, he would be locked away for many years. His grown son and his three young boys would live, as he had, without the presence of a father. The little ones—eleven-year-old twins and a ten-year-old—would be adults when he got out. When he met with his state-appointed attorney, the lawyer, like most state-appointed attorneys, pushed him to accept a plea bargain, one that would see him behind bars for at least the next decade. Brown pulled the pictures of his children out of his wallet, laid the pictures carefully on the table in front of the lawyer, looked at the faces of his children, and broke down in tears. He shook and sobbed. It was a hard thing to do for a man who stands nearly six feet tall, weighs 210 pounds, and has coped with a lot in his life.

"I didn't do nothing," he choked out to the lawyer.

He refused the plea bargain offer. He sat in jail for the next two years before getting a trial. It was a time of deep despair. Jail had changed since he had last been incarcerated. The facilities were overcrowded, with inmates sleeping in corridors and on the floor. The gangs taunted those who, like Brown, were not affiliated with a gang. Gang members knocked trays of food to the floor. They pissed on mattresses. They stole canteen items and commissary orders. And there was nothing the victims could do about it.

"See this?" he says to me in a dimly lit coffee shop in downtown Trenton as he rolls up the right sleeve of his T-shirt. "It's the grim reaper. I got it in jail. I was so scared. I was scared I wouldn't get out this time. I was scared I would not see my kids grow up. They make their own tattoo guns in jail with a toothbrush, a staple, and the motor of a Walkman. It cost me fifteen dollars–well, not really dollars. I had to give him about ten soups and a package of cigarettes. On the street this would be three or four hundred dollars."

Under the tattoo of the scythe-wielding, hooded figure are the words *Death Awaits*.

He had a trial after two years in jail and was found not guilty. The sheriff's deputies in the courtroom said as he was walking out that they "had never seen anything like this." He reaches into his baggy jeans and pulls out his thin brown wallet. He opens it to show me a folded piece of paper. The paper says, "Verdict: Defendant found not guilty on all charges." It is dated January 31, 2008.

But innocence and guilt are funny things in America. If you are rich and guilty, if you have defrauded banks and customers and investment firms of billions of dollars, as AIG or Citibank has, if you wear fancy suits and have degrees from elite universities that cost more per year than Brown used to make, you get taxpayer money. You get lots of it. You maintain the lavish lifestyle of jets and spas and million-dollar bonuses. You live a life of unchecked greed and have too much in a world where most have too little. If you are moral scum in America, we take care of you. But if you are poor, if you are, say, Tearyan Brown and African American and thirty-nine years old now, with four kids and no job, and you live in the inner city, you are in trouble. No one comes to help you. You don't get a second chance. This is what being poor means.

Brown found that life had changed when he got out. He had lost his job as a forklift operator. And there were no new jobs to be found. He had faithfully paid child support until his arrest, but, with no income, he could not pay from jail, and now he was being hauled into court by the state every few weeks for being in arrears for $13,000. The mother of his three youngest boys goes to court with him. She explains that he paid regularly while he had work. She explains that when she works on the weekends Brown takes the kids. She asks that he be forgiven until he can get a job and begin paying again. But there are no jobs.

"I would not be in arrears in child support if I had not been incarcerated for something I didn't do," he says. "I will never get above ground owing $13,000. How can I pay $120 a week when I don't have a job?"

Brown lives on $200 a month in food stamps and $40 in cash. Welfare will pay his apartment for another four months. He is barely making it. I ask him what he will do when he loses the rent subsidy.

"I'll be homeless," he says.

"My son says come down to Texas," he adds. "Start a new life with me. But what about my three little boys? I can't leave them. I can't leave them in Trenton. They need a father."

Brown works out every day. He does calisthenics. He is a vegetarian. He volunteers at a food pantry. He attends the Jerusalem Baptist Church with his little boys. "They are church kids," he tells me proudly. "They are pretty much raised by the church."

He is trying to keep himself together. But he lives in a world that is falling apart. The gangs on the streets of Trenton carry Glock nine-millimeter pistols and AK-47 assault rifles. When the Trenton police stop a car or raid a house filled with suspected gang members, they approach with loaded M16s. A local newspaper, the *Trentonian*, reports the daily chronicle of crime, decay, and neglect. The lead story in the day's paper, which Brown has with him, is about a young man named James Deonte James, whose street name is "Lurch." James was charged in the death of a thirteen-year-old girl during a gang shooting. He is reputed to be a "five-star general in the Sex Money Murder set of the Bloods street gang."

In another story, an ex-con and reputed mobster, Michael "Mickey Rome" DiMattia, was arrested in his car after a woman behind the wheel was seen driving erratically. Mickey Rome, dressed in a black bathrobe with a red scarf around his neck, was found to be wearing a bulletproof vest, with three guns stuck in his waistband, and a crack pipe, crack cocaine, and prescription pills in his pockets. He had been convicted in 1990 of killing a seventeen-year-old boy with a shotgun blast to the head. He served less than three years for the murder.

A feature story on page four of the paper is about a man with AIDS who raped his girlfriend's son fifty-five times and infected the boy with the virus. The boy was nine when the rapes took place.

"There are thousands more guns out there than when I was on the street," Brown says. "It is easier to buy a gun than get liquor from a liquor store."

He says he rarely goes out at night, even to the corner store. It is too dangerous.

The desperation is palpable. People don't know where to turn. Benefits are running out. More and more people are out of work.

"You see things getting worse and worse," he says. "You see people who wonder how they are going to eat and take care of themselves and their kids. You see people starting to do anything to get food, to hustle or rob, to go back to doing things they do not want to do. Good people start doin' bad things. People are getting eviler."

He pauses.

"All things are better with God," he says softly, looking down at the tabletop.

He is reading a book about the Bible. It is about Jesus and God. It is about learning to trust in God's help. In America that is about all the poor have left. And when God fails them, they are on their own.

The Man in the Mirror

JULY 13, 2009

In celebrity culture we destroy what we worship. The commercial exploitation of Michael Jackson's death was orchestrated by the corporate forces that rendered Jackson insane. Jackson, robbed of his childhood and surrounded by vultures who preyed on his fears and weaknesses, was so consumed by self-loathing he carved his African American face into an ever-changing Caucasian death mask and hid his apparent pedophilia behind a Peter Pan illusion of eternal childhood. He could not disentangle his public and his private self. He became a commodity, a product, one to be sold, used, and manipulated. He was infected by the moral nihilism and personal disintegration at the core of our corporate culture. And his fantasies of eternal youth, delusions of majesty, and desperate, disfiguring quests for physical transformation were expressions of our own yearning. He was a reflection of us in the extreme.

His memorial service—a variety show with a coffin—had an estimated 31.1 million television viewers. The ceremony, which featured performances or tributes from Stevie Wonder, Brooke Shields, and other celebrities, was carried live on nineteen networks, including the major broadcast and cable news outlets. It was the final episode of the long-running Michael Jackson series. And it concluded with Jackson's daughter, Paris, being prodded to stand in front of a microphone to speak about her father. Before the girl could get a few words out, Michael's sister Janet Jackson told Paris to "speak up." As the child broke down, the adults around her adjusted the microphone so we could hear the sobs. The crowd clapped. It was a haunting echo of what destroyed her father.

The stories we like best are "real-life" stories—early fame, wild success, and then a long, bizarre, and macabre emotional train wreck. O.J. Simpson offered a tamer version of the same plot. So does Britney Spears. Jackson, by the end, was heavily in debt and had weathered a $22 million out-of-court settlement payment to Jordy Chandler, as well as seven counts of child sexual abuse and two counts of administering an intoxicating agent in order to commit a felony. We fed on his physical and psychological disintegration, especially since many Americans are struggling with their own descent into overwhelming debt, loss of status, and personal disintegration.

The lurid drama of Jackson's personal life meshed perfectly with the ongoing dramas on television, in movies, and in the news. News thrives on "real-life" stories, especially those involving celebrities. News reports on television are minidramas complete with a star, a villain, a supporting cast, a good-looking host, and a dramatic, if often unexpected, ending. The public greedily consumed "news" about Jackson, especially in his exile and decline, that often outdid most works of fiction. In *Fahrenheit 451*, Ray Bradbury's novel about a future dystopia, people spend most of the day watching giant television screens that show endless scenes of police chases and criminal apprehensions. Bradbury understood that life, once it was packaged, scripted, given a narrative, and filmed, became the most compelling form of entertainment. And Jackson was a great show. He deserved a great finale.

Those who created Jackson's public persona and turned him into a piece of property, first as a child and finally as a corpse encased in a $15,000 gold-plated casket, are the agents, publicists, marketing people, promoters, scriptwriters, television and movie producers, advertisers, video technicians, photographers, bodyguards, recording executives, wardrobe consultants, fitness trainers, pollsters, public announcers, and television news personalities who create the vast stage of celebrity for profit. They are the puppet masters. No one achieves celebrity status, no cultural illusion is swallowed as reality, without these armies of cultural enablers and intermediaries. The producers at the Staples Center in Los Angeles made sure the eighteen thousand attendees and the television audience (even the BBC devoted three hours to the tribute) watched a funeral that was turned into another maudlin form of up-lifting popular entertainment.

The memorial service for Jackson was a celebration of celebrity. There was the queasy sight of groups of children, including his own, singing over the coffin. Magic Johnson put in a plug for Kentucky Fried Chicken. Shields, fighting back tears, recalled how she and a thirty-three-year-old Jackson—who always maintained that he was straight—broke into Elizabeth Taylor's room the night before her last wedding to "get the first peek of the [wedding] dress." Shields and Jackson, at Taylor's wedding, then joked that they were "the mother and father of the bride."

"Yes, it may have seemed very odd to the outside," Shields said, "but we made it fun and we made it real."

There were photo montages in which a shot of Jackson shaking hands with Nelson Mandela was immediately followed by one of him with Kermit the Frog. Fame reduces all of the famous to the same level. Fame is its own denominator. And every anecdote seemed to confirm that when you spend your life as a celebrity, you have no idea who you are.

We measure our lives by these celebrities. We seek to be like them. We emulate their look and behavior. We escape the messiness of real life through the fantasy of their stardom. We, too, long to attract admiring audiences for our grand, ongoing life movie. We try to see ourselves moving through our lives as a camera would see us, mindful of how we hold ourselves, how we dress, what we say. We invent movies that play inside our heads with us as stars. We wonder how an audience would react. Celebrity culture has taught us, almost unconsciously, to generate interior personal screenplays. We have learned ways of speaking and thinking that grossly disfigure the way we relate to the world and those around us. Neal Gabler, who has written wisely about this, argues that celebrity culture is not a convergence of consumer culture and religion so much as a hostile takeover of religion by consumer culture.

Jackson desperately feared growing old. He believed he could control race and gender. He transformed himself through surgery and perhaps female hormones from a brown-skinned African American male to a chalk-faced androgynous ghoul with no clear sexual identity. And while he pushed these boundaries to the extreme, he did only what many Americans do. Twelve million cosmetic plastic surgery procedures were performed last year in the United States. They were performed because, in America, most human beings, rich and poor, famous and obscure, have been conditioned to view themselves as marketable commodities. They are objects, like consumer products. They have no intrinsic value. They must look fabulous and live on fabulous sets. They must remain young. They must achieve notoriety and money, or the illusion of them, to be a success. And it does not matter how they get there.

The moral nihilism of our culture licenses a dark voyeurism into other people's humiliation, pain, weakness, and betrayal. Education, community-building skills, honesty, transparency, and sharing are qualities that will see you, in a gross perversion of democracy and morality, ridiculed and voted off any reality show. Fellow competitors for prize money and a chance for fleeting fame elect to "disappear" the unwanted. In the final credits of the reality show *America's Next Top Model*, a picture of the woman expelled during the episode vanishes from the group portrait on the screen. Those cast aside become, at least to the television audience, nonpersons. Celebrities who can no longer generate publicity, good or bad, vanish. Life, these shows teach, is a brutal world of unadulterated competition and constant quest for notoriety and attention. And life is about the personal humiliation of those who oppose us. Those who win are the best. Those who lose deserve to be erased. Those who fail, those who are ugly or poor, are belittled and mocked. In a commodity culture, human beings are used, betrayed, and discarded—which is pretty much the story of Jackson's life, although he experienced the equivalent of celebrity resurrection. This story arc has been very good for his music sales and perhaps for his father's new recording company, which Joe Jackson made sure to plug at public events after his son's death. Compassion, competence, intelligence, and solidarity are useless assets when human beings are commodities. Those who do not achieve celebrity status, who do not win the prize money or make millions in Wall Street firms, deserve their fate.

The cult of self, which Jackson embodied, dominates our culture. This cult stresses and cultivates traits that are much the same as the classic traits of psychopaths: superficial charm, grandiosity, and self-importance; a need for constant stimulation; a penchant for lying, deception, and manipulation; and the incapacity for remorse or guilt. Jackson, from his phony marriages to his questionable relationships with young boys, had all these qualities. This is also the ethic promoted by corporations. It is the ethic of unfettered capitalism. It is the misguided belief that personal style and personal advancement, mistaken for individualism, are the same as democratic equality. It is the celebration of image over substance.

We have a right, in the cult of the self, to get whatever we desire. We can do anything, even belittle and destroy those around us, including our friends, to make money, to be happy, and to become famous. Once fame and wealth are achieved, they become their own justification, their own morality. How one gets there is irrelevant. It is this perverted ethic that gave us Wall Street banks and investment houses that willfully trashed the nation's economy, that stole money from tens of millions of small shareholders who had bought stocks to finance their retirement or the college expenses of their children. The heads of these corporations, like the winners on a reality television program who lied and manipulated others to succeed, walked away with hundreds of millions of dollars in compensation and bonuses. The ethic of Wall Street is the ethic of celebrity.

The saturation coverage of Jackson's death is an example of our collective flight into illusion. The obsession with the trivia of his life conceals the despair, meaninglessness, and emptiness of our own lives. It deflects the moral questions arising from mounting social injustice, growing inequalities, costly imperial wars, economic collapse, and political corruption. The wild pursuit of status, wealth, and fame has destroyed our souls, as it destroyed Jackson, and it has destroyed our economy.

The fame of celebrities masks the identities of those who possess true power—corporations and the oligarchic elite. And as we sink into an economic and political morass, as we barrel toward a crisis that will create more misery than the Great Depression, we are controlled, manipulated, and distracted by the celluloid shadows on the wall of Plato's cave. The fantasy of celebrity culture is not designed simply to entertain. It is designed to drain us emotionally, confuse us about our identity, make us blame ourselves for our predicament, condition us to chase illusions of fame and happiness, and keep us from fighting back. And in the end, that is all the Jackson coverage was really about: another tawdry and tasteless spectacle to divert a dying culture from the howling wolf at the gate.

So Much for the Promised Land

AUGUST 3, 2009

LeAlan Jones, the thirty-year-old Green Party candidate for Barack Obama's old Senate seat in Illinois, is as angry at injustice as he is at the African American intellectual and political class that accommodates it. He does not buy Obama's "post-racial" ideology or have much patience with African American leaders who, hungry for prestige, power, and money, have, in his eyes, forgotten the people they are supposed to represent. They have confused a personal ability to be heard and earn a comfortable living with justice.

"The selflessness of leaders like Malcolm X, Dr. Martin Luther King, Harold Washington, and Medgar Evers has produced selfishness within the elite African American leadership," Jones told me by phone from Chicago.

"This is the only thing I can do to have peace of mind," he said when I asked him why he was running for office:

> I am looking at a community that is suffering because of a lack of genuine concern from their leaders. This isn't about a contract. This isn't about a grant. This isn't about who gets to stand behind the political elite at a press conference. This is about who is going to stand behind the people. What these leaders talk about and what needs to happen in the community is disjointed.

Jones began his career as a boy making radio documentaries about life in Chicago's public housing projects on the South Side, including the acclaimed *Ghetto Life 101*. He knows the world of which he speaks. He lives in the troubled Chicago neighborhood of Englewood, where he works as a freelance journalist and a high school football coach. He is the legal guardian of a sixteen-year-old nephew. And he often echoes the denunciations of black leaders by the historian Houston A. Baker Jr., who wrote the book *Betrayal: How Black Intellectuals Have Abandoned the Ideals of the Civil Rights Era.*

Baker excoriates leading public intellectuals, including Michael Eric Dyson, Henry Louis Gates Jr., Shelby Steele, Yale law professor Stephen Carter, and Manhattan Institute fellow John McWhorter, saying they pander to the powerful. He argues they have lost touch with the reality of most African Americans. Professor Gates' statement after his July 16 arrest that "what it made me realize was how vulnerable all black men are, how vulnerable are all poor people to capricious forces like a rogue policemen" was a stunning example of how distant from black reality many successful African American figures like Gates have become. These elite African American figures, Baker argues, long ago placed personal gain and career advancement over the interests of the black majority. They espouse positions palatable to a white audience, positions that ignore the radicalism and structural critiques of inequality by W. E. B. Du Bois, Martin Luther King Jr., and Malcolm X. And in a time when, as the poet Yusef Komunyakaa has said, "the cell block has replaced the auction block," they do not express the rage, frustration, and despair of the black underclass.[11]

Conditions for black men and women in America are sliding backward, with huge numbers of impoverished and unemployed removed from society and locked up. Baker acidly calls this "the disappearing" of blacks. The unemployment rate in most inner cities is in the double digits, and segregation, especially in city schools and wealthy states like New Jersey, is the norm. African American communities are more likely than others to be redlined (declared poor-risk areas from whose inhabitants loans should be withheld) by banks and preyed on by unscrupulous mortgage lenders, which is why such a high percentage of foreclosures are in blighted, urban neighborhoods. The *Village Voice*'s recent exposé that detailed brutal and sometimes fatal beatings of black and Hispanic prisoners by guards at New York's Rikers Island was a window into a daily reality usually not seen or acknowledged by the white mainstream.

"I have three people within my immediate family that are men that have come home within the last twenty-four to thirty-six months from being incarcerated," Jones said:

> They are tired of going to jail. They don't want to go to jail any-more. But there are no jobs. What service can they provide? My be-lief is those individuals coming home, these ex-felons, have more credibility to stop the violence in the inner city than the police do. It is their sons and nephews and their immediate families that are being the provocateurs of that violence. But if we are asking them to stop crime, what incentive are we providing them to do that?

"How much money did the American economy lose because of the derivatives and the credit default swaps?" he asked:

> There have been only two men prosecuted for that level of crime: Bernard Madoff and Allen Stanford. How much is the drug indus-try worth in the United States? It is not worth $45 trillion. How many African American and Hispanic men are incarcerated for being the same kind of capitalist? If we swap dope for derivatives, there wouldn't be a Wall Street because they would be behind bars. If we prosecute derivatives the same way you prosecute dope, which is not different in how it undermines a family, Wall Street wouldn't exist.

"A bunch of guys on Wall Street have done more to devastate the white community than any black man ever could," he added:

> I would have bailed out the pension funds, retirement funds, 401(k)s and funds attached to everyday people. If Wall Street and the banks couldn't survive, they couldn't survive, but the people's money would not have been impacted. If you would have killed personal wealth, you would have killed personal wealth. They took the pension funds of state, city, and local governments and misappropriated that capi-

tal. How can you reward them on the front end when they messed up the people's money on the front end?

"The only difference between the world of high finance and drug dealers are the commodities they deal," he added. "The mentality is the same."

The most prominent faces of color, such as Obama and his attorney general, Eric Holder, mask an insidious new racism that, in essence, tells blacks they have enough, that progress has been made, and that it is up to them to take advantage of what society offers them. And black politicians and intellectuals, including Obama and Gates, are the delivery systems for the message. We blame the victims, those for whom jobs and opportunities do not exist, while we orchestrate the largest transfer of wealth upward in American history. We sustain with taxpayer dollars a power elite and oligarchy responsible for dismantling the manufacturing-base and social-service programs that once gave workers and their families hope. Apologists for the system call their demands for black personal responsibility "tough love." But the stance, music to the ears of the white elite, is to Baker and Jones morally indefensible. It ignores the harsh reality visited on the poor by the cruelty of unfettered capitalism. It ignores the institutional racism that makes sure the poor remain poor.

"The most published and publicized blacks on the American public scene today are well-dressed, comfortably educated, sagaciously articulate, avowedly New Age, and resolutely middle class," Baker wrote. "The evolution of their relationship to the black majority during the past three decades can be summed up in a single word: good-bye!"[12]

"Things are deteriorating," Jones said of the inner city:

There are no natural relationships because of the decentralization of the street gangs. You don't have a leadership structure that can be talked to by members of the community to bring peace. You have basically guerrilla warfare going on in the inner city of Chicago. There is no structure or hierarchy where you can go talk to one person in the neighborhood that can then go down the pecking order to bring peace. You have different groups that have different motivations, and that factionalism is at the base of the violence. But there is no alternative when you don't have jobs, when you have an educational system that has failed and bad home environments.

Jones said Obama's silence was illustrated during a recent fund-raising trip to Chicago. The president called Chicago White Sox pitcher Mark Buehrle to congratulate him for pitching a perfect game. Obama made no comment, however, about the shooting of nine people in Chicago, including a nine-year-old girl, a few days earlier.

"When Barack Obama does not speak to these issues, it is almost a double devastation to a certain degree," Jones said. "It is different if President Bush doesn't say anything or Bill Clinton doesn't say anything. But when Barack Obama can't say the obvious, it does a double devastation to those young men who wanted to hope and wanted to believe in the system to redress these issues."

August Wilson wrote his last play, *Radio Golf*, about the black elite that sold out the African American community in exchange for personal power and wealth. He portrayed them as tools and puppets of the white mainstream. It was the final salvo from one of the country's most courageous playwrights on behalf of the forgotten. The show, despite being named best American play by the New York Drama Critics' Circle and earning a Tony nomination for best play, was one of the least attended shows on Broadway and closed after less than two months. There are African American leaders and writers with Wilson's integrity who have refused to accommodate an economic and political system that increasingly punishes the poor, especially the poor of color, but you do not see them on CNN or writing op-ed pieces in the *New York Times*. Dick Gregory, James Cone of Union Theological Seminary, Thulani Davis, Komunyakaa, Angela Davis, Baker, and Ishmael Reed still harbor the radical fire of our greatest civil-rights leaders.

And, of course, there is Harry Belafonte, whose invitation to speak at the funeral of Coretta Scott King was withdrawn so President George W. Bush, whom Belafonte had called a "terrorist," would not be offended when he spoke there. This last slight illustrates how craven many in the black elite, including some of King's children, have become and how hard it is to hear the anguished cries of those being beaten down in the age of Obama.

Courtiers come in different colors in America, but their function is the same. They are hedonists of power. They are invited into the inner circles of the elite, including the White House and Harvard University, as long as they faithfully serve the system. They are offered comfort and privilege, but they pay with their souls.

"Loose and easy language about equality, resonant resolutions about brotherhood fall pleasantly on the ear," Martin Luther King Jr. once said, "but for the Negro, there is a credibility gap he cannot overlook. He remembers that with each modest advance, the white population promptly raises the argument that the Negro has come far enough. Each step forward accents an ever-present tendency to backlash."[13]

Nader Was Right: Liberals Are Going Nowhere With Obama

AUGUST 10, 2009

The American empire has not altered under Barack Obama. It kills as brutally and indiscriminately in Iraq, Afghanistan, and Pakistan as it did under George W. Bush. It steals from the U.S. Treasury to enrich the corporate elite as rapaciously. It will not give us universal health care, abolish the Bush secrecy laws, end torture or "extraordinary rendition," restore habeas corpus, or halt the warrantless wiretapping and monitoring of citizens. It will not push through significant environmental reform, regulate Wall Street, or end our relationship with private contractors that provide mercenary armies to fight our imperial wars and produce useless and costly weapons systems.

The sad reality is that all the well-meaning groups and individuals who challenge our permanent war economy and the doctrine of pre-emptive war, who care about sustainable energy, fight for civil liberties, and want corporate malfeasance to end, were once again suckered by the Democratic Party. They were had. It is not a new story. The Democrats have been doing this to us since Bill Clinton. It is the same old merry-go-round, only with Obama branding. And if we have not learned by now that the system is broken, that as citizens we do not matter to our political elite, or that we live in a corporate state where our welfare and our interests are irrelevant, we are in serious trouble. Our last hope is to step outside of the two-party system and build movements that defy the Democrats and the Republicans. If we fail to do this, we will continue to undergo a slow-motion corporate coup d'état that will end in feudalism.

We owe Ralph Nader, Cynthia McKinney, and the Green Party an apology. They were right. If a few million of us had had the temerity to stand behind our ideals rather than our illusions and the empty slogans peddled by the Obama campaign, we would have a platform. We forgot that social reform never comes from accommodating the power structure but from frightening it. The Liberty Party that fought slavery, the suffragists who battled for women's rights, the labor movement, and the civil-rights movement knew that the question was not how we get good people to rule—those attracted to power tend to be venal mediocrities—but how we limit the damage the powerful do to us. These mass movements were the engines for social reform, the correctives to our democracy, and the true protectors of the rights of citizens. We have surrendered this power. It is vital to reclaim it. Where is the foreclosure movement? Where is the robust universal health-care or antiwar movement? Where is the militant movement for sustainable energy?

"Something is broken," Nader said when I reached him at his family home in Connecticut:

> We are not at the Bangladesh level in terms of passivity, but we are getting there. No one sees anything changing. There is no new political party to give people a choice. The progressive forces have no hammer. When they abandoned our campaign, they told the Democrats we have nowhere to go and will take whatever you give us. The Democrats are under no heat in the electoral arena from the Left.

"There comes a point when the public imbibes the ultimatum of the plutocracy," Nader said when asked about public apathy. "They have bought into the belief that if it protests, it will be brutalized by the police. If they have Muslim names, they will be subjected to Patriot Act treatment. This has scared the hell out of the underclass. They will be called terrorists."

"This is the third television generation," Nader said. "They have grown up watching screens. They have not gone to rallies. Those are history now. They hear their parents and grandparents talk about marches and rallies. They have little toys and gizmos that they hold in their hands. They have no idea of any public protest or activity. It is a tapestry of passivity.

"They have been broken," Nader said of the working class:

How many times have their employers threatened them with going abroad? How many times have they threatened the workers with outsourcing? The polls on job insecurity are record-high by those who have employment. And the liberal intelligentsia have failed them. They [the intellectuals] have bought into carping and making lecture fees as the senior fellow at the institute of so-and-so. Look at the top fifty intelligentsia—not one of them supported our campaign, not one of them has urged for street action and marches.

Our task is to build movements that can act as a counterweight to the corporate rape of America. We must opt out of the mainstream. We must articulate and stand behind a viable and uncompromising socialism, one that is firmly and unequivocally on the side of working men and women. We must give up the self-delusion that we can influence the power elite from the inside. We must become as militant as those who are seeking our enslavement. If we remain passive as we undergo the largest transference of wealth upward in American history, our open society will die. The working class is being plunged into desperation that will soon rival the misery endured by the working classes in China and India. And the Democratic Party, including Obama, is a willing accomplice.

"Obama is squandering his positive response around the world," Nader said. "In terms of foreign and military policy, it is a distinct continuity with Bush. Iraq, Afghanistan, the militarization of foreign policy, the continued expansion of the Pentagon budget, and pursuing more globalized trade agreements are the same."

This is an assessment neoconservatives now gleefully share. Eliot A. Cohen, writing in the *Wall Street Journal*, made the same pronouncement. "Mostly . . . the underlying structure of the policy remains the same," Cohen wrote in an August 2, 2009, opinion piece titled "What's Different About the Obama Foreign Policy?"

Nor should this surprise us: The United States has interests dictated by its physical location, its economy, its alliances, and above all, its values. Naïve realists, a large tribe, fail to understand that ideals will inevitably guide American foreign policy, even if they do not always determine it. Moreover, because the Obama foreign and defense policy senior team consists of centrist experts from the Democratic Party, it is unlikely to make radically different judgments about the world, and about American interests in it, than its predecessors.[14]

Nader said that Obama should gradually steer the country away from imperial and corporate tyranny. "You don't just put out policy statements of congeniality, but statements of gradual redirection," he said:

You incorporate in that statement not just demilitarization, not just ascension of smart diplomacy, but the enlargement of the U.S. as a humanitarian superpower, and cut out these Soviet-era weapons systems and start rapid response for disasters like earthquakes and tsunamis. You expand infectious disease programs, which the [United Nations] says can be done for $50 billion a year in Third-World countries on nutrition, minimal health care, and minimal shelter.

Obama has expanded the assistance to our class of Wall Street extortionists through subsidies, loan guarantees, and backup declarations to financial conglomerates such as Citigroup. His stimulus package does not address the crisis in our public works infrastructure; instead, it doles out funds to Medicaid and unemployment compensation. There will be no huge public works program to remodel the country. The president refuses to acknowledge the obvious: We can no longer afford our empire.

"Obama could raise a call to 'Come home, America, from the military budget abroad,'" Nader suggested. "He could create a new constituency that does not exist because everything is so fragmented, scattered, haphazard, and slapdash with the stimulus. He could get the local labor unions, the local Chambers of Commerce, and the mayors to say, 'The more we cut the military budget, the more you get in terms of public works.'"

Administration leaders "don't see the distinction between public power and corporate power," Nader said. "This is their time in history to reassert public values represented by workers, consumers, taxpayers, and communities. They are creating a jobless recovery, the worst of the worst, with the clear specter of inflation on the horizon. We are heading for deep water."

Massive borrowing acts as an anesthetic. It prevents us from facing the new limitations we must learn to cope with domestically and abroad. It allows us to live in the illusion that we are not in a state of irrevocable crisis, that our decline is not real, and that catastrophe has been averted. But running up the national debt can work only so long.

"No one can predict the future," Nader added hopefully. "No one knows the variables. No one predicted the move on tobacco. No one predicted gay rights. No one predicted the Berkeley student rebellion. The students were supine. You never know what will light the fire. You have to keep the pressure on. I know only one thing for sure: The whole liberal-progressive constituency is going nowhere."

This Isn't Reform, It's Robbery

AUGUST 24, 2009

> Percentage change since 2002 in average premiums paid to large US health-insurance companies: +87%
>
> Percentage change in the profits of the top ten insurance companies: +428%
>
> Chances that an American bankrupted by medical bills has health insurance: 7 in 10
>
> —HARPER'S INDEX, SEPTEMBER 2009

Capitalists, as my friend Father Michael Doyle says, should never be allowed near a health-care system. They hold sick children hostage as they force parents to bankrupt themselves in the desperate scramble to pay for medical care. The sick do not have a choice. Medical care is not a consumable good. We can choose to buy a used car or a new car, shop at a boutique or a thrift store, but there is no choice between illness and health. And any debate about health care must acknowledge that the for-profit health-care industry is the problem and must be destroyed. This is an industry that hires doctors and analysts to deny care to patients in order to increase profits. It is an industry that causes half of all bankruptcies. And the twenty thousand Americans who died last year because they did not receive adequate care condemn these corporations as complicit in murder.

The current health-care debate in Congress has nothing to do with death panels or public options or socialized medicine. The real debate, the only one that counts, is how much money our blood-sucking insurance, pharmaceutical, and for-profit health services are going to be able to siphon off from new health-care legislation. The proposed plans rattling around Congress all ensure that the profits for these corporations will increase and the misery for ordinary Americans will be compounded. The corporate state, enabled by both Democrats and Republicans, is yet again cannibalizing the Treasury. It is yet again pushing Americans, especially the poor and the working class, into levels of despair and rage that will continue to fuel the violent, proto-fascist movements leaping up around the edges of American society. And the traditional watchdogs—those in public office, the press and citizens groups—are as useless as the perfumed fops of another era who busied their days with court intrigue at Versailles. Canada never looked so good.

The Democrats are collaborating with lobbyists for the insurance industry, the pharmaceutical industry, and for-profit health-care providers to craft the current health-care reform legislation. "Corporate and industry players are inside the tent this time," says David Merritt, project director at Newt Gingrich's Center for Health Transformation, "so there is a vacuum on the outside." And these lobbyists have already killed a viable public option and made sure nothing in the bills will impede their growing profits and capacity for abuse.

"It will basically be a government law that says you have to buy their defective product," says Dr. David Himmelstein, a professor at Harvard Medical School and a founder of Physicians for a National Health Plan. "Next the government will tell us a Pinto in every garage, a lead-coated toy to every child, and melamine-laced Puppy Chow for every dog."

"Health insurance is not a race to the top; it is a race to the bottom," he told me from Cambridge, Massachusetts:

The way you make money is by abusing people. And if a public-option plan is not ready and willing to abuse patients, it is stuck with the expensive patients. The premiums will go up until it is noncompetitive. The conditions that have now been set for the plans include a hobbled public option. Under the best-case scenario, there will be tens of millions [who] will remain uninsured at the outset, and the number will climb as more and more people are priced out of the insurance market.

The inclusion of these corporations in the crafting of health-care legislation has not stopped figures like Rick Scott, the former head of the Columbia/HCA health-care company, from attempting to sabotage any plan. Scott's company was forced to pay a $1.7 billion fraud settlement—the largest health-care fraud settlement in U.S. history—for stealing hundreds of millions from taxpayers by overbilling for medical care. Scott, who made his money primarily from Medicare, is now saturating the airwaves in a reputed $20 million ad campaign that is stoking the anger and fear of many Americans. His ads are coordinated by CRC Public Relations, the group that masterminded the "swift boat" attacks against 2004 Democratic presidential candidate Senator John Kerry.

"They are using our money to campaign against us," Himmelstein told me:

> The money for these commercials came from health-care interests that collect fees from American patients. We experienced this before in Massachusetts. We ran a ballot initiative for universal health care in 2000, and the insurance industry spent $5 million on it, including the insurance company I am insured by. They used my premiums to smear an idea that seventy percent in Massachusetts, according to polls, favored before this smear campaign. Universal health care was narrowly defeated.

The bills now in Congress will, at best, impose on the country the failed model in Massachusetts. That model will demand that Americans buy health insurance from private insurers. There will be some subsidies for the very poor, but not for anyone above a modest income. Insurers will be allowed to continue to jack up premiums, including for the elderly. Bankruptcies due to medical bills and swelling premiums will mount along with rising deductibles and co-payments. Health care will be beyond the reach of many families. In Massachusetts, one in six people who have mandated insurance still say they cannot afford care, and thirty thousand people were evicted from the state program this month because of budget cuts. Expect the same debacle nationwide.

"For someone my age who is making $40,000 a year, you are required to lay out $5,000 for an insurance premium for coverage that covers nothing until you have spent $2,000 out of pocket," Himmelstein said. "You are $7,000 out of pocket before you have any coverage at all. For most people, that means you are already bankrupt before you have insurance. If anything, that has made them worse off. Instead of having that $5,000 to cover some of their medical expenses, they have laid it out in premiums."

The United States spends twice as much as other industrialized nations on health care—$7,129 per capita—although 45.7 million Americans remain without health coverage and millions more are inadequately covered. Fourteen thousand Americans now lose their health care each day. A report in the journal *Health Affairs* estimates that, if the system is left unchanged, one of every five dollars spent by Americans in 2017 will go to health coverage.[15] Private insurance bureaucracy and paperwork consume nearly one-third, thirty-one percent, of every health-care dollar. Streamlining payment through a single nonprofit payer would save more than $400 billion per year, enough, Physicians for a National Health Plan points out, to provide comprehensive, high-quality coverage for all Americans. But the proposed America's Affordable Health Choices Act of 2009 (House Resolution 3200) will, rather than cut costs, add an estimated $239 billion over ten years to the federal deficit. This is very good for the corporations. It is very bad for us.

The lobbyists have, as they did with the obscene bailouts for banks and investment firms, hijacked legislation in order to fleece the citizen. The five largest private health insurers and their trade group, America's Health Insurance Plans, spent more than $6 million on lobbying in the first quarter of 2009. Pfizer, the world's biggest drug maker, spent more than $9 million during the last quarter of 2008 and the first three months of this year. The *Washington Post* reported that up to thirty members of Congress from both parties who hold key committee memberships have major investments in health-care companies totaling between $11 million and $27 million.[16] President Barack Obama's director of health care policy, who will not discuss single-payer as an option, has served on the boards of several health care corporations.

Obama and the congressional leadership have shut out advocates of single-payer. The media, including papers such as the *New York Times*, treats single-payer as a fringe movement. The television networks rarely mention it. And yet between 45 and 60 percent of doctors favor single-payer. Between 40 and 62 percent of the American people, including 80 percent of registered Democrats, want universal, single-payer, not-for-profit health care for all Americans. The ability of the corporations to discredit and silence voices that represent at least half of the population is another sad testament to the power of our corporate state.

"We are considering a variety of striking efforts for early in the fall," Himmelstein said, "including protests outside state capitols by doctors around the country, video links of conferences in seventy or eighty cities around the country, with protests and potential doctors chaining themselves to the fence of the White House."

Make sure you join them.

Go to Pittsburgh, Young Man, and Defy Your Empire

AUGUST 31, 2009

Globalization and unfettered capitalism have been swept into the history books along with the open-market theory of the 1920s, the experiments of fascism and communism, and the New Deal. It is time for a new economic and political paradigm. It is time for a new language to address our reality. The voices of change, those who speak in powerful and yet unfamiliar words, will cry out on September 25 and 26 in Pittsburgh, when protesters from around the country gather to defy the heads of state, bankers, and finance ministers from the world's twenty-two largest economies who are convening for a meeting of the G-20. If we heed these dissident voices we have a future. If we do not we will commit collective suicide.

The international power elites will go to Pittsburgh to preach the mantra that globalization is inevitable and eternal. They will discuss a corpse as if it were living. They will urge us to remain in suspended animation and place our trust in the inept bankers and politicians who orchestrated the crisis. This is the usual tactic of bankrupt elites clinging to power. They denigrate and push to the margins the realists—none of whom will be inside their security perimeters—who give words to our disintegration and demand a new, unfamiliar course. The powerful discredit dissent and protest. But human history, as Erich Fromm wrote, always begins anew with disobedience.[17] This disobedience is the first step toward freedom. It makes possible the recovery of reason.

The longer we speak in the language of global capitalism, the longer we utter platitudes about the free market—even as we funnel hundreds of billions of taxpayer dollars into the accounts of large corporations—the longer we live in a state of collective self-delusion. Our power elite, who profess to hate government and government involvement in the free market, who claim they are the defenders of competition and individualism, have been stealing hundreds of billions of dollars of our money to nationalize mismanaged corporations and save them from bankruptcy. We hear angry and confused citizens, their minds warped by hate talk-radio and television, condemn socialized medicine although we have become, at least for corporations, the most socialized nation on Earth. The schizophrenia between what we profess and what we actually embrace has rendered us incapable of confronting reality. The longer we speak in the old language of markets, capitalism, free trade, and globalization, the longer the entities that created this collapse will cannibalize the nation.

What are we now? What do we believe? What economic model explains the irrationality of looting the U.S. Treasury to permit speculators at Goldman Sachs to make obscene profits? How can Barack Obama's chief economic adviser, Lawrence Summers, tout a "jobless recovery"? How much longer can we believe the fantasy that global markets will replace nation states and that economics will permit us to create a utopian world where we will all share the same happy goals? When will we denounce the lie that globalization fosters democracy, enlightenment, worldwide prosperity and stability? When we will we realize that unfettered global trade and corporate profit are the bitter enemies of freedom and the common good?

Corporations are pushing through legislation in the United States that will force us to buy defective, for-profit health insurance, a plan that will expand corporate monopolies and profits at our expense and leave tens of millions without adequate care. Corporations are blocking all attempts to move to renewable and sustainable energy to protect the staggering profits of the oil, natural gas, and coal industries. Corporations are plunging us deeper and deeper as a nation into debt to feed the permanent war economy and swell the military budget, which consumes half of all discretionary spending. Corporations use lobbyists and campaign contributions to maintain arcane tax codes that offer them tax havens and tax evasions. Corporations are draining the Treasury while the working class sheds jobs, sees homes foreclosed, and struggles to survive in a new and terrifying global serfdom. This has been the awful price of complacency.

Protests will begin several days before the summit. Many of the activities are being coordinated by Pittsburgh's Thomas Merton Center. There will be a march on September 25 for anyone who, as Jessica Benner of the center's Antiwar Committee stated, "has lost a job, a home, a loved one to war, lost value to a retirement plan, gotten sick from environmental pollution, or lived without adequate health care, water, or food." There will be at least three tent cities, in addition to a Music Camp beginning September 18 that will be situated at the South Side Riverfront Park near 18th Street. Unemployed workers will set up one tent city at the Monumental Baptist Church on September 20, and five days later they will march on the Convention Center. The encampment and the march are being organized by the Bail Out the People Movement. The Institute for Policy Studies, the *Nation* magazine, the United Electrical, Radio and Machine Workers of America, Pittsburgh United, and other organizations will host events including a panel on corporate globalization featuring former World Bank President Joseph Stiglitz, along with a "People's Tribunal." There will be a religious procession calling for social justice and a concert organized by Students for a Democratic Society.

But expect difficulties. The Secret Service has so far denied protesters permits while it determines the size of the "security perimeter" it will impose around the world leaders. Pittsburgh has contracted to bring in an extra four thousand police officers at an estimated cost of $9.5 million. Activist groups have reported incidents of surveillance and harassment. The struggle to thwart the voices of citizens will be as fierce as the struggle to amplify the voices of the criminal class that is trashing the world's economy. These elites will appear from behind closed doors with their communiqués and resolutions to address us in their specialized jargon of power and expertise. They will attempt to convince us they have not lost control. Recommitments to free-trade agreements in the General Agreement on Tariffs and Trade (GATT) will come from the World Trade Organization and NAFTA, which have all thrust a knife into the backs of the working class. They will insist that the world can be managed and understood exclusively through their distorted lens of economics. But their day is over. They are the apostles of a dead system. They maintain power through fraud and force. Do not expect them to go without a struggle. But they have nothing left to say to us.

"Those who profess to favor freedom, yet deprecate agitation, are men who want crops without plowing up the ground," Frederick Douglass wrote:

> They want rain without thunder and lightning. They want the ocean without the awful roar of its many waters. This struggle may be a moral one; or it may be a physical one; or it may be both moral and physical; but it must be a struggle. Power concedes nothing without a demand. It never did and it never will.[18]

If you can, go to Pittsburgh. This is an opportunity to defy the titans of the corporate state and speak in words that describe our reality. The power elite fear these words. If these words seep into the population, if they become part of our common vernacular, the elite and the systems they defend will be unmasked. Our collective self-delusion will be shattered. These words of defiance expose the lies and crimes the elite use to barrel us toward neofeudalism. And these words, when they become real, propel men and women to resist.

"The end of something often resembles the beginning," the philosopher John Ralston Saul wrote in his book *Voltaire's Bastards*:

> More often than not our nose-to-the-glass view makes us believe that the end we are living is in fact a new beginning. This confusion is typical of an old civilization's self-confidence—limited by circumstances and by an absence of memory—and in many ways resembling the sort often produced by senility. Our rational need to control understanding and therefore memory has simply accentuated the confusion. . . . Nothing seems more permanent than a long-established government about to lose power, nothing more invincible than a grand army on the morning of its annihilation.[19]

Food Is Power, and the Powerful Are Poisoning Us

SEPTEMBER 7, 2009

Our most potent political weapon is food. If we take back our agriculture, if we buy and raise produce locally, we can begin to break the grip of corporations that control a food system as fragile, unsafe, and destined for collapse as our financial system. If we continue to allow corporations to determine what we eat, as well as how food is harvested and distributed, then we will become captive to rising prices and shortages and increasingly dependent on cheap, mass-produced food filled with sugar and fat. Food, along with energy, will be the most pressing issue of our age. And if we do not build alternative food networks soon, the social and political ramifications of shortages and hunger will be devastating.

The effects of climate change, especially with widespread droughts in Australia, Africa, California and the Midwest, coupled with the rising cost of fossil fuels, have already blighted the environments of millions. The poor can often no longer afford a balanced diet. Global food prices have increased an average of forty-three percent since 2007, according to the International Monetary Fund. These increases have been horrific for the approximately one billion people—one-sixth of the world's population—who subsist on less than a dollar per day. And 162 million of these people survive on less than fifty cents per day. The global poor spend as much as sixty percent of their income on food, according to the International Food Policy Research Institute.

There have been food riots in many parts of the world, including Austria, Hungary, Mexico, Namibia, Zimbabwe, Morocco, Yemen,

Mauritania, Senegal, and Uzbekistan. Russia and Pakistan have introduced food rationing. Pakistani troops guard imported wheat. India has banned the export of rice, except for high-end basmati. And the shortages and price increases are being felt in the industrialized world as we continue to shed hundreds of thousands of jobs and food prices climb. There are 33.2 million Americans, or one in nine, who depend on food stamps. And in twenty states as many as one in eight are on the food stamp program, according to the Food Research Center. The average monthly benefit was $113.87 per person, leaving many, even with government assistance, without adequate food. The USDA says 36.2 million Americans, or eleven percent of households, struggle to get enough food, and one-third of them sometimes have to skip or cut back on meals. Congress allocated some $54 billion for food stamps this fiscal year, up from $39 billion last year. In the new fiscal year beginning October 1, costs will be $60 billion, according to estimates.

Food shortages have been tinder for social upheaval throughout history. But this time around, because we have lost the skills to feed and clothe ourselves, it will be much harder for most of us to become self-sustaining. The large agribusinesses have largely wiped out small farmers. They have poisoned our soil with pesticides and contaminated animals in filthy and overcrowded stockyards with high doses of antibiotics and steroids. They have pumped nutrients and phosphorus into water systems, causing algae bloom and fish die-off in our rivers and streams. Crop yields, under the onslaught of changing weather patterns and chemical pollution, are declining in the Northeast, where a blight has nearly wiped out the tomato crop. The draconian Food Modernization Safety Act, another gift from our governing elite to corporations, means small farms will only continue to dwindle in number. Web sites such as La Via Campesina do a good job of tracking these disturbing global trends.

"The entire economy built around food is unsafe and unethical," activist Henry Harris of the Food Security Roundtable told me. The group builds distribution systems between independent farmers and city residents.

"Food is the greatest place for communities to start taking back power," he said. "The national food system is collapsing by degrees.

More than fifty percent of what we eat comes from the Central Valley of California. What happens when gasoline becomes $5 a gallon or drought sweeps across the cropland? The monolithic system of food production is highly unstable. It has to be replaced very soon with small, diverse sources that provide greater food security."

Cornell University recently did a study to determine whether New York State could feed itself. The research is described in two articles published in 2006 and 2008 by the journal *Renewable Agriculture and Food Systems*.[20] If all agricultural land were in use, and food distribution were optimized to minimize the total distance that food travels, New York state could, the researchers found, have thirty-four percent of its food needs met from within its boundaries. This is not encouraging news to those who live in New York City. New York once relied on New Jersey, still known as the Garden State, instead of having food shipped from across the country. But New Jersey farms have largely given way to soulless housing developments. Farming communities upstate, their downtowns boarded up and desolate, have been gutted by industrial farming.

The ties most Americans had to rural communities during the Great Depression kept many alive. A barter economy replaced the formal economy. Families could grow food or had relatives to feed them. But in a world where we do not know where our food comes from, or how to produce it, we have become vulnerable. And many will be forced, as food prices continue to rise, to shift to a diet of cheap, fatty, mass-produced foods, already a staple of the nation's poor. Junk food, a major factor in obesity, diabetes, and heart disease, is often the only food those in the inner city can buy because supermarkets and nutritious food are geographically and financially beyond reach. As the economy continues to deteriorate, the middle class will soon join them.

"And it is clear to anyone who looks carefully at any crowd that we are wasting our bodies exactly as we are wasting our land," Wendell Berry observed in *The Unsettling of America*:

> Our bodies are fat, weak, joyless, sickly, ugly, the virtual prey of the manufacturers of medicine and cosmetics. Our bodies have become marginal; they are growing useless like our "marginal land" because we have less and less use for them. After the games and idle flour-

ishes of modern youth, we use them only as shipping cartons to transport our brains and our few employable muscles back and forth to work.[21]

Berry, who lives on a farm in Kentucky where his family has farmed for generations, argues that local farming is fundamental to sustaining communities. Industrial farming, he says, has estranged us from the land. It has rendered us powerless to provide for ourselves. It has left us complicit in the corporate destruction of the ecosystem. Its moral cost, Berry argues, has been as devastating as its physical cost.

"The people will eat what the corporations decide for them to eat," writes Berry:

> They will be detached and remote from the sources of their life, joined to them only by corporate tolerance. They will have become consumers purely—consumptive machines—which is to say, the slaves of producers. What . . . model farms very powerfully suggest, then, is that the concept of total control may be impossible to confine within the boundaries of the specialist enterprise—that it is impossible to mechanize production without mechanizing consumption, impossible to make machines of soil, plants, and animals without making machines also of people.[22]

The nascent effort by communities to reclaim local food production is the first step toward reclaiming lives severed and fragmented by corporate culture. It is more than a return to local food production. It is a return to community. It brings us back to the values that sustain community. It is a return to the recognition of the fragility, interconnectedness, and sacredness of all living systems and our dependence on each other. It turns back to an ethic that can save us.

"[The commercial] revolution . . . ," writes Berry, "did not stop with the subjugation of the Indians, but went on to impose substantially the same catastrophe upon the small farms and the farm communities, upon the shops of small local tradesmen of all sorts, upon the workshops of independent craftsmen, and upon the households of citizens":

It is a revolution that is still going on. The economy is still substantially that of the fur trade, still based on the same general kinds of commercial items: technology, weapons, ornaments, novelties, and drugs. The one great difference is that by now the revolution has deprived the mass of consumers of any independent access to the staples of life: clothing, shelter, food, even water. Air remains the only necessity that the average user can still get for himself, and the revolution has imposed a heavy tax on that by way of pollution. Commercial conquest is far more thorough and final than military defeat.

"The inevitable result of such an economy," Berry adds, "is that no farm or any other usable property can safely be regarded by anyone as a home, no home is ultimately worthy of our loyalty, nothing is ultimately worth doing, and no place or task or person is worth a lifetime's devotion. 'Waste,' in such an economy, must eventually include several categories of humans—the unborn, the old, 'disinvested' farmers, the unemployed, the 'unemployable.' Indeed, once our homeland, our source, is regarded as a resource, we are all sliding downward toward the ash heap or the dump."[23]

Liberals Are Useless

DECEMBER 7, 2009

Liberals are a useless lot. They talk about peace and do nothing to challenge our permanent war economy. They claim to support the working class, and vote for candidates that glibly defend the North American Free Trade Agreement. They insist they believe in welfare, the right to organize, universal health care, and a host of other socially progressive causes, and will not risk stepping out of the mainstream to fight for them. The only talent they seem to possess is the ability to write abject, cloying letters to Barack Obama—as if he reads them—asking the president to come back to his "true" self. This sterile moral posturing, which is not only useless but also humiliating, has made America's liberal class an object of public derision.

I am not disappointed in Obama. I don't feel betrayed. I don't wonder when he is going to be Obama. I did not vote for the man. I vote socialist, which in my case meant Ralph Nader, but could have meant Cynthia McKinney. How can an organization with the oxymoronic title Progressives for Obama even exist? Liberal groups like these make political satire obsolete. Obama was and is a brand. He is a product of the Chicago political machine. He has been skillfully packaged as the new face of the corporate state. I don't dislike Obama—I would much rather listen to him than his smug and venal predecessor—though I expected nothing but a continuation of the corporate rape of the country. And that is what he has delivered.

"You have a tug of war with one side pulling," Ralph Nader told me when we met on a recent afternoon:

The corporate interests pull on the Democratic Party the way they pull on the Republican Party. If you are a "least-worst" voter you don't want to disturb John Kerry on the war, so you call off the antiwar demonstrations in 2004. You don't want to disturb Obama because McCain is worse. And every four years both parties get worse. There is no pull. That is the dilemma of the *Nation* and the *Progressive* and other similar publications. There is no breaking point. What is the breaking point? The criminal war of aggression in Iraq? The escalation of the war in Afghanistan? Forty-five thousand people dying a year because they can't afford health insurance? The hollowing out of communities and sending the jobs to fascist and communist regimes overseas that know how to put the workers in their place? There is no breaking point. And when there is no breaking point you do not have a moral compass.

I save my anger for our bankrupt liberal intelligentsia, of which, sadly, I guess I am a member. Liberals are the defeated, self-absorbed Mouse Man in Dostoevsky's *Notes From Underground*. They embrace cynicism, a cloak for their cowardice and impotence. They, like Dostoevsky's depraved character, have come to believe that the "conscious inertia" of the underground surpasses all other forms of existence. They too use inaction and empty moral posturing, not to effect change but rather to engage in an orgy of self-adulation and self-pity. They too refuse to act or engage with anyone not cowering in the underground. This choice does not satisfy the Mouse Man, as it does not satisfy our liberal class, but neither has the strength to change. The gravest danger we face as a nation is not from the far Right, although it may well inherit power, but from a bankrupt liberal class that has lost the will to fight and the moral courage to stand up for what it espouses.

Anyone who says he or she cares about the working class in this country should have walked out on the Democratic Party in 1994 with the passage of NAFTA. And it has been only downhill since. If welfare reform, the 1999 Financial Services Modernization Act, which gutted the 1933 Glass-Steagall Act—designed to prevent the kind of banking crisis we are now undergoing—and the craven decision by the Democratic Congress to continue to fund and expand our imperial wars were not enough to make you revolt, how about the refusal to restore habeas corpus, end torture in our offshore penal colonies, abolish George W.

Bush's secrecy laws, or halt the warrantless wiretapping and monitoring of American citizens? The imperial projects and the corporate state have not altered under Obama. The state kills as ruthlessly and indiscriminately in Iraq, Afghanistan, and Pakistan as it did under Bush. It, too, bows before the conservative Israel lobby, refuses to enact serious environmental or health-care reform, regulate Wall Street, end our relationship with private mercenary contractors, or stop handing obscene sums of money, some $1 trillion a year, to the military and arms industry. At what point do we stop being a doormat? At what point do we fight back? We may lose if we step outside the mainstream, but at least we will salvage our self-esteem and integrity.

I learned to dislike liberals when I lived in Roxbury, the inner city in Boston, as a seminary student at Harvard Divinity School. I commuted into Cambridge to hear professors and students talk about empowering people they never met. It was the time of the leftist Sandinista government in Nicaragua. Spending two weeks picking coffee in that country and then coming back and talking about it for the rest of the semester was the best way to "credentialize" yourself as a revolutionary. But few of these "revolutionaries" found the time to spend twenty minutes on the Green Line to see where human beings in their own city were being warehoused little better than animals. They liked the poor, but they did not like the smell of the poor. It was a lesson I never forgot.

I was also at the time a member of the Greater Boston YMCA boxing team. We fought on Saturday nights for $25 in arenas in working-class neighborhoods like Charlestown. My closest friends were construction workers and pot washers. They worked hard. They believed in unions. They wanted a better life, which few of them ever got. We used to run five miles after our nightly training, passing through the Mission Main and Mission Extension Housing Projects, and they would joke, "I hope we get mugged." They knew precisely what to do with people who abused them. They may not have been liberal, they may not have finished high school, but they were far more grounded than most of those I studied with across the Charles River. They would have felt awkward, and would have been made to feel awkward, at the little gatherings of progressive and liberal intellectuals at Harvard, but you could trust and rely on them.

I went on to spend two decades as a war correspondent. The qualities inherent in good soldiers or Marines, like the qualities I found among those boxers, are qualities I admire—self-sacrifice, courage, the ability to make decisions under stress, the capacity to endure physical discomfort, and a fierce loyalty to those around you, even if it puts you in greater danger. If liberals had even a bit of their fortitude, we could have avoided this mess. But they don't. So here we are again, begging Obama to be Obama. He is Obama. Obama is not the problem. We are.

The Creed of Objectivity
Killed the News

FEBRUARY 1, 2010

Reporters who witness the worst of human suffering and return to newsrooms angry see their compassion washed out or severely muted by the layers of editors who stand between the reporter and the reader. The creed of objectivity and balance, formulated at the beginning of the nineteenth century by newspaper owners to generate greater profits from advertisers, disarms and cripples the press.

And the creed of objectivity becomes a convenient and profitable vehicle with which to avoid confronting unpleasant truths or angering a power structure on which news organizations depend for access and profits. This creed transforms reporters into neutral observers or voyeurs. It banishes empathy, passion, and a quest for justice. Reporters are permitted to watch but not to feel or to speak in their own voices. They function as "professionals" and see themselves as dispassionate and disinterested social scientists. This vaunted lack of bias, enforced by bloodless hierarchies of bureaucrats, is the disease of American journalism.

"The very notion that on any given story all you have to do is report what both sides say and you've done a fine job of objective journalism debilitates the press," the late columnist Molly Ivins once wrote:

> There is no such thing as objectivity, and the truth, that slippery little bugger, has the oddest habit of being way to hell off on one side or the other: it seldom nestles neatly halfway between any two opposing points of view. The smug complacency of much of the

press—I have heard many an editor say, "Well, we're being attacked by both sides so we must be right"—stems from the curious notion that if you get a quote from both sides, preferably in an official position, you've done the job. In the first place, most stories aren't two-sided, they're 17-sided at least. In the second place, it's of no help to either the readers or the truth to quote one side saying, "Cat," and the other side saying "Dog," while the truth is there's an elephant crashing around out there in the bushes.[24]

Ivins went on to write that "the press's most serious failures are not its sins of commission, but its sins of omission—the stories we miss, the stories we don't see, the stories that don't hold press conferences, the stories that don't come from 'reliable sources.'"[25]

This abject moral failing has left the growing numbers of Americans shunted aside by our corporate state without a voice. It has also, with the rise of a ruthless American oligarchy, left the traditional press on the wrong side of our growing class divide. The elitism, distrust and lack of credibility of the media—and here I speak of the dwindling institutions that attempt to report news—come directly from this steady and willful disintegration of the media's moral core.

This moral void has been effectively exploited by the twenty-four-hour cable news shows and trash talk-radio programs. The failure of the fact-based press to express empathy or outrage for our growing underclass has permitted the disastrous rise of "faith-based" reporting. The bloodless and soulless journalism of the traditional media has bolstered the popularity of partisan outlets that present a view of the world that often has no relation to the real, but responds very effectively to the emotional needs of viewers. Fox News is, in some sense, no more objective than the *New York Times*, but there is one crucial and vital difference. Fox News and most of the other cable outlets do not feel constrained by verifiable facts. Within the traditional news establishment, facts may have been self-selected or skillfully stage-managed by public relations specialists, but what was not verifiable was not publishable.

The cable news channels have cleverly seized on the creed of objectivity and redefined it in populist terms. They attack news based on verifiable fact for its liberal bias, for, in essence, failing to be objective, and promise a return to "genuine" objectivity. Fox's Bill O'Reilly argues, "If Fox News is a conservative channel—and I'm going to use the word *if*—so what? . . . You've got fifty other media that are blatantly left. Now, I don't think Fox is a conservative channel. I think it's a traditional channel. There's a difference. We are willing to hear points of view that you'll never hear on ABC, CBS or NBC."

O'Reilly is not wrong in suggesting that the objectivity of the traditional media has an inherent political bias. But it is a bias that caters to the power elite and it is a bias that is confined by fact. The traditional quest for "objectivity" is, as James Carey wrote, also based on an ethnocentric conceit: "It pretended to discover Universal Truth, to proclaim Universal Laws, and to describe a Universal Man. Upon inspection it appeared, however, that its Universal Man resembled a type found around Cambridge, Massachusetts, or Cambridge, England; its Universal Laws resembled those felt to be useful by Congress and Parliament; and its Universal Truth bore English and American accents."[26]

Objectivity creates the formula of quoting Establishment specialists or experts within the narrow confines of the power elite who debate policy nuance like medieval theologians. As long as one viewpoint is balanced by another, usually no more than what Sigmund Freud would term "the narcissism of minor difference," the job of a reporter is deemed complete. But this is more often a way to obscure rather than expose truth.

Reporting, while it is presented to the public as neutral, objective and unbiased, is always highly interpretive. It is defined by rigid stylistic parameters. I have written, like most other reporters, hundreds of news stories. Reporters begin with a collection of facts, statements, positions, and anecdotes and then select those that create the "balance" permitted by the formula of daily journalism. The closer reporters get to official sources, for example those covering Wall Street, Congress, the White House, or the State Department, the more constraints they endure. When reporting depends heavily on access, it becomes very difficult to challenge those who grant or deny that access. This craven desire for access has turned huge sections of the Washington media, along with most business reporters, into courtiers. The need to be included in news briefings and background interviews with government or business officials, as well as the desire for leaks and early access to official documents, obliterates journalistic autonomy.

"Record the fury of a Palestinian whose land has been taken from him by Israeli settlers—but always refer to Israel's 'security needs' and its 'war on terror,'" Robert Fisk writes:

> If Americans are accused of "torture," call it "abuse." If Israel assassinates a Palestinian, call it a "targeted killing." If Armenians lament their Holocaust of 1,500,000 souls in 1915, remind readers that Turkey denies this all too real and fully documented genocide. If Iraq has become a hell on earth for its people, recall how awful Saddam was. If a dictator is on our side, call him a "strongman." If he's our enemy, call him a tyrant, or part of the "axis of evil." And above all else, use the word *terrorist*. Terror, terror, terror, terror, terror, terror, terror. Seven days a week.[27]

"Ask 'how' and 'who'—but not 'why,'" Fisk adds:

> Source everything to officials: "American officials," "intelligence officials," "official sources," anonymous policemen, or Army officers. And if these institutions charged with our protection abuse their power, then remind readers and listeners and viewers of the dangerous age in which we now live, the age of terror—which means that we must live in the Age of the Warrior, someone whose business and profession and vocation and mere existence is to destroy our enemies.[28]

"In the classic example, a refugee from Nazi Germany who appears on television saying monstrous things are happening in his homeland must be followed by a Nazi spokesman saying Adolf Hitler is the greatest boon to humanity since pasteurized milk," the former *New York Times* columnist Russell Baker wrote:

> Real objectivity would require not only hard work by news people to determine which report was accurate, but also a willingness to put up with the abuse certain to follow publication of an objectively

formed judgment. To escape the hard work or the abuse, if one man says Hitler is an ogre, we instantly give you another to say Hitler is a prince. A man says the rockets won't work? We give you another who says they will. The public may not learn much about these fairly sensitive matters, but neither does it get another excuse to denounce the media for unfairness and lack of objectivity. In brief, society is teeming with people who become furious if told what the score is.[29]

Journalists, because of their training and distaste for shattering their own exalted notion of themselves, lack the inclination and vocabulary to discuss ethics. They will, when pressed, mumble something about telling the truth and serving the public. They prefer not to face the fact that my truth is not your truth. News is a signal, a "blip," an alarm that something is happening beyond our small circle of existence, as Walter Lippmann noted in his book *Public Opinion*. Journalism does not point us toward truth, since, as Lippmann understood, there is always a vast divide between truth and news. Ethical questions open journalism to the nebulous world of interpretation and philosophy, and for this reason journalists flee from ethical inquiry like a herd of frightened sheep.

Journalists, while they like to promote the image of themselves as fierce individualists, are in the end another species of corporate employees. They claim as their clients an amorphous public. They seek their moral justification in the service of this nameless, faceless mass and speak little about the vast influence of the power elite to shape and determine reporting. Does a public even exist in a society as fragmented and divided as ours? Or is the public, as Walter Lippmann wrote, now so deeply uninformed and divorced from the inner workings of power and diplomacy as to make it a clean slate on which our armies of skilled propagandists can, often through the media, leave a message?

The symbiotic relationship between the media and the power elite worked for nearly a century. It worked as long as our power elite, no matter how ruthless or insensitive, was competent. But once our power elite became incompetent and morally bankrupt, the media, along with the power elite, lost their final vestige of credibility. The media became, as seen in the Iraq war and the aftermath of the financial upheavals, a class of courtiers. The media, which has always written and spoken from presuppositions and principles that reflect the elite consensus, now peddle a consensus that is flagrantly artificial. Our elite oversaw the dismantling of the country's manufacturing base and the betrayal of the working class with the passage of NAFTA, and the media dutifully trumpeted this as a form of growth. Our elite deregulated the banking industry, leading to nationwide bank collapses, and the media extolled the value of the free market. Our elite corrupted the levers of power to advance the interests of corporations, and the media naively conflated freedom with the free market. This reporting may have been "objective" and "impartial," but it defied common sense. The harsh reality of shuttered former steel-producing towns and growing human misery should have, in the hands of any good cop reporter, exposed the fantasies. But the media long ago stopped thinking and lost nearly all its moral autonomy.

Real reporting, grounded in a commitment to justice and empathy, could have informed and empowered the public as we underwent a slow-motion corporate coup d'état. It could have stimulated a radical debate about structures, laws, privilege, power, and justice. But the traditional media, by clinging to an outdated etiquette designed to serve corrupt power structures, lost their social function. Corporations, which once made many of these news outlets very rich, have turned to more effective forms of advertising. Profits have plummeted. And yet these media courtiers, lost in the fantasy of their own righteousness and moral probity, cling to the hollow morality of "objectivity" with comic ferocity.

The world will not be a better place when these fact-based news organizations die. We will be propelled into a culture where facts and opinions will be interchangeable, where lies will become true, and where fantasy will be peddled as news. I will lament the loss of traditional news. It will unmoor us from reality. The tragedy is that the moral void of the news business contributed as much to its own annihilation as the protofascists who feed on its carcass.

Calling All Rebels

MARCH 8, 2010

There are no constraints left to halt America's slide into a totalitarian capitalism. Electoral politics are a sham. The media have been debased and defanged by corporate owners. The working class has been impoverished and is now being plunged into profound despair. The legal system has been corrupted to serve corporate interests. Popular institutions, from labor unions to political parties, have been destroyed or emasculated by corporate power. And any form of protest, no matter how tepid, is blocked by an internal security apparatus that is starting to rival that of the East German secret police. The mounting anger and hatred, coursing through the bloodstream of the body politic, make violence and counterviolence inevitable. Brace yourself. The American empire is over. And the descent is going to be horrifying.

Those singled out as internal enemies will include people of color, immigrants, gays, intellectuals, feminists, Jews, Muslims, union leaders, and those defined as "liberals." They will be condemned as anti-American and blamed for our decline. The economic collapse, which remains mysterious and enigmatic to most Americans, will be pinned by demagogues and hate-mongers on these hapless scapegoats. Random acts of violence, already leaping up around the fringes of American society, will justify harsh measures of internal control that will snuff out the final vestiges of our democracy. The corporate forces that destroyed the country will use the information systems they control to mask their culpability. The old game of blaming the weak and the marginal, a staple of despotic regimes, will empower the dark undercurrents of sadism and violence in American society and deflect attention from the corporate vampires who have drained the blood of the country.

"We are going to be poorer," David Cay Johnston told me. Johnston was the tax reporter of the *New York Times* for thirteen years and has written on how the corporate state rigged the system against us. His book *Free Lunch* concerns hidden subsidies, rigged markets, and corporate socialism. "Health care is going to eat up more and more of our income." He says,

> We are going to have less and less for other things. We are going to have some huge disasters sooner or later caused by our failure to invest. Dams and bridges will break. Buildings will collapse. There are water mains that are twenty-five to fifty feet wide. There will be huge infrastructure disasters. Our intellectual resources are in decline. We are failing to educate young people and instill in them rigor. We are going to continue to pour money into the military. I think it is possible, I do not say it is probable, that we will have a revolution, a civil war that will see the end of the United States of America.[30]

"If we see the end of this country, it will come from the right and our failure to provide people with the basic necessities of life," said Johnston:

> Revolutions occur when young men see the present as worse than the unknown future. We are not there. But it will not take a lot to get there. The politicians running for office who are denigrating the government, who are saying there are traitors in Congress, who say we do not need the IRS, this when no government in the history of the world has existed without a tax enforcement agency, are sowing the seeds for the destruction of the country. A lot of the people on the right hate the United States of America. They would say they hate the people they are arrayed against. But the whole idea of the United States is that we criticize the government. We remake it to serve our interests. They do not want that kind of society. They reject, as Aristotle said, the idea that democracy is to rule and to be ruled in turns. They see a world where they are right and that is it. If we do not want to do it their way, we should be vanquished. This is not the idea on which the United States was founded.[31]

It is hard to see how these events can be prevented. The engines of social reform are dead. Liberal apologists, who long ago should have abandoned the Democratic Party, continue to make pathetic appeals to a tone-deaf corporate state and Barack Obama while the working and middle class are ruthlessly stripped of rights, income, and jobs. Liberals self-righteously condemn imperial wars and Wall Street greed, but not the Democrats who are responsible. And the longer the liberal class dithers and speaks in the bloodless language of policies and programs, the more hated and irrelevant it becomes. No one has discredited American liberalism more than liberals themselves. And I do not hold out any hope for their reform. We have entered an age in which, as William Butler Yeats wrote, "the best lack all conviction and the worst / Are full of passionate intensity."[32]

"If we end up with violence in the streets on a large scale, not random riots, but insurrection and things break down, there will be a coup d'état from the right," Johnston said. "We have already had an economic coup d'état. It will not take much to go further."[33]

How do we resist? How, if this descent is inevitable, as I believe it is, do we fight back? Why should we resist at all? Why not give in to cynicism and despair? Why not carve out as comfortable a niche as possible within the embrace of the corporate state and spend our lives attempting to satiate our private needs? The power elite, including most of those who graduate from our top universities and our liberal and intellectual classes, have sold out for personal comfort. Why not us?

The French moral philosopher Albert Camus argued that we are separated from one another. Our lives are meaningless. We cannot influence fate. We will all die and our individual beings will be obliterated. And yet Camus wrote that "one of the only coherent philosophical positions is revolt. It is a constant confrontation between man and his obscurity. It is not aspiration, for it is devoid of hope. That revolt is the certainty of a crushing fate, without the resignation that ought to accompany it."[34]

"A living man can be enslaved and reduced to the historic condition of an object," Camus warned. "But if he dies in refusing to be enslaved, he reaffirms the existence of another kind of human nature which refuses to be classified as an object."[35]

The rebel, for Camus, stands with the oppressed—the unemployed workers thrust into impoverishment and misery by the corporate state, the Palestinians in Gaza, the civilians in Iraq and Afghanistan, the disappeared held in our global black sites, the poor in our inner cities and depressed rural communities, immigrants, and those locked away in our prison system. To stand with them does not mean to collaborate with parties, such as the Democrats, who can mouth the words of justice while carrying out acts of oppression. It means open and direct defiance.

The power structure and its liberal apologists dismiss the rebel as impractical and see the rebel's outsider stance as counterproductive. They condemn the rebel for expressing anger at injustice. The elites and their apologists call for calm and patience. They use the hypocritical language of spirituality, compromise, generosity, and compassion to argue that the only alternative is to accept and work with the systems of power. The rebel, however, is beholden to a moral commitment that makes it impossible to stand with the power elite. The rebel refuses to be bought off with foundation grants, invitations to the White House, television appearances, book contracts, academic appointments or empty rhetoric. The rebel is not concerned with self-promotion or public opinion. The rebel knows that, as Augustine wrote, hope has two beautiful daughters, anger and courage—anger at the way things are and the courage to see that they do not remain the way they are. The rebel is aware that virtue is not rewarded. The act of rebellion defines itself.

"You do not become a 'dissident' just because you decide one day to take up this most unusual career," Václav Havel said when he battled the communist regime in Czechoslovakia.

You are thrown into it by your personal sense of responsibility, combined with a complex set of external circumstances. You are cast out of the existing structures and placed in a position of conflict with them. It begins as an attempt to do your work well, and ends with being branded an enemy of society. . . . The dissident does not operate in the realm of genuine power at all. He is not seeking power. He has no desire for office and does not gather votes. He does not attempt to charm the public. He offers nothing and promises nothing. He can offer, if anything, only his own skin—and he offers it solely because he has no other way of affirming the truth he stands for. His actions simply articulate his dignity as a citizen, regardless of the cost.[36]

Those in power have disarmed the liberal class. They do not argue that the current system is just or good, because they cannot, but they have convinced liberals that there is no alternative. But we are not slaves. We have a choice. We can refuse to be either a victim or an executioner. We have the moral capacity to say no, to refuse to cooperate. Any boycott or demonstration, any occupation or sit-in, any strike, any act of obstruction or sabotage, any refusal to pay taxes, any fast, any popular movement, and any act of civil disobedience ignites the soul of the rebel and exposes the dead hand of authority. "There is beauty and there are the humiliated," Camus wrote. "Whatever difficulties the enterprise may present, I should like never to be unfaithful either to the second or the first."[37]

"There is a time when the operation of the machine becomes so odious, makes you so sick at heart, that you can't take part; you can't even passively take part, and you've got to put your bodies upon the gears and upon the wheels, upon the levers, upon all the apparatus, and you've got to make it stop," Mario Savio said on the steps of Sproul Hall at Berkeley during a sit-in on December 2, 1964. "And you've got to indicate to the people who run it, to the people who own it, that unless you're free, the machine will be prevented from working at all."[38]

The capacity to exercise moral autonomy, the capacity to refuse to cooperate, offers us the only route left to personal freedom and a life with meaning. Rebellion is its own justification. Those of us who come out of the religious left have no quarrel with Camus. Camus is right about the absurdity of existence, right about finding worth in the act of rebellion rather than some bizarre dream of an afterlife or Sunday School fantasy that God rewards the just and the good. "Oh my soul," the ancient Greek poet Pindar wrote, "do not aspire to immortal life, but exhaust the limits of the possible."[39]

We differ with Camus only in that we have faith that rebellion is not ultimately meaningless. Rebellion allows us to be free and independent human beings, but rebellion also chips away, however imperceptibly, at the edifice of the oppressor and sustains the dim flames of hope and love. And in moments of profound human despair these flames are never insignificant. They keep alive the capacity to be human. We must become, as Camus said, so absolutely free that "existence is an act of rebellion."[40] Those who do not rebel in our age of totalitarian capitalism and who convince themselves that there is no alternative to collaboration are complicit in their own enslavement. They commit spiritual and moral suicide.

How the Corporations Broke
Ralph Nader and America, Too

APRIL 5, 2010

Ralph Nader's descent from being one of the most respected and powerful men in the country to being a pariah illustrates the totality of the corporate coup. Nader's marginalization was not accidental. It was orchestrated to thwart the legislation that Nader and his allies—who once consisted of many in the Democratic Party—enacted to prevent corporate abuse, fraud, and control. He was targeted to be destroyed. And by the time he was shut out of the political process with the election of Ronald Reagan, the government was in the hands of corporations. Nader's fate mirrors our own.

"The press discovered citizen investigators around the mid-1960s," Nader told me when we spoke:

> I was one of them. I would go down with the press releases, the findings, the story suggestions and the internal documents and give it to a variety of reporters. I would go to Congress and generate hearings. Oftentimes I would be the lead witness. What was interesting was the novelty; the press gravitates to novelty. They achieved great things. There was collaboration. We provided the newsworthy material. They covered it. The legislation passed. Regulations were issued. Lives were saved. Other civic movements began to flower.

Nader was singled out for destruction, as Henriette Mantel and Stephen Skrovan point out in *An Unreasonable Man*, their engaging documentary movie on Nader. General Motors had him followed in an attempt to blackmail him. It sent an attractive woman to his neighborhood

Safeway supermarket in a bid to meet him while he was shopping and then seduce him; the attempt failed, and GM, when exposed, had to issue a public apology.

But far from ending their effort to destroy Nader, corporations unleashed a much more sophisticated and well-funded attack. In 1971, the corporate lawyer and future U.S. Supreme Court Justice Lewis Powell wrote an eight-page memo titled "Attack on American Free Enterprise System," in which he named Nader as the chief nemesis of corporations. It became the blueprint for corporate resurgence. Powell's memo led to the establishment of the Business Roundtable, which amassed enough money and power to direct government policy and mold public opinion. The Powell memo outlined ways corporations could shut out those who, in "the college campus, the pulpit, the media, the intellectual and literary journals," were hostile to corporate interests. Powell called for the establishment of lavishly funded think tanks and conservative institutes to churn out ideological tracts that attacked government regulation and environmental protection. His memo led to the successful effort to place corporate-friendly academics and economists in universities and on the airwaves, as well as drive out those in the public sphere who questioned the rise of unchecked corporate power and deregulation. It saw the establishment of organizations to monitor and pressure the media to report favorably on issues that furthered corporate interests. And it led to the building of legal organizations to promote corporate interests in the courts and appoint of sympathetic judges to the bench.[41]

"It was off to the races," Nader said:

> You could hardly keep count of the number of right-wing, corporate-funded think tanks. These think tanks specialized, especially against the tort system. We struggled through the Nixon and early Ford years, when inflation was a big issue. Nixon did things that horrified conservatives. He signed into law OSHA, the Environmental Protection Agency, and air and water pollution acts because he was afraid of the people from the rumble that came out of the 1960s. He was the last Republican president to be afraid of liberals.

The corporations carefully studied and emulated the tactics of the consumer advocate they wanted to destroy. "Ralph Nader came along and did serious journalism; that is what his early stuff was, such as *Unsafe at Any Speed*," David Cay Johnston told me:

> The big books they [Nader and associates] put out were serious, first-rate journalism. Corporate America was terrified by this. They went to school on Nader. They said, "We see how you do this. You gather material, you get people who are articulate, you hone how you present this," and the corporations copycatted him, with one big difference: they had no regard for the truth. Nader may have had a consumer ideology, but he was not trying to sell you a product. He is trying to tell the truth as best as he can determine it. It does not mean it is the truth. It means it is the truth as best as he and his people can determine the truth. And he told you where he was coming from.

Between 1966 and 1973, Congress passed 25 pieces of consumer legislation, nearly all of which Nader had a hand in authoring. The auto and highway safety laws, the meat and poultry inspection laws, the oil pipeline safety laws, the product safety laws, the update on flammable fabric laws, the Clean Air Act and Clean Water Act of 1970, the creation of the Environmental Protection Agency, the Occupational Safety and Health Administration, and the Environmental Council in the White House transformed the political landscape. By 1973 Nader was named the fourth most influential person in the country after Richard Nixon, Supreme Court Justice Earl Warren, and the labor leader George Meany.

"Then something very interesting happened," Nader said.

> The pressure of these meetings by the corporations like General Motors, the oil companies, and the drug companies with the editorial people, and probably with the publishers, coincided with the emergence of the most destructive force to the citizen movement: Abe Rosenthal, the editor of the *New York Times*. Rosenthal was a right-winger from Canada who hated communism, came here, and hated

progressivism. The *Times* was not doing that well at the time. Rosenthal was commissioned to expand his suburban sections, which required a lot of advertising. He was very receptive to the entreaties of corporations, and he did not like me. I would give material to Jack Morris in the Washington bureau, and it would not get in the paper.

Rosenthal, who banned social critics such as Noam Chomsky from being quoted in the paper and met frequently for lunch with conservative icon William F. Buckley, demanded that no story built around Nader's research could be published unless there was a corporate response. Corporations, informed of Rosenthal's dictate, refused to comment on Nader's research. This tactic meant the stories were never published. The authority of the *Times* set the agenda for national news coverage. Once Nader disappeared from the *Times*, other major papers and the networks did not feel compelled to report on his investigations. It was harder and harder to be heard.

"There was, before we were silenced, a brief, golden age of journalism," Nader lamented. "We worked with the press to expose corporate abuse on behalf of the public. We saved lives. This is what journalism should be about; it should be about making the world a better and safer place for our families and our children, but then it ended and we were shut out."

"We were thrown on the defensive, and once we were on the defensive it was difficult to recover," Nader said:

The break came in 1979, when they deregulated natural gas. Our last national stand was for the Consumer Protection Agency. We put everything we had on that. We would pass it during the 1970s in the House on one year, then the Senate during the next session, then the House later on. It Ping-ponged. Each time we would lose ground. We lost it because [Jimmy] Carter, although he campaigned on it, did not lift a finger compared to what he did to deregulate natural gas. We lost it by twenty votes in the House, although we had a two-thirds majority in the Senate waiting for it. That was the real beginning of the decline. Then Reagan was elected. We tried to be the watchdog. We put out investigative reports. They would not be covered.

"The press in the 1980s would say, 'Why should we cover you?'" Nader went on:

"Who is your base in Congress?" I used to be known as someone who could trigger a congressional hearing pretty fast in the House and Senate. They started looking towards the neoliberals and neo-cons and the deregulation mania. We put out two reports on the ben-efits of regulation, and they, too, disappeared. They did not get covered at all. This was about the same time that [former U.S. Rep-resentative] Tony Coelho taught the Democrats, starting in 1979 when he was head of the House Campaign Finance Committee, to start raising big-time money from corporate interests. And they did. It had a magical influence. It is the best example I have of the impact of money. The more money they raised, the less interested they were in any of these popular issues. They made more money when they screwed up the tax system. There were a few little gains here and there; we got the Freedom of Information [Act] through in 1974. And even in the 1980s we would get some things done, [General Services Administration,] buying airbag-equipped cars, the drive for standardized air bags. We would defeat some things here and there, block a tax loophole and defeat a deregulatory move. We were suc-cessful in staunching some of the deregulatory efforts.

Nader, locked out of the legislative process, decided to send a message to the Democrats. He went to New Hampshire and Massachusetts during the 1992 primaries and ran as "none of the above." In 1996 he allowed the Green Party to put his name on the ballot before running hard in 2000 in an effort that spooked the Democratic Party. The Democrats, fearful of his grassroots campaign, blamed him for the election of George W. Bush, an absurdity that found fertile ground among those who had abandoned rational inquiry for the thought-terminating clichés of television.

Nader's status as a pariah corresponded with an unchecked assault by corporations on the working class. The long-term unemployment rate, which in reality is close to twenty percent, the millions of foreclosures, the crippling personal debts that plague households, the personal bank-ruptcies, Wall Street's looting of the U.S. Treasury, the evaporation of savings and retirement accounts, and the crumbling of the country's vital infrastructure are taking place as billions in taxpayer subsidies, obscene profits, bonuses, and compensation are enjoyed by the corporate overlords. We will soon be forced to buy the defective products of the government-subsidized drug and health insurance companies, which will remain free to raise co-payments and premiums, especially if policyholders get seriously ill. The oil, gas, coal and nuclear power companies have made a mockery of Barack Obama's promises to promote clean, renewable energy. And we are rapidly becoming a third-world country, cannibalized by corporations, with two-thirds of the population facing financial difficulty and poverty.

The system is broken. And the consumer advocate who represented the best of our democracy was broken with it. As Nader pointed out after he published *Unsafe at Any Speed* in 1965, it took nine months to federally regulate the auto industry for safety and fuel efficiency. Two years after the collapse of Bear Stearns, there is still no financial reform. The large hedge funds and banks are using billions in taxpayer subsidies to engage once again in the speculative games that triggered the first financial crisis and will almost certainly trigger a second. The corporate media that abet our vast historical amnesia do nothing to remind us how we got here. They speak in the hollow and empty slogans handed to them by public relations firms, their corporate paymasters, and the sound-bite society.

"If you organize one percent of the people in this country along progressive lines, you can turn the country around, as long as you give them infrastructure," Nader said:

> They represent a large percentage of the population. Take all the conservatives who work in Wal-Mart: How many would be against a living wage? Take all the conservatives who have preexisting conditions: How many would be for single-payer, not-for-profit health insurance? When you get down to the concrete, when you have an active movement that is visible and media-savvy, when you have a community, a lot of people will join. And lots more will support it. The problem is that most liberals are estranged from the working class. They largely have the good jobs. They are not hurting.

"The real tragedy is that citizens' movements should not have to rely on the commercial media, and public television and radio are disgraceful—if anything, they are worse," Nader said:

> In thirty-some years, [Bill] Moyers has had me on [only] twice. We can't rely on the public media. We do what we can with Amy [Goodman] on *Democracy Now!* and Pacifica stations. When I go to local areas I get very good press, TV, and newspapers, but that doesn't have the impact, even locally. The national press has enormous impact on the issues. It is not pleasant having to say this. You don't want to telegraph that you have been blacked out, but on the other hand you can't keep it quiet. The right wing has won through intimidation.

Noam Chomsky Has Never Seen Anything Like This

APRIL 19, 2010

Noam Chomsky is America's greatest intellectual. His massive body of work, which includes nearly one hundred books, has for decades deflated and exposed the lies of the power elite and the myths they perpetrate. Chomsky has done this despite being blacklisted by the commercial media, turned into a pariah by the academy, and, by his own admission, being a pedantic and at times slightly boring speaker. He combines moral autonomy with rigorous scholarship, a remarkable grasp of detail, and a searing intellect. He curtly dismisses our two-party system as a mirage orchestrated by the corporate state, excoriates the liberal intelligentsia for being fops and courtiers, and describes the drivel of the commercial media as a form of "brainwashing." And as our nation's most prescient critic of unregulated capitalism, globalization and the poison of empire, he enters his eighty-first year warning us that we have little time left to save our anemic democracy.

"It is very similar to late Weimar Germany," Chomsky told me when I called him at his office in Cambridge, Massachusetts:

> The parallels are striking. There was also tremendous disillusionment with the parliamentary system. The most striking fact about Weimar was not that the Nazis managed to destroy the Social Democrats and the Communists, but that the traditional parties, the Conservative and Liberal parties, were hated and disappeared. It left a vacuum which the Nazis very cleverly and intelligently managed to take over.

"The United States is extremely lucky that no honest, charismatic figure has arisen," Chomsky went on:

Every charismatic figure is such an obvious crook that he destroys himself, like McCarthy or Nixon or the evangelist preachers. If somebody comes along who is charismatic and honest, this country is in real trouble because of the frustration, disillusionment, the justified anger, and the absence of any coherent response. What are people supposed to think if someone says, "I have got an answer: We have an enemy"? There it was the Jews. Here it will be the illegal immigrants and the blacks. We will be told that white males are a persecuted minority. We will be told we have to defend ourselves and the honor of the nation. Military force will be exalted. People will be beaten up. This could become an overwhelming force. And if it happens it will be more dangerous than Germany. The United States is the world power. Germany was powerful but had more powerful antagonists. I don't think all this is very far away. If the polls are accurate it is not the Republicans but the right-wing Republicans, the crazed Republicans, who will sweep the next election.

"I have never seen anything like this in my lifetime," Chomsky added:

I am old enough to remember the 1930s. My whole family was unemployed. There were far more desperate conditions than today. But it was hopeful. People had hope. The [Congress of Industrial Organizations] was organizing. No one wants to say it anymore, but the Communist Party was the spearhead for labor and civil-rights organizing. Even things like giving my unemployed seamstress aunt a week in the country. It was a life. There is nothing like that now. The mood of the country is frightening. The level of anger, frustration, and hatred of institutions is not organized in a constructive way. It is going off into self-destructive fantasies.

"I listen to talk radio," Chomsky said:

I don't want to hear Rush Limbaugh. I want to hear the people calling in. They are like [suicide pilot] Joe Stack, [who crashed a plane into an Austin, Texas, government building on February 18, 2010]: "What is happening to me? I have done all the right things. I am a God-fearing Christian. I work hard for my family. I have a gun. I believe in the values of the country, and my life is collapsing."

Chomsky has, more than any other American intellectual, charted the downward spiral of the American political and economic system, in works such as *On Power and Ideology: The Managua Lectures; Rethinking Camelot: JFK, the Vietnam War, and U.S. Political Culture; A New Generation Draws the Line: Kosovo, East Timor and the Standards of the West; Understanding Power: The Indispensable Chomsky; Manufacturing Consent;* and *Letters From Lexington: Reflections on Propaganda.* He reminds us that genuine intellectual inquiry is always subversive. It challenges cultural and political assumptions. It critiques structures. It is relentlessly self-critical. It explodes the self-indulgent myths and stereotypes we use to elevate ourselves and ignore our complicity in acts of violence and oppression. And it makes the powerful, as well as their liberal apologists, deeply uncomfortable.

Chomsky reserves his fiercest venom for the liberal elite in the media, the universities, and the political system, which serve as smoke screens for the cruelty of unchecked capitalism and imperial war. He exposes their moral and intellectual posturing as a fraud. And this is why Chomsky is hated, and perhaps feared, more among liberal elites than among the right wing he also excoriates. When Christopher Hitchens decided to become a windup doll for the Bush administration after the attacks of 9/11, one of the first things he did was write a vicious article attacking Chomsky. Hitchens, unlike most of those he served, knew which intellectual in America mattered.

"I don't bother writing about Fox News," Chomsky said:

It is too easy. What I talk about are the liberal intellectuals, the ones who portray themselves and perceive themselves as challenging power, as courageous, as standing up for truth and justice. They are basically the guardians of the faith. They set the limits. They tell us how far we can go. They say, "Look how courageous I am." But do not go one millimeter beyond that. At least for the educated sectors, they are the most dangerous in supporting power.

Chomsky, because he steps outside of every group and eschews all ideologies, has been crucial to American discourse for decades, from his work on the Vietnam War to his criticisms of the Obama administration. He stubbornly maintains his position as an iconoclast, one who distrusts power in any form.

"Most intellectuals have a self-understanding of themselves as the conscience of humanity," said the Middle East scholar Norman Finkelstein:

> They revel in and admire someone like Václav Havel. Chomsky is contemptuous of Havel. Chomsky embraces the Julien Benda view of the world. There are two sets of principles. They are the principles of power and privilege and the principles of truth and justice. If you pursue truth and justice, it will always mean a diminution of power and privilege. If you pursue power and privilege, it will always be at the expense of truth and justice. Benda says that the credo of any true intellectual has to be, as Christ said, "My kingdom is not of this world." Chomsky exposes the pretenses of those who claim to be the bearers of truth and justice. He shows that in fact these intellectuals are the bearers of power and privilege and all the evil that attends it.[42]

"Some of Chomsky's books will consist of things like analyzing the misrepresentations of the Arias plan in Central America, and he will devote two hundred pages to it," Finkelstein said:

> And two years later, who will have heard of Óscar Arias? It causes you to wonder: Would Chomsky have been wiser to write things on a grander scale, things with a more enduring quality, so that you read them forty or sixty years later? This is what [Bertrand] Russell did in books like *Marriage and Morals*. Can you even read any longer what Chomsky wrote on Vietnam and Central America? The

answer has to often be no. This tells you something about him. He is not writing for ego. If he were writing for ego he would have written in a grand style that would have buttressed his legacy. He is writing because he wants to effect political change. He cares about the lives of people, and there the details count. He is trying to refute the daily lies spewed out by the establishment media. He could have devoted his time to writing philosophical treatises that would have endured like [Immanuel] Kant or Russell. But he invested in the tiny details which make a difference to win a political battle.[43]

"I try to encourage people to think for themselves, to question standard assumptions," Chomsky said when asked about his goals:

Don't take assumptions for granted. Begin by taking a skeptical attitude toward anything that is conventional wisdom. Make it justify itself. It usually can't. Be willing to ask questions about what is taken for granted. Try to think things through for yourself. There is plenty of information. You have got to learn how to judge, evaluate, and compare it with other things. You have to take some things on trust or you can't survive. But if there is something significant and important, don't take it on trust. As soon as you read anything that is anonymous, you should immediately distrust it. If you read in the newspapers that Iran is defying the international community, ask, "Who is the international community?" India is opposed to sanctions. China is opposed to sanctions. Brazil is opposed to sanctions. The Non-Aligned Movement is vigorously opposed to sanctions and has been for years. Who is the international community? It is Washington and anyone who happens to agree with it. You can figure that out, but you have to do work. It is the same on issue after issue.

Chomsky's courage to speak on behalf of those, such as the Palestinians, whose suffering is often minimized or ignored in mass culture, holds up the possibility of the moral life. And, perhaps even more than his scholarship, his example of intellectual and moral independence sustains all who defy the cant of the crowd to speak the truth.

"I cannot tell you how many people, myself included, and this is not hyperbole, whose lives were changed by him," said Finkelstein, who has been driven out of several university posts for his intellectual courage and independence:

Were it not for Chomsky I would have long ago succumbed. I was beaten and battered in my professional life. It was only the knowledge that one of the greatest minds in human history has faith in me that compensates for this constant, relentless, and vicious battering. There are many people who are considered nonentities, the so-called little people of this world, who suddenly get an e-mail from Noam Chomsky. It breathes new life into you. Chomsky has stirred many, many people to realize a level of their potential that would forever be lost.[44]

BP and the Little Eichmanns

MAY 17, 2010

Cultures that do not recognize that human life and the natural world have a sacred dimension, an intrinsic value beyond monetary value, cannibalize themselves until they die. They ruthlessly exploit the natural world and the members of their society in the name of progress until exhaustion or collapse, blind to the fury of their own self-destruction. The oil pouring into the Gulf of Mexico, estimated to be perhaps as much as 100,000 barrels a day, is part of our foolish death march. It is one more blow delivered by the corporate state, the trade of life for gold. But this time collapse, when it comes, will not be confined to the geography of a decayed civilization. It will be global.

Those who carry out this global genocide—men like BP's chief executive Tony Hayward, who, during the Gulf oil crisis, when millions of gallons of oil leaked from a distressed well, polluting the Gulf, assured us that "The Gulf of Mexico is a very big ocean. The amount of oil and dispersant we are putting into it is tiny in relation to the total water volume"—are, to steal a line from Ward Churchill, "little Eichmanns." They serve Thanatos, the forces of death, the dark instinct Sigmund Freud identified within human beings that propels us to annihilate all living things, including ourselves. These deformed individuals lack the capacity for empathy. They are at once banal and dangerous. They possess the peculiar ability to organize vast, destructive bureaucracies and yet remain blind to the ramifications. The death they dispense, whether in the pollutants and carcinogens that have made cancer an epidemic, the dead zone rapidly being created in the Gulf of Mexico, the melting polar ice caps, or the deaths last year of forty-five thousand Americans who could not afford proper medical care, is part of the cold and rational exchange of life for money.

The corporations, and those who run them, consume, pollute, oppress, and kill. The little Eichmanns who manage them reside in a parallel universe of staggering wealth, luxury, and splendid isolation that rivals that of the closed court of Versailles. The elite, sheltered and enriched, continue to prosper even as the rest of us and the natural world start to die. They are numb. They will drain the last drop of profit from us until there is nothing left. And our business schools and elite universities churn out tens of thousands of these deaf, dumb, and blind systems managers, who are endowed with sophisticated management skills and the incapacity for common sense, compassion, or remorse. These technocrats mistake the art of manipulation with knowledge.

"The longer one listened to him, the more obvious it became that his inability to speak was closely connected with an inability to think, namely, to think from the standpoint of somebody else," Hannah Arendt wrote of Adolf Eichmann in her book *Eichmann in Jerusalem: A Report on the Banality of Evil.* "No communication was possible with him, not because he lied but because he was surrounded by the most reliable of all safeguards against words and the presence of others, and hence against reality as such."[45]

Our ruling class of technocrats, as John Ralston Saul points out, is effectively illiterate. "One of the reasons that he is unable to recognize the necessary relationship between power and morality is that moral traditions are the product of civilization and he has little knowledge of his own civilization," Saul writes of the technocrat. Saul calls these technocrats "hedonists of power," and warns that their "obsession with structures and their inability or unwillingness to link these to the public good make this power an abstract force—a force that works, more often than not, at cross-purposes to the real needs of a painfully real world."[46]

BP, which made $6.1 billion in profits in the first quarter of this year, never obtained permits from the National Oceanic and Atmospheric Administration before putting its pollution well in place. The protection of the ecosystem did not matter. But BP is hardly alone. Drilling with utter disregard to the ecosystem is common practice among oil companies, according to a report in the *New York Times*.[47] Our corporate state has gutted environmental regulation as tenaciously as it has gutted financial regulation. Corporations make no distinction between our personal impoverishment and the impoverishment of the ecosystem that sustains the human species. And the abuse, of us and the natural world, is as rampant under Barack Obama as it was under George W. Bush. The branded figure who sits in the White House is a puppet, a face used to mask an insidious system under which we as citizens have been disempowered and under which we become, along with the natural world, collateral damage. As Karl Marx understood, unfettered capitalism is a revolutionary force. And this force is consuming us.

In his book *The Great Transformation*, written in 1944, Karl Polanyi laid out the devastating consequences—the depressions, wars and totalitarianism—that grow out of a so-called self-regulated free market. He grasped that "fascism, like socialism, was rooted in a market society that refused to function." He warned that a financial system always devolved, without heavy government control, into a Mafia capitalism—and a Mafia political system—which is a good description of our corporate government. Polanyi warned that when nature and human beings are objects whose worth is determined by the market, then human beings and nature are destroyed. Speculative excesses and growing inequality, he wrote, always dynamite the foundation for a continued prosperity and ensure "the demolition of society."

"In disposing of a man's labor power the system would, incidentally, dispose of the physical, psychological, and moral entity 'man' attached to that tag," Polanyi wrote:

Robbed of the protective covering of cultural institutions, human beings would perish from the effects of social exposure; they would die as victims of acute social dislocation through vice, perversion, crime, and starvation. Nature would be reduced to its elements, neighborhoods and landscapes defiled, rivers polluted, military safety jeopardized, the power to produce food and raw materials destroyed. Finally, the market administration of purchasing power would periodically liquidate business enterprise, for shortages and surfeits of money would prove as disastrous to business as floods and droughts in primitive society. Undoubtedly, labor, land, and money markets are essential to a market economy. But no society could stand the effects of such a system of crude fictions even for the shortest stretch of time unless its human and natural substance as well as its business organizations was protected against the ravages of this satanic mill.[48]

The corporate state is a runaway freight train. It shreds the Copenhagen Accords signed as part of the Kyoto climate protocols. It plunders the U.S. Treasury so speculators can continue to gamble with billions in taxpayer subsidies in our perverted system of casino capitalism. It disenfranchises our working class, decimates our manufacturing sector, and denies us funds to sustain our infrastructure, our public schools, and our social services. It poisons the planet. We are losing, every year across the globe, an area of farmland greater than Scotland to erosion and urban sprawl. An estimated twenty-five people die every day somewhere in the world because of contaminated water. And some twenty million children are mentally impaired each year by malnourishment.

America is dying in the manner in which all imperial projects die. Joseph Tainter, in his book *The Collapse of Complex Societies*, argues that the costs of running and defending an empire eventually become so burdensome, and the elite becomes so calcified, that it becomes more efficient to dismantle the imperial superstructures and return to local forms of organization. At that point the great monuments to empire, from the Sumerian and Mayan temples to the Roman bath complexes, are abandoned, fall into disuse, and are overgrown. But this time around, Tainter warns, because we have nowhere left to migrate and expand, "world civilization will disintegrate as a whole."[49] This time around we will take the planet down with us.

"We in the lucky countries of the West now regard our two-century bubble of freedom and affluence as normal and inevitable; it has even been called the 'end' of history, in both a temporal and teleological sense," writes Ronald Wright in *A Short History of Progress*:

Yet this new order is an anomaly: the opposite of what usually happens as civilizations grow. Our age was bankrolled by the seizing of half the planet, extended by taking over most of the remaining half, and has been sustained by spending down new forms of natural capital, especially fossil fuels. In the New World, the West hit the biggest bonanza of all time. And there won't be another like it—not unless we find the civilized Martians of H.G. Wells, complete with the vulnerability to our germs that undid them in his *War of the Worlds*.[50]

The moral and physical contamination is matched by a cultural contamination. Our political and civil discourse has become gibberish. It is dominated by elaborate spectacles, celebrity gossip, the lies of advertising and scandal. The tawdry and the salacious occupy our time and energy. We do not see the walls falling around us. We invest our intellectual and emotional energy in the inane and the absurd, the empty amusements that preoccupy a degenerate culture, so that when the final collapse arrives we can be herded, uncomprehending and fearful, into the inferno.

This Country Needs a Few Good Communists

MAY 31, 2010

The witch hunts against communists in the United States were used to silence socialists, anarchists, pacifists, and all those who defied the abuses of capitalism. Those "anti-Red" actions were devastating blows to the political health of the country. The communists spoke the language of class struggle. They understood that Wall Street, along with corporations such as BP, is the enemy. They offered a broad social vision that allowed even the noncommunist Left to employ a vocabulary that made sense of the destructive impulses of capitalism. But once the Communist Party, along with other radical movements, was eradicated as a social and political force, once the liberal class took government-imposed loyalty oaths and collaborated in the witch hunts for phantom communist agents, we were robbed of the ability to make sense of our struggle. We became fearful, timid, and ineffectual. We lost our voice and became part of the corporate structure we should have been dismantling.

Hope in this age of bankrupt capitalism will come with the return of the language of class conflict. It does not mean we have to agree with Karl Marx, who advocated violence and whose worship of the state as a utopian mechanism led to another form of enslavement of the working class, but we have to speak in the vocabulary Marx employed. We have to grasp, as Marx did, that corporations are not concerned with the common good. They exploit, pollute, impoverish, repress, kill, and lie to make money. They throw poor families out of homes, let the uninsured die, wage useless wars to make profits, poison and pollute the ecosystem, slash social assistance programs, gut public education, trash the global economy, and crush all popular movements that seek justice for working men and women. They worship only money and power. And, as Marx knew, unfettered capitalism is a revolutionary force that consumes greater and greater numbers of human lives until it finally consumes itself. The nightmare in the Gulf of Mexico is the perfect metaphor for the corporate state. It is the same nightmare seen in postindustrial pockets from the old mill towns in New England to the abandoned steel mills in Ohio. It is a nightmare that Iraqis, Pakistanis, and Afghans, mourning their dead, live each day.

Capitalism was once viewed in America as a system that had to be fought. But capitalism is no longer challenged. And so, even as Wall Street steals billions of taxpayer dollars and the Gulf of Mexico is turned into a toxic swamp, we do not know what to do or say. We decry the excesses of capitalism without demanding a dismantling of the corporate state. The liberal class has a misguided loyalty, illustrated by environmental groups that have refused to excoriate the Obama White House over the ecological catastrophe in the Gulf of Mexico. Liberals bow before a Democratic Party that ignores them and does the bidding of corporations. The reflexive deference to the Democrats by the liberal class is the result of cowardice and fear. It is also the result of an infantile understanding of the mechanisms of power. The divide is not between Republican and Democrat. It is a divide between the corporate state and the citizen. It is a divide between capitalists and workers. And, for all the failings of the communists, they got it.

Unions, organizations formerly steeped in the doctrine of class struggle and filled with those who sought broad social and political rights for the working class, have been transformed into domesticated partners of the capitalist class. They have been reduced to simple bartering tools. The social demands of unions early in the twentieth century that gave the working class weekends off, the right to strike, the eight-hour day, and Social Security have been abandoned. Universities, especially in political science and economics departments, parrot the discredited ideology of unregulated capitalism and have no new ideas. Artistic expression, along with most religious worship, is largely self-absorbed narcissism. The Democratic Party and the media have become corporate servants. The loss of radicals within the labor movement, the Democratic Party, the arts, the church, and the universities has obliterated one of the most important counterweights to the corporate state. And the purging of those radicals has left us unable to make sense of what is happening to us.

The fear of communism, like the fear of Islamic terrorism, has resulted in the steady suspension of civil liberties, including freedom of speech, habeas corpus, and the right to organize, values the liberal class claims to support. It was the orchestration of fear that permitted the capitalist class to ram through the Taft-Hartley Act in 1948 in the name of anticommunism, the most destructive legislative blow to the working class until NAFTA. It was fear that created the Patriot Act, extraordinary rendition, offshore penal colonies where we torture, and the endless wars in the Middle East. And it was fear that was used to silence us as we were fleeced by Wall Street. If we do not stop being afraid and name our enemy, we will continue toward a state of neofeudalism.

The robber barons of the late nineteenth century used goons and thugs to beat up workers and retain control. The corporations, employing the science of public relations, have used actors, artists, writers, scholars, and filmmakers to manipulate and shape public opinion. Corporations employ the college-educated, liberal elite to saturate the culture with lies. The liberal class should have defied the emasculation of radical organizations, including the Communist Party. Instead, it was lured into the corporate embrace. It became a class of collaborators. National cohesion, because our intellectual life has become so impoverished, revolves around the empty pursuits of mass culture, brands, consumption, status, and the bland uniformity of opinions disseminated by corporate-friendly courtiers. We speak and think in the empty slogans and clichés we are given. And they are given to us by the liberal class.

The "idea of the intellectual vocation," as Irving Howe pointed out in his essay "The Age of Conformity," "the idea of a life dedicated to values that cannot possibly be realized by a commercial civilization—has gradually lost its allure. And, it is this, rather than the abandonment of a particular program, which constitutes our rout." The belief that capitalism is the unassailable engine of human progress, Howe added, "is trumpeted through every medium of communication: official propaganda, institutional advertising and scholarly writings of people who, until a few years ago, were its major opponents."[51]

"The truly powerless people are those intellectuals—the new realists—who attach themselves to the seats of power, where they surrender their freedom of expression without gaining any significance as political figures," Howe wrote:

> For it is crucial to the history of the American intellectuals in the past few decades—as well as to the relationship between "wealth" and "intellect"—that whenever they become absorbed into the accredited institutions of society they not only lose their traditional rebelliousness but to one extent or another *they cease to function as intellectuals*. The institutional world needs intellectuals because they are intellectuals but it does not want them as intellectuals. It beckons to them *because* of what they are but it will not allow them, at least within its sphere of articulation, either to remain or entirely cease being what they are. It needs them for their knowledge, their talent, their inclinations and passions; it insists that they retain a measure of these endowments, which it means to employ for its own ends, and without which the intellectuals would be of no use to it whatever. A simplified but useful equation suggests itself: the relation of the institutional world to the intellectuals is as the relation of middlebrow culture to serious culture, the one battens on the other, absorbs and raids it with increasing frequency and skill, subsidizes and encourages it enough to make further raids possible—at times the parasite will support its victim. Surely this relationship must be one reason for the high incidence of neurosis that is supposed to prevail among intellectuals. A total estrangement from the sources of power and prestige, even a blind unreasoning rejection of every aspect of our culture, would be far healthier if only because it would permit a free discharge of aggression.[52]

The liberal class prefers comfort to confrontation. It will not challenge the decaying structures of the corporate state. It is intolerant within its ranks of those who do. It clings pathetically to the carcass of the Obama presidency. It has been exposed as a dead force in American politics. We must find our way back to the old radicals, to the discredited Marxists, socialists, and anarchists, including Dwight Macdonald and Dorothy Day. Language is our first step toward salvation. We cannot fight what we cannot describe.

Freedom in the Grace of the World

JULY 5, 2010

Earl Shaffer, adrift after serving in the South Pacific in World War II and struggling with the loss of his childhood friend Walter Winemiller during the assault on Iwo Jima, made his way to Mount Oglethorpe in Georgia in 1947. He headed north toward Mount Katahdin in Maine, and for the next 124 days, averaging 16.5 miles a day, beat back the demons of war. His goal, he said, was to "walk the Army out of my system." He was the first person to hike the full length of the Appalachian Trail.

The beauty and tranquility of the old-growth forests, the vistas that stretch for miles over unbroken treetops, the waterfalls and rivers, the severance from the noise and electronic hallucinations of modern existence, become, if you stay out long enough, a balm to wounds. It is in solitude, contemplation, and a connection with nature that we transcend the frenzied and desperate existence imposed on us by the distortions of a commodity culture.

The mountains that loom on the northern part of the trail in New Hampshire and Maine, most of them in the White Mountain National Forest, are also forbidding, even in summer, when winds can routinely reach sixty or seventy miles per hour accompanied by lashing rain. The highest surface wind speed recorded on the planet, 231 miles per hour, was measured on April 12, 1934, at the Mount Washington Observatory. Boulders and steep inclines become slippery and treacherous when wet and shrouded in dense fog. Thunderstorms, racing across treeless ridgelines with the speed of a freight train, turn the razorbacked peaks into lightning rods. The Penacooks, one of two Native American tribes that dominated the area, called Mount Washington, the highest peak in the Northeast, Agiochook or "Place of the Great Spirit."

The Penacooks, fearing the power of Agiochook to inflict death, did not climb to its summit. The fury you bring into the mountains is overpowered by the fury of nature itself. Nature always extracts justice. Defy nature and it obliterates the human species. The more we divorce ourselves from nature, the more we permit the natural world to be exploited and polluted by corporations for profit, the more estranged we become from the essence of life. Corporate systems, which grow our food and ship it across country in trucks, which drill deep into the ocean to extract diminishing fossil fuels and send container ships to bring us piles of electronics and clothes from China, have created fragile, unsustainable man-made infrastructures that will collapse. Corporations have, at the same time, destroyed sustainable local communities. We do not know how to grow our own food. We do not know how to make our own clothes. We are helpless appendages of the corporate state. We are fooled by virtual mirages into mistaking the busy, corporate hives of human activity and the salacious images and gossip that clog our minds as real. The natural world, the real world on which our life depends, is walled off from view as it is systematically slaughtered. The oil gushing into the Gulf of Mexico is one assault. There are thousands more, including the coal-burning power plants dumping gases into our atmosphere that are largely unseen. Left unchecked, this arrogant defiance of nature will kill us.

"We have reached a point at which we must either consciously desire and choose and determine the future of the Earth or submit to such an involvement in our destructiveness that the Earth, and ourselves with it, must certainly be destroyed," farmer-poet Wendell Berry warns. "And we have come to this at a time when it is hard, if not impossible, to foresee a future that is not terrifying."[53]

Year after year I returned to these forbidding peaks from conflicts in Central America, the Middle East, Africa, and the Balkans. I had a house in Maine on an eight-hundred-foot hill with no television, cell phone, or Internet service. The phone number was unlisted. It rarely rang. I refused to give the number to my employer, the *New York Times*. I brought with me the stench of death, the cries of the wounded, the bloated bodies on the side of the road, the fear, the paranoia, the alienation, the insomnia, the anger, and the despair and threw it at these mountains. I strapped my pack on in the pounding rain at trailheads and drove myself, and later my son, up mountains. I rarely stopped. Once, in a bitter rain, I crested the peak of Mount Madison in August and was immediately thrown backward by howling winds whipping across the ridge and pelting hailstones. It was impossible to reach the summit. On a hike in the remote Pemigewasset Wilderness I made a wrong turn and, fearing hypothermia, walked all night. By the time the sun rose my blisters had turned to open sores. I wrung the blood out of my socks. I go to the mountains to at once spend this fury and seek renewal, to be reminded of my tiny, insignificant place in the universe and to confront mystery. Berry writes in "The Peace of Wild Things":

> When despair for the world grows in me
> and I wake in the night at the least sound
> in fear of what my life and my children's lives may be,
> I go and lie down where the wood drake
> rests in his beauty on the water, and the great heron feeds.
> I come into the peace of wild things
> who do not tax their lives with forethought
> of grief. I come into the presence of still water.
> And I feel above me the day-blind stars
> waiting with their light. For a time
> I rest in the grace of the world, and am free.[54]

I climbed my first mountain in the White Mountain National Forest when I was seven. It was Mount Chocorua. The mountain, capped with a rocky dome and perhaps the most beautiful in the park, is named for a legendary Pequawket chief who refused to flee with his tribe to Canada and was supposedly pursued to its summit by white settlers, where he leapt to his death. It is a climb I have repeated nearly every year, now with my children. I guided trips in the mountains in college. I would lie, years later, awake in San Salvador, Gaza, Juba, or Sarajevo and try to recall the sound of the wind, the smell of the pine forests, and the cacophony of bird song. To know the forests and mountains were there, to know I would return to them, gave me a psychological and physical refuge. And as my two older children grew to adulthood, I dragged them up one peak after another, pushing them perhaps too hard. My college-age son is deeply connected to the mountains. He works in the summer as a guide and has spent upward of seven weeks at a time backpacking on the Appalachian Trail. My teenage daughter, perhaps reflecting her sanity, is reticent to enter the mountains with the two of us.

I stood a few days ago in a parking lot at Crawford Notch with Rick Sullivan, an Army captain and Afghanistan war veteran. It was the end of our weeklong hike in the White Mountains. Sullivan noticed a man with a T-shirt that read "Operation Iraqi Freedom." The shirt had Arabic and English script warning motorists not to come too close or risk being shot. The man, an Iraqi veteran, was putting on a pack and told us that he was the caretaker of a campsite. He said he left the Army a year ago, drifted, drank too much, and worked at a bar as a bouncer. His life was unraveling. He then answered an ad for a park caretaker. The clouds hovering on the peaks above us were an ominous gray. The caretaker said he planned to beat the rain back to the tent site. I thought of Earl Shaffer.

"You try and forget the war but you carry pieces of it with you anyway," the caretaker said. "In the mountains, at least, I can finally sleep."

Obama's Health Care Bill Is Enough to Make You Sick

JULY 12, 2010

A close reading of the new health-care legislation, which will conveniently take effect in 2014 after the next presidential election, is deeply depressing. The legislation not only mocks the lofty promises made by President Barack Obama, exposing most as lies, but sadly reconfirms that our nation is hostage to unchecked corporate greed and abuse. The simple truth, that single-payer, nonprofit health care for all Americans would dramatically reduce costs and save lives, that the for-profit health care system is the problem and must be destroyed, is censored out of the public debate by media that rely on these corporations as major advertisers and sponsors, as well as a morally bankrupt Democratic Party that is as bought off by corporations as the Republicans.

The two-thousand-page piece of legislation, according to figures compiled by Physicians for a National Health Plan (PNHP), will leave at least twenty-three million people without insurance, a figure that translates into an estimated twenty-three thousand unnecessary deaths a year among people who cannot afford care. It will permit prices to climb so that many of us will soon be paying close to ten percent of our annual income to buy commercial health insurance, although this coverage will pay for only about seventy percent of our medical expenses. Those who become seriously ill, lose their incomes, and cannot pay skyrocketing premiums will be denied coverage. And at least $447 billion in taxpayer subsidies will now be handed to insurance firms. We will be forced by law to buy their defective products. There is no check in the new legislation to halt rising health-care costs. The elderly can be charged three times the rates provided to the young. Companies with predominantly female workforces can be charged higher gender-based rates. The dizzying array of technical loopholes in the bill—written in by armies of insurance and pharmaceutical lobbyists—means that these companies, which profit off human sickness, suffering, and death, can continue their grim game of trading away human life for money.

"They named this legislation the Patient Protection and Affordable Care Act, and as the tradition of this nation goes, any words they put into the name of a piece of legislation means the opposite," said single-payer activist Margaret Flowers when I heard her and Helen Redmond dissect the legislation in Chicago at the Socialism 2010 Conference in June 2010. "It neither protects patients nor leads to affordable care.

"This legislation moves us further in the direction of the commodification of health care," Flowers went on:

> It requires people to purchase health insurance. It takes public dollars to subsidize the purchase of that private insurance. It not only forces people to purchase this private product, but uses public dollars and gives them directly to these corporations. In return, there are no caps on premiums. Insurance companies can continue to raise premiums. We estimate that because they are required to cover people with preexisting conditions, although we will see if this happens, they will argue that they will have to raise premiums.

The legislation included a few tiny improvements used as bait to sell it to the public. The bill promises, for example, to expand community health centers and increase access to primary-care doctors. It allows children to stay on their parents' plan until they turn twenty-six. It will include those with preexisting conditions in insurance plans, although Flowers warns that many technicalities and loopholes make it easy for insurance companies to drop patients. Most of the more than thirty million people currently without insurance, and the forty-five thousand who die each year because they lack medical care, essentially remain left out in the cold, and things will not get better for the rest of us.

"We are still a nation full of health-care hostages," Redmond said:

We live in fear of losing our health care. Millions of people have lost their health care. We fear bankruptcy. The inability to pay medical bills is the number one cause of bankruptcy. We fear not being able to afford medications. Millions of people skip medications. They skip these medications to the detriment of their health. We are not free. And we won't be free until health care is a human right, until health care is not tied to a job, because we still have an employment-based system, and until health care has nothing to do with immigration status. We don't care if you are documented or undocumented. It should not matter what your health-care status is, if you have a disease or you don't. It should not matter how much money you have or don't, because many of our programs are based on income eligibility rules. Until we abolish the private, for-profit health insurance industry in this county we are not free. Until we take the profit motive out of health care, we cannot live in the way we want to live. This legislation doesn't do any of that. It doesn't change those basic facts of our health-care system.

Redmond held up a syringe.
"I take a medication that costs $1,700 every single month," she said:

I inject this medication. It costs $425 a week for fifty milligrams of medication. I would do almost anything to get this medication because without it I don't have much of a life. The pharmaceutical industry knows this. They price these drugs accordingly to the level of desperation that people feel. Billy Tauzin, the former CEO of [the Pharmaceutical Research and Manufacturers Association, the trade organization of] Big Pharma, negotiated a secret deal with President Obama to extend the patents of biologics, this new revolutionary class of drugs, for twelve years. And Obama also promised in this deal that he would not negotiate drug prices for Medicare.

Obama's numerous betrayals—from his failure to implement serious environmental reform at Copenhagen, to his expansion of the current wars, to his refusal to create jobs for our desperate class of unemployed and underemployed, to his gutting of public education, to his callous disregard for the rights of workers and funneling of trillions in taxpayer money to banks—is a shameful list. Passing universal, single-payer, nonprofit health care for all Americans might have delivered to Obama, who may well be a one-term president, at least one worthwhile achievement. Single-payer, nonprofit health care has widespread popular support, with nearly two-thirds of the public behind it. It is backed by fifty-nine percent of doctors. And it would have helped roll back, at least a bit, the corporate assault on the citizenry.

Medical bills lead to sixty-two percent of personal bankruptcies, and nearly eighty percent of these people had insurance. The United States spends twice as much as other industrialized nations on health care, $8,160 per capita. Private insurance, bureaucracy, and paperwork consume thirty-one percent of every health-care dollar. Streamlining payment through a single nonprofit payer would save more than $400 billion per year—enough, PNHP estimates, to provide comprehensive, high-quality coverage for all Americans.

Candidate Obama promised to protect women's rights under *Roe v. Wade*, something this legislation does not do. He told voters he would create a public option and then refused to consider it. The health-care reform bill, to quote a statement released by PNHP, has instead "saddled Americans with an expensive package of onerous individual mandates, new taxes on workers' health plans, countless sweetheart deals with the insurers and Big Pharma, and a perpetuation of the fragmented, dysfunctional, and unsustainable system that is taking such a heavy toll on our health and economy today."

"Obama said he was going to have everybody at the table," Redmond said, "but that was a lie:

> Our voice was not allowed to be there. There was a blackout on our movement. We did not get media attention. We did actions all over the country, but we could not get coverage. We had the "Mad as Hell Doctors" go across the country in a caravan, and they had rallies and meetings. If that had been a bunch of AMA Republican doctors, Anderson Cooper would have been on the caravan reporting live.

NPR would have done a series. Instead, they did not get much coverage. And neither did the sit-ins and arrests at insurance companies, although we have never seen that level of activity. They turned us into a fringe movement, although poll after poll shows that the majority of people want some kind of single-payer system.

Our for-profit health system is driven by insurance companies whose goal is to avoid covering the elderly and the sick. These groups, most in need of medical care, diminish profits. Medicare, paid for by the government, removes responsibility for many of the old. Medicaid, also paid for by the government, removes the poor people, who have a greater tendency to have chronic health problems. Hefty premiums, which those who are seriously ill and lose their jobs often cannot pay, remove the very sick. If you are healthy and employed, which means you are less likely to need expensive or complex treatment, the insurance companies swoop down like birds of prey. These corporations need to control our perceptions of health care. Patients must be viewed as consumers. Doctors, identified as "health-care providers," must be seen as salespeople.

Insurance companies, which will soon be able to use billions in taxpayer dollars to bolster their lobbying efforts and campaign contributions, know that single-payer, nonprofit insurance means their extinction. And they will employ considerable resources to make sure single-payer, nonprofit coverage is denied to the public. They correctly see this as a battle for their lives. And if human beings have to die so they can survive, they are willing to make us pay this price.

The for-profit health-care industry, along with the Democratic Party, consciously set out to confuse the public debate. It created Health Care for America NOW! in 2008 and provided it with tens of millions of dollars, supposedly to build a public campaign for a public option. But the organization had no intention of permitting a public option. The organization was, as Flowers said, "a very clever way to distract members of the single-payer movement and co-opt some of them. They told them that the public option would become single-payer, that it was a back door to single-payer, although there was no evidence that was true."

Physicians for a National Health Plan attempted to fight back. It worked with a number of organizations under a coalition called the Leadership Conference for Guaranteed Health Care. The group, which included the National Nurses Union and Health Care Now, sought meetings with members of Congress. Flowers and other advocates asked Congress members to include them in committee debates about the health-care bill. But when the first debate on health-care reform took place in the Senate Finance Committee, chaired by Senator Max Baucus, a politician who gets more than eighty percent of his campaign contributions from outside his home state of Montana, they were locked out. Baucus invited forty-one people to testify. None backed single-payer.

The Leadership Conference, which represents more than twenty million people, again requested that one of their members testify. Baucus again refused. When the second committee meeting took place, Flowers and seven other activists stood one by one in the room and asked why the voices of the patients and the health-care providers were not being heard. The eight were arrested and removed from the committee hearing.

Single-payer advocates were eventually heard by a few of the House and Senate committees. But the hearings were a charade, part of Washington's cynical political theater. It was the insurance and pharmaceutical lobbyists who were in charge. They dominated the public debate. They wrote the legislation. They determined who received lavish campaign contributions and who did not. And they won.

"We are talking about life and death, about the difference between living your life and dying," Redmond said. "And once again it came down to the Democratic Party trumping the needs of the people."

Calling All Future Eaters

JULY 19, 2010

The human species during its brief time on Earth has exhibited a remarkable capacity to kill itself off. The Cro-Magnons dispatched the gentler Neanderthals. The conquistadors, with the help of smallpox, decimated the native populations in the Americas. Modern industrial warfare in the twentieth century took at least one hundred million lives, most of them civilians. And now we sit passive and dumb as corporations and the leaders of industrialized nations ensure that climate change will accelerate to levels that could mean the extinction of our species. *Homo sapiens*, as the biologist Tim Flannery points out, are the "future-eaters."[55]

In the past, when civilizations went belly up through greed, mismanagement and the exhaustion of natural resources, human beings migrated somewhere else to pillage anew. But this time the game is over. There is nowhere else to go. The industrialized nations spent the last century seizing half the planet and dominating most of the other half. We giddily exhausted our natural capital, especially fossil fuel, to engage in an orgy of consumption and waste that poisoned the Earth and attacked the ecosystem on which human life depends. It was quite a party if you were a member of the industrialized elite. But it was pretty stupid.

Collapse this time around will be global. We will disintegrate together. And there is no way out. The ten-thousand-year experiment of settled life is about to come to a crashing halt. And humankind, which thought it was given dominion over the Earth and all living things, will be taught a painful lesson in the necessity of balance, restraint, and humility. There is almost no human monument or city ruin that is more than five thousand years old. Civilization, as Ronald Wright notes in *A*

Short History of Progress, "occupies a mere 0.2 percent of the two and a half million years since our first ancestor sharpened a stone."[56] Bye-bye, Paris. Bye-bye, New York. Bye-bye, Tokyo. Welcome to the new experience of human existence, in which rooting around for grubs on islands in northern latitudes is the prerequisite for survival.

We view ourselves as rational creatures. But is it rational to wait like sheep in a pen as oil and natural gas companies, coal companies, chemical industries, plastics manufacturers, the automotive industry, arms manufacturers, and the leaders of the industrial world, as they did in Copenhagen, take us to mass extinction? It is too late to prevent profound climate change. But why add fuel to the fire? Why allow our ruling elite, driven by the lust for profits, to accelerate the death spiral? Why continue to obey the laws and dictates of our executioners?

The news is grim. The accelerating disintegration of Arctic Ocean sea ice means that summer ice will probably disappear within the next decade. The open water will absorb more solar radiation, significantly increasing the rate of global warming. The Siberian permafrost will disappear, sending up plumes of methane gas from underground. The Greenland ice sheet and the Himalayan-Tibetan glaciers will melt. Jay Zwally, a NASA climate scientist, declared in December 2007: "The Arctic is often cited as the canary in the coal mine for climate warming. Now, as a sign of climate warming, the canary has died. It is time to start getting out of the coal mines."[57]

But reality is rarely an impediment to human folly. The world's greenhouse gases have continued to grow since Zwally's statement. Global emissions of carbon dioxide (CO_2) from burning fossil fuels since 2000 have increased by three percent a year. At that rate annual emissions will double every twenty-five years. James Hansen, the head of NASA's Goddard Institute for Space Studies and one of the world's foremost climate experts, has warned that if we keep warming the planet it will be "a recipe for global disaster." The safe level of CO_2 in the atmosphere, Hansen estimates, is no more than 350 parts per million (ppm). The current level of CO_2 is 385 ppm and climbing.[58] These levels already guarantee terrible consequences, even if we act immediately to cut carbon emissions.

For three million years, the natural carbon cycle has ensured that the atmosphere contained less than 300 ppm of CO_2, which sustained the wide variety of life on the planet. The idea now championed by our corporate elite, at least those in contact with the reality of global warming, is that we will intentionally overshoot 350 ppm and then return to a safer climate through rapid and dramatic emission cuts. This, of course, is a theory designed to absolve the elite from doing anything *now*. But as Clive Hamilton writes in his book *Requiem for a Species: Why We Resist the Truth About Climate Change*, even "if carbon dioxide concentrations reach 550 ppm, after which emissions fell to zero, the global temperatures would continue to rise for at least another century."[59]

Copenhagen was perhaps the last chance to save ourselves. Barack Obama and the other leaders of the industrialized nations blew it. Radical climate change is certain. It is only a question now of how bad it will become. The engines of climate change will, climate scientists have warned, soon create a domino effect that could thrust the Earth into a chaotic state for thousands of years before it regains equilibrium. "Whether human beings would still be a force on the planet, or even survive, is a moot point," Hamilton writes. "One thing is certain: there will be far fewer of us."[60]

We have fallen prey to the illusion that we can modify and control our environment, that human ingenuity ensures the inevitability of human progress, and that our secular god of science will save us. The "intoxicating belief that we can conquer all has come up against a greater force, the Earth itself," Hamilton writes. "The prospect of runaway climate change challenges our technological hubris, our Enlightenment faith in reason and the whole modernist project. The Earth may soon demonstrate that, ultimately, it cannot be tamed and that the human urge to master nature has only roused a slumbering beast."[61]

We face a terrible political truth. Those who hold power will not act with the urgency required to protect human life and the ecosystem. Decisions about the fate of the planet and human civilization are in the hands of moral and intellectual trolls such as BP's Tony Hayward. These political and corporate masters are driven by a craven desire to accumulate wealth at the expense of human life. They showed this drive everywhere in their handling of the mess they created in the Gulf of Mexico. They do this in the southern Chinese province of Guangdong, where the export-oriented industry is booming. China's transformation into totalitarian capitalism, done so world markets can be flooded with cheap consumer goods, is contributing to a dramatic rise in carbon dioxide emissions, which in China are expected to more than double by 2030, from a little over five billion metric tons to just under 12 billion.

This degradation of the planet by corporations is accompanied by a degradation of human beings. In the factories in Guangdong we see the face of our adversaries. The sociologist Ching Kwan Lee found "satanic mills" in China's industrial southeast that run "at such a nerve-racking pace that worker's physical limits and bodily strength are put to the test on a daily basis." Some employees put in workdays of fourteen to sixteen hours, with no rest day during the month until payday. In these factories it is normal for an employee to work four hundred hours or more a month, especially those in the garment industry. Most workers, Lee found, endure unpaid wages, illegal deductions, and substandard wage rates. They are often physically abused at work and do not receive compensation if they are injured on the job. Every year a dozen or more workers die from overwork in the city of Shenzhen alone. In Lee's words, the working conditions "go beyond the Marxist notions of exploitation and alienation." A survey published in 2003 by the official China News Agency, cited in Lee's book *Against the Law: Labor Protests in China's Rustbelt and Sunbelt*, found that three in four migrant workers had trouble collecting their pay. Each year scores of workers threaten to commit suicide, Lee writes, by jumping off high-rises or setting themselves on fire over unpaid wages. "If getting paid for one's labor is a fundamental feature of capitalist employment relations, strictly speaking many Chinese workers are not yet laborers," Lee writes.[62]

The leaders of these corporations now determine our fate. They are not endowed with human decency or compassion. Yet their lobbyists make the laws. Their public relations firms craft the propaganda and trivia pumped out through systems of mass communication. Their money determines elections. Their greed turns workers into global serfs and our planet into a wasteland.

As climate change advances, we will face a choice between obeying the rules put in place by corporations or rebellion. Those who work human beings to death in overcrowded factories in China and turn the Gulf of Mexico into a dead zone are the enemy. They serve systems of death. They cannot be reformed or trusted.

The climate crisis is a political crisis. We will either defy the corporate elite, which will mean civil disobedience, a rejection of traditional politics for a new radicalism, and the systematic breaking of laws, or see ourselves consumed. Time is not on our side. The longer we wait, the more assured our destruction becomes. The future, if we remain passive, will be wrested from us by events. Our moral obligation is not to structures of power, but to life.

Do Not Pity the Democrats

SEPTEMBER 13, 2010

There are no longer any major institutions in American society, including the media, the educational system, the financial sector, labor unions, the arts, religious institutions, and our dysfunctional political parties, that can be considered democratic. The intent, design, and function of these institutions, controlled by corporate money, are to bolster the hierarchical and antidemocratic power of the corporate state. These institutions, often mouthing liberal values, abet and perpetuate mounting inequality. They operate increasingly in secrecy. They ignore suffering or sacrifice human lives for profit. They control and manipulate all levers of power and mass communication. They have muzzled the voices and concerns of citizens. They use entertainment, celebrity gossip, and emotionally laden public-relations lies to seduce us into believing in a Disneyworld fantasy of democracy.

The menace we face does not come from the insane wing of the Republican Party, set, as I write, to make huge inroads in coming elections, but from the institutions tasked with protecting democratic participation. Do not fear Glenn Beck or Sarah Palin. Do not fear the Tea Party movement, the "birthers," the legions of conspiracy theorists, or the militias. Fear the underlying corporate power structure, which no one, from Barack Obama to the right-wing nut cases who pollute the airwaves, can alter. If the hegemony of the corporate state is not soon broken, we will descend into a technologically enhanced age of barbarism.

Investing emotional and intellectual energy in electoral politics is a waste of time. Resistance means a radical break with the formal structures of American society. We must cut as many ties with consumer society and corporations as possible. We must build a new political and economic consciousness centered on the tangible issues of sustainable agriculture, self-sufficiency, and radical environmental reform. The democratic system, like the liberal institutions that once made piecemeal reform possible, is dead. It exists only in name. It is no longer a viable mechanism for change. And the longer we play our scripted and absurd role in this charade, the worse it will get. Do not pity Barack Obama and the Democratic Party. They will get what they deserve. They sold the citizens out for cash and power. They lied. They manipulated and deceived the public, from the bailouts to the abandonment of universal health care, to serve corporate interests. They refused to halt the wanton corporate destruction of the ecosystem on which all life depends. They betrayed the ideals of democracy. And they, as much as the Republicans, are the problem.

"It is like being in a pit," Ralph Nader told me when we spoke September 11. "If you are four feet in the pit, you have a chance to grab the top and hoist yourself up. If you are thirty feet in the pit, you have to start on a different scale."

All resistance will take place outside the arena of electoral politics. The more we expand community credit unions, community health clinics, and food cooperatives, and build alternative energy systems, the more empowered we will become.

"To the extent that these organizations expand and get into communities where they do not exist, we will weaken the multinational goliath, from the banks to the agribusinesses to the HMO giants and hospital chains," Nader said.

The failure of liberals to defend the interests of working men and women as our manufacturing sector was dismantled, labor unions were destroyed, and social services were slashed has proved to be a disastrous and fatal misjudgment. Liberals, who betrayed the working class, have no credibility. This is one of the principal reasons the antiwar movement cannot attract the families whose sons and daughters are fighting and dying in Iraq and Afghanistan. And liberal hypocrisy has opened the door for a virulent right wing. If we are to reconnect with the working class we will have to begin from zero. We will have to rebuild the ties with the poor and the working class the liberal establishment has severed. We will have to condemn the liberal class as vociferously as we condemn the right wing. And we will have to remain true to the moral imperative to foster the common good and the tangible needs of housing, health care, jobs, education, and food.

We will, once again, be bombarded in this election cycle with messages of fear from the Democratic Party—designed, in the end, to serve corporate interests. "Better Barack Obama than Sarah Palin," we will be told. Better the sane technocrats like Larry Summers than half-wits like John Bolton. But this time we must resist. If we express the legitimate rage of the dispossessed working class as our own, if we denounce and refuse to cooperate with the Democratic Party, we can begin to impede the march of the right-wing trolls who seem destined to inherit power. If we again prove compliant we will discredit the socialism we should be offering as an alternative to a perverted Christian and corporate fascism.

The Tea Party movement is, as Nader points out, "a conviction revolt." Most of the participants in the Tea Party rallies are not poor. They are small-business people and professionals. They feel that something is wrong. They see that the two parties are equally responsible for the subsidies and bailouts, the wars and the deficits. They know these parties must be replaced. The corporate state, whose interests are being championed by Tea Party leaders such as Palin and Dick Armey, is working hard to make sure the anger of the movement is directed toward government rather than corporations and Wall Street. And if these corporate apologists succeed, a more overt form of corporate fascism will emerge without a socialist counterweight.

"Poor people do not organize," Nader lamented:

They never have. It has always been people who have fairly good jobs. You don't see Wal-Mart workers massing anywhere. The people who are the most militant are the people who had the best blue-collar jobs. Their expectation level was high. When they felt their jobs were being jeopardized, they got really angry. But when you are at $7.25 an hour you want to hang on to $7.25 an hour. It is a strange thing.

"People have institutionalized oppressive power in the form of surrender," Nader said:

It is not that they like it. But what are you going to do about it? You make the best of it. The system of control is staggeringly dictatorial. It breaks new ground and innovates in ways no one in human history has ever innovated. You start in American history where these corporations have influence. Then they have lobbyists. Then they run candidates. Then they put their appointments in top government positions. Now, they are actually operating the government. Look at Halliburton and Blackwater. Yesterday someone in our office called the Office of Pipeline Safety apropos the San Bruno explosion in California. The press woman answered. The guy in our office saw on the screen that she had CTR next to her name. He said, "What is CTR?" She said, "I am a contractor." He said, "This is the press office at the Department of Transportation. They contracted out the press office?" "Yes," she said, "but that's OK, I come to work here every day."

"The corporate state is the ultimate maturation of American-type fascism," Nader said:

They leave wide areas of personal freedom so that people can confuse personal freedom with civic freedom—the freedom to go where you want, eat where you want, associate with who you want, buy what you want, work where you want, sleep when you want, play when you want. If people have given up on any civic or political role for themselves, there is a sufficient amount of elbow room to get through the day. They do not have the freedom to participate in the decisions about war, foreign policy, domestic health and safety issues, taxes or transportation. That is its genius. But one of its Achilles' heels is that the price of the corporate state is a deteriorating political economy. They can't stop their greed from getting the next morsel. The question is, at what point are enough people going to have a breaking point in terms of their own economic plight? At what point will they say enough is enough? When that happens, is a Tea Party type enough or [Senator Robert M.] La Follette or Eugene Debs type enough?

It is anticorporate movements as exemplified by the Scandinavian energy firm Kraft&Kultur that we must emulate. Kraft&Kultur sells electricity exclusively from solar and water power. It has begun to merge clean energy activities with cultural events, bookstores, and a political consciousness that actively defies corporate hegemony.

The failure by the Obama administration to use the bailout and stimulus money to build public works such as schools, libraries, roads, clinics, highways, public transit; to reclaim dams, and to create green jobs, has snuffed out any hope of serious economic, political, or environmental reform coming from the centralized bureaucracy of the corporate state. And since the government did not hire enough auditors and examiners to monitor how the hundreds of billions in taxpayer funds funneled to Wall Street are being spent, we will soon see reports of widespread mismanagement and corruption. The rot and corruption at the top levels of our financial and political systems, coupled with the increasing deprivation felt by tens of millions of Americans, are volatile tinder for a horrific right-wing backlash in the absence of a committed socialist alternative.

"If you took a day off and did nothing but listen to [Sean] Hannity, Beck, and Limbaugh and realized that this goes on 260 days a year, you would see that it is overwhelming," Nader said:

> You have to almost have a genetic resistance in your mind and body not to be affected by it. These guys are very good. They are clever. They are funny. They are emotional. It beats me how Air America didn't make it, except it went after [it criticized] corporations, and corporations advertise. These right-wingers go after government, and government doesn't advertise. And that is the difference. It isn't that their message appeals more. Air America starved because it could not get ads.

We do not have much time left. And the longer we refuse to confront corporate power, the more impotent we become as society breaks down. The game of electoral politics, given legitimacy by the right and the so-called left on the cable news shows, is just that—a game. It diverts us from what should be our daily task: dismantling, piece by piece, the iron grip that corporations hold over our lives. Hope is a word that is applicable only to those who grasp reality, however bleak, and do something meaningful to fight back—which does not include the farce of elections and involvement in mainstream political parties. Hope involves fighting against the real forces of destruction, not chanting "Yes We Can!" in rallies orchestrated by marketing experts, television crews, pollsters, and propagandists, or begging Obama to be Obama. Hope, in the hands of realists, spreads fear into the black heart of the corporate elite. But hope, real hope, remains thwarted by our collective self-delusion.

ISRAEL AND PALESTINE

Mutually Assured Destruction

JULY 14, 2006

Israel's air, land, and sea blockade of Lebanon, which includes jet fighter strikes against the airport in Beirut, presages a new era in the Middle East, one in which the center has collapsed and Muslim and Jewish extremists, capable only of the language of violence, determine the parameters of existence. These strikes, like the suicide bombings carried out by Islamic militants in Iraq or Israel, expose the Ahab-like self-immolation that now inflects the region. And unless it is halted soon, unless those fueling these conflicts learn to speak another language, unless they break free from an indulgence in collective necrophilia, the Middle East will slip into a death spiral.

This crisis has been a long time coming. The Bush administration never had any interest in helping broker Middle East peace agreements. This willful negligence was seen as befriending Israel, along with the bizarre demands of the Christian Right. In fact, the administration befriended only an extreme political wing in Israel that, since the death of Yitzhak Rabin, has done a pretty effective job of endangering the Jewish state by dismantling all mechanisms for peace and turning Israel into an international pariah. As the machinery of Middle East diplomacy rusted shut with disuse, it was gleefully replaced by harsher Israeli closures, curfews, shelling, and air strikes. Palestinians have, since Bush arrived in office, been reduced by Israel to a subsistence existence matched only by that in the poorer African countries. And the tools of repression against Palestinians now match those once imposed on South African blacks by the apartheid regime, with the exception that the South African government never sent warplanes to bomb the townships.

And why should this not be so? In this binary worldview, force is the only thing Arabs understand. This logic only fuels those in the Arab world who also speak exclusively in the language of violence. The escalating repression by Israel, like the escalating repression by the U.S. occupiers in Iraq, has become the most potent recruiting tool for Islamic extremists. It has rendered each side deaf and dumb. As those under the boot of Israel or the United States lose all hope for justice, as they give up on peaceful recourses to ameliorate their plight, as they fall into despair, despair throws them, by default, into the hands of extremists. And as the extremists grow and their attacks became more deadly, this despair likewise helps silence those in Israel and the United States who call for compassion, restraint, and understanding. It is difficult to argue with those holding up bloodied corpses. Each side finds it useful to keep the supply coming.

In this demented world, friend and foe need each other. Hamas and Hezbollah yearn, on some level, for Israeli air strikes against civilians just as the hard Right in Israel yearns, in some dark way, for suicide bombers. The indiscriminate violence of one justifies the indiscriminate violence of the other. The violence stokes the fear that is the driving force behind all messianic, violent movements—American, Jewish, and Muslim. And since these groups have nothing to offer other than violence, they need fear to keep those around them compliant. The atrocities committed by one, real or imagined, make possible the atrocities of the other.

Does anyone in the Israeli government really believe that attacking Lebanon and killing more than sixty Lebanese civilians will ensure the freedom of the two captured Israeli soldiers? Hostages, including Israeli hostages, have been taken captive in Lebanon before, and most have been freed through long and painful negotiations. If the Israelis do believe in the violent path they have taken, it is a sad indication of how out of touch they are with the world that opposes them.

We cannot ascribe equal amounts of moral blame to all sides. Israel is the oppressor in Gaza, the West Bank, and now Lebanon. The United States is the oppressor in Iraq. And there can be no hope for a peaceful resolution to these conflicts until Iraqis are freed from U.S. occupation and Palestinians are allowed to build a viable state. The distorting and dehumanizing effects of occupation made possible the proliferation of extremist groups that, albeit on a smaller scale, simply hand back to the occupiers some of their own medicine. The numbers, after all, make clear that most of the victims are Palestinian, Iraqi, and now Lebanese civilians, although the numbers game can also obscure the fact that the murder of any innocent by any group is indefensible.

This is the world of the apocalypse. It is the world where those on either extreme become indistinguishable. And if we do not find a new way to speak, and soon, there will be untold suffering—not only for many innocents in the Middle East but also eventually innocents at home. It was the Israeli occupation of southern Lebanon that spawned and empowered Hezbollah. It was the decades-long occupation and humiliation of Palestinians in Gaza and the West Bank by Israel that spawned and empowered Hamas, and it is the brutal U.S. occupation that has bred the legions of extremists in Iraq. And when Hezbollah leader Hassan Nasrallah promises "open war" against Israel, as he did in an address shortly after his Beirut offices were bombed, and Israeli prime minister Ehud Olmert says he won't cease his attack until Israel is secure, it is time to run for cover, especially when George W. Bush is our best hope for peace.

Israel's Barrier to Peace

JULY 25, 2006

There is a twenty-five-foot-high concrete wall in Nuhayla Auynaf's front yard. The gray mass, punctuated by cylindrical guard towers with narrow window slits for Israeli soldiers, appears from her steps like the side of a docked ocean liner. It is massive, cold, and alien. The dwarfed shrubs and bushes and the stunted fruit trees seem to huddle before it in supplication. I struggle to make sense of it, the way I struggled to make sense of the smoldering rubble that was the World Trade Center a few hours after the planes hit. We do not speak. Auynaf lives with the wall. She is as drawn to it as she is repelled by it. It absorbs her. She goes out on her second-floor balcony every morning and looks at it. She implores it for answers, as if it is a Sphinx that will answer the riddle of her new existence.

"My old life ended with the wall," she tells me.

The wall, built by Israel a year before, blocked her from the neighboring Israeli town of Kfar Saba, where she used to shop. It cut her off from Israel. It made it hard to reach the rest of the West Bank. The lone Israeli checkpoint with its guard towers, floodlights, concrete barriers, dust, stench, crowds, special pass cards, intrusive searches, and rude remarks by border police, were more than she could bear.

She tried to pass through once.

"I could not stand the humiliation," she says. "I turned back. I went home. Now I never leave."

The wall reduces her world to its ugly perimeter. Her five boys beg to go to the seaside. The wall makes this impossible. No one goes to the sea anymore. There are days when the checkpoint is sealed, days after suicide bombings, or days when the Israeli soldiers shut it down abruptly without explanation. On those days she sometimes gathers up her children and walks the empty streets, wandering like prisoners in a circle. Other families do the same. It gives her a sense of movement. Families pass each other two, three, four times in an afternoon. All are thinking the same thoughts.

"The town would rent buses to go to the sea," she says. "We would go for the day. We would stand in the water. We would look at the rocks and the waves. This was before."

The house is pleasant. It was finished at the start of the uprising, when business was good and peace seemed possible. The floors are marble. The kitchen has a counter and white appliances. The sofa and chairs have muted blue and beige striped fabric. We sit in the living room. A large window fan, set on the floor in front of the open door, provides a weak breeze. The door frame is filled with the expressionless gray face of the wall. It draws our eyes to it, the way a muted television screen distracts me during conversations. Sometimes we turn to look at it, as if it is a presence in the room, someone who should be offered sweet tea or a glass of water . . . or asked to leave. We want it to speak to us.

Her son Ibrahim, six, sits on her lap. He has a scar on his leg. He was shot two years ago by Israeli soldiers. It happened at dusk. The soldiers were firing at a group of Palestinian workers trying to slip into or out of Israel without proper work permits. He was watching from the front yard when a bullet went astray. He stays close to his mother, especially when he hears the sounds of gunshots. He does not like to leave home. The world frightens him.

The family was one of the wealthiest in Qalqilyah before the wall ruined them. They spent $200,000 on their home, with its sloping terra-cotta tiled roof, its pleasant garden. It looks like the homes in the middle-class suburbs outside Tel Aviv. Once the wall went up, the family's car parts business was wiped out. Auynaf's husband makes less than ten percent of what he once earned. He has trouble shipping car parts into the walled enclosure. He often cannot reach suppliers. Customers, those in Israel and those in other areas of the West Bank, can no longer get to his store. He does not have a permit to drive the family car through the checkpoint. He must stand in line, often for several hours, to go in and out. He is away now. He is trying to salvage his business, but it cannot go on like this. She hopes he will be home tonight. But she does not know. The lines are long. Sometimes the soldiers get tired or bored or surly and turn people away until the next morning.

"We talk about how we are going to survive, what we are going to do," she said.

She hangs laundry on the balcony. Her only view is the wall. The other morning she was hanging laundry to dry and she heard singing. The song was by Fadel Shaker, a popular Arab singer. The singer had a sweet voice.

"You who are far away, why do you forget those who love you?" the words go. "When I fall asleep I think only of your eyes. I think only of you."

Her five boys were in the yard. They began to sing. There was a chorus of voices, the sweet voice and the voices of the children. She peered up into the glaring sunlight to see the singer. She saw an Israeli soldier in his green uniform standing on top of the earthen mound on the Israeli side of the wall, the mound the army drives jeeps up to peer down on those below. He looked like an Olympian god. She thinks he was a Druze, the tiny, nominally Muslim sect that lives near the border with Syria and serves in the Israeli army and border police.

"He waved when the song finished," she says. "The children waved back. Then he disappeared behind the wall."

She was on the balcony a few days later. She was pinning up clothes on the line. The wooden shutters were open into the house. She looked up and saw a soldier watching her from the top of the mound. There was no singing. His raspy voice crackled over the megaphone mounted on the jeep. He ordered her to go inside and close the shutters. She obeyed. Her wet laundry lay behind in the basket.

"I live in a zoo," she says. "They come and watch me. I am a caged animal. They have the freedom to come and go, to look or not look, to be kind or cruel. I have no freedom."

She fears madness. She points to an elderly woman 200 feet away squatting under a fig tree.

"The wall was the end," she says. "When it was finished she went mad."

We watch the woman. She is keening slightly. People are being destroyed by the serpent's teeth of the wall, springing up from the soil of the West Bank like the evil warriors sown by Cadmus. This for me is the story, not the amount of concrete or coils of razor wire or razed olive groves and villages, but what all this is doing to human souls.

I walk down the road to the elderly woman. I kneel in the shade beside her. She is missing many teeth. Her dirty hair, platted and uncombed, is thick and white. Her name is Fatme Khalil al-Bas. She is 72. Her husband died a few years ago. Next to us are the shattered walls of an old stone house. It was her house. She was born in it and lived there until Israeli tanks blew it up in the 1967 war. She and her family continued to work the fields around the wreck of a home, never rebuilding. When the Israelis built the wall they seized her land. She was left with a small garden lot. Her fields, the ones where she worked as a girl, as a mother and a grandmother, are inaccessible. They are overgrown and untended on the other side of the wall. They belong to Israel now. She left her small apartment to sleep under the fig tree. She has built a shelter out of old boards placed across the branches. In the small patch of land she grows tomatoes and cucumbers.

Much of what she says is incoherent. She rails against her husband's second wife and then says softly, "He was a good man." She spits out the names of Ariel Sharon and George Bush and Yasir Arafat, hissing with anger. She vows to protect her little plot with her life, even though she says she is afraid at night, "afraid as a woman to sleep alone on the ground, afraid for my honor."

I stand to leave. She looks at me with plaintive eyes. I turn and see Auynaf watching us.

"I am a bird in a net," the old woman whispers.

Qalqilyah is a ghetto. It is completely surrounded by the wall. There is one Israeli military checkpoint to let people into the West Bank or back home again. Only those with special Israeli-issued permits can go in and out of Qalqilyah. It is not the Łódź ghetto or the Warsaw ghetto, but it is a ghetto that would be recognizable to the Jews herded into walled enclaves by Pope IV in 1555 and stranded there for generations. Qalqilyah, like all ghettos, is dying. And it is being joined by dozens of other ringed ghettos as the serpentine barrier snaking its way up and down two sides of the West Bank gobbles up Palestinian land and lays down nooses around Palestinian cities, towns, villages, and fields.

Construction began on the barrier in 2002 with the purported intent of safeguarding Israel from suicide bombers and other types of attacks. Although it nominally runs along the Green Line, established after the 1949 Jordanian-Israeli armistice, which demarcates the boundary between Israel and the Palestinian-held West Bank, around eighty percent of the barrier actually cuts into Palestinian territories—at some points by as much as twenty kilometers.

If and when the barrier is completed, several years from now, it will see the West Bank cut up into three large enclaves and numerous small, ringed ghettos. The three large enclaves will include in the south the Bethlehem/Hebron area and in the north the Jenin/Nablus and Ramallah areas.

B'Tselem, a leading Israeli human-rights organization that documents conditions in the occupied territories, recently estimated that the barrier will eventually stretch 703 miles around the West Bank, about 450 of which are already completed or under construction. (The Berlin Wall, for comparison, ran ninety-six miles.) B'Tselem also estimates that half a million West Bank residents will be directly affected by the barrier (by virtue of residing in areas completely encircled by the wall; by virtue of residing west of the barrier and thus in de facto Israeli territory; or by virtue of residing in East Jerusalem, where Palestinians effectively cannot cross into West Jerusalem).

I stand on Qalqilyah's main street. There is little traffic. Shop after shop is shuttered and closed. The heavy metal doors are secured to the ground with thick padlocks. There are signs in Hebrew and Arabic, fading reminders of a time when commerce was possible. There were, before the wall was built, forty-two thousand people living here. Mayor Maa'rouf Zahran says at least six thousand have left. Many more, with the unemployment rate close to seventy percent, will follow. Over the tip of the wall, in the distance, I can see the tops of the skyscrapers in Tel Aviv. It feels as if it is a plague town, quarantined. Israeli officials, after a few suicide bombers slipped into Israel from Qalqilyah, began to refer to the town as a "hotel for terrorists."

There are hundreds of acres of farmland on the other side of the wall, some of the best farmland in the West Bank, harder and harder to reach given the gates, checkpoints and closures. There are some thirty-two farming villages on the outskirts of Qalqilyah, cut off from their land, sinking into poverty and despair. Olive groves, with trees hundreds of years old, have been uprooted and bulldozed into the ground. The barrier is wiping out the middle class in the West Bank, the last bulwark against Islamic fundamentalism. It is plunging the West Bank into the squalor that defines life in the Gaza Strip, where Palestinians struggle to live on less than $2 a day. It is the Africanization of Palestinian land.

It is also ethnic cleansing, less overtly violent than that I watched carried out by the Serbs in Bosnia, but as effective. Thousands of Palestinians have left, never to return. Cities such as Bethlehem are emptying. This, Palestinians say, is the real goal: to make life impossible and force them to leave.

The Israelis, who have thought hard about making the project as linguistically benign as possible, call the barrier "the seam line." They insist it is not meant to be a border. They say it will make Israel more secure. They said that once Gaza was enclosed, suicide attacks from the Gaza Strip would end. They promise that once the West Bank is sealed off, terrorists will not be able to cross into Israel. The promise of security for the weary Israeli populace is like manna from heaven.

This assumes, of course, that the barrier will separate Palestinians from Jews. It ignores the one million Israeli Arabs living inside Israel, some of whom have already elected to use their bodies as weapons. It ignores the presence of Jewish settlers in some two hundred settlements who often live within yards of Palestinians. But most ominously, it ignores the consequences of total enclosure. The West Bank, like Gaza, will erupt with high-octane rage. Hamas was an insignificant group with little following in 1988 when I first reported from Gaza. The Islamist radicals are now the vanguard of the resistance. Every pillar of concrete driven into the soil of the West Bank will bring forth screeching bands of killers. It happened in Gaza. It will happen here. Security will never come with the barrier, but then, security is not the point. What is happening is much more insidious.

If the barrier is being built for security, why is so much of the West Bank being confiscated by Israel? Why is the barrier plunging in deep loops into the West Bank to draw far-flung settlements into Israel? Why are thousands of acres of the most fertile farmland and so many of the West Bank's aquifers being seized by Israel?

The barrier does not run along the old 1967 border or the 1949 armistice line between Israel and the Arab states, which, in the eyes of the United Nations, delineates Israel from the West Bank. It will contain at least fifty percent of the West Bank, including the whole of the Western Mountain Aquifer, which supplies the West Bank Palestinians with more than half their water. The barrier is the most catastrophic blow to the Palestinians since the 1967 occupation of the West Bank and Gaza.

The barrier itself mocks any claim that it is temporary. It costs $1 million per mile and will run more than $2 billion by the time it is completed. It will cut the entire 224-mile length of the West Bank off from Israel, but because of its diversions into the West Bank to incorporate Palestinian land, it will be about 400 miles in length. A second barrier is being built on the Jordan River side of the West Bank. To look at a map of the barrier is to miss the point. The barrier interconnects with every other piece of Israeli-stolen real estate in Palestinian territory. And when all the pieces are in place, the Israelis will no doubt offer up the little ringed puddles of poverty and despair and misery to the world as a Palestinian state.

I traveled along the completed parts of the barrier for ten days. It is being built in sections. When I go into and out of the West Bank, often passing through multiple Israeli checkpoints, it takes three or four hours. The northern sections were completed in July 2003, although Israel's Ministry of Defense was still razing houses and fields along the barrier in the north for a buffer zone when I visited. Bulldozers, trucks, and backhoes belch diesel smoke and lumber across the landscape. Where there is no barrier there is often a wide dirt track being graded and smoothed for construction. On either side of the emerging barrier are the dynamited remains of markets or homes and the blackened stumps of destroyed olive groves. It is one of the most ambitious construction projects ever undertaken by the state, certainly one of the most costly.

The small town of Mas'ha lies in the path of the barrier. It has been in decline since the start of the uprising three years ago, when Israel blocked the road leading from the town to Tel Aviv. The closure ended the businesses of the dozens of fruit and vegetable sellers who lined the road with shops and markets. The closure trapped most Palestinians inside the West Bank, and because of this the barrier for Israelis is an abstraction. It does not slice through any Israeli land. It does not change Israeli life. It only solidifies the status quo.

The Baddya Market on either side of the small asphalt road is empty, the tin-roofed sheds and warehouses that once held piles of fruits and vegetables for sale abandoned. The town's population has fallen from seven thousand to two thousand since the closure of the road.

I stand on top of one of the two dirt mounds that block the road to Tel Aviv. There is an army base on a hilltop in front of me. An electric fence runs around a settlement a hundred yards up the road on my left. Two green Israeli army jeeps lie parked at an angle, blocking the road a few feet beyond the second mound. The two dirt mounds and strip of empty road between them are filled with old cardboard boxes, broken bottles, empty wooden vegetable crates, cans, plastic Coke bottles, tires, shredded remnants of plastic bags, a broken chair, and the twisted remains of a child's stroller.

A young boy is loading three cardboard boxes into a shopping cart. An elderly woman, standing on the mound a few feet from me, is helping him. When the cart is full the boy begins to push it to the other mound about fifty feet away. The woman follows. When they get to the other side, he lifts out the boxes for her. She drops a silver shekel in his hand for payment. He goes back to the other mound to wait. He does this all day. It is the only way goods move up and down this road.

I walk into a small shed where a man is seated at a table. The shelves around him are bare. He has two boxes of tomatoes in front of him. There are cold drinks in a large refrigerated case with glass doors. A single light bulb hangs from a wire, casting a soft hue over the gray stubble on his face. Fat, languid flies buzz nosily. It is the only sound I hear. I ask him if he will speak to me. There is a long silence.

"Why?" he finally says. "It won't do any good."

I walk up the road, over the two mounds, and turn left to go up through the opening in a post fence with loops of barbed wire. A rainbow flag flies from a post planted in the ground along the fence. The dirt in the yard is pitted and gouged with tread marks from heavy earth-moving equipment. I hear the squelch, grunts, and guttural moans of engines at work. I cannot see the machinery. The sky is clear, that searing, crystalline clearness that makes the light of the Middle East unforgiving and overpowering.

There are tarps in the yard in front of the house. Under the tarps are a collection of dirty mattresses and foam pads. Piled around the mattresses are backpacks, some with tickets from European airlines. A blue backpack has a tag with the letters SAS. There are plastic water coolers under the tarp. Plastic cups are scattered on the ground. Several young men and women, many in sandals and baggy cotton pants, lounge on the mattresses speaking quietly. Some are asleep.

I go to the door of the house. Munira Ibrahim Amer, who lives there, takes me upstairs to the flat roof where laundry is hanging and there is a large water tank. The heat on the roof is withering. I edge my way under a narrow eave to capture some shade. A young woman with glasses and short blond hair holds a video camera. She is wearing a green T-shirt and green cargo pants. She has a small pouch strapped around her waist. She says her name is Maria. She says she does not want to give me her last name.

"Thousands of us have been denied entry visas by the Israelis at the airport," she says with what I suspect is a German accent. "Many of us who get picked up are deported. If I give you my name I will be on their blacklist. They will not let me in. They will put a 'No Entry' stamp in my passport."

She has been in and out of Palestine, she says, for more than a year. She was one of the first internationals to get into the Jenin refugee camp after the April 2002 Israeli attack against armed militants that left scores dead and sections of the camp destroyed.

"I could not breathe because of the smell of the dead bodies," she says. "I saw children collect body parts of their parents. None of us could eat. It was terrible. And the world stood by and did nothing."

She was an Islamic studies major. She speaks Arabic. She became involved in protests in Italy against the occupation. She joined a group called International Women's Peace Service, which sends activists to protest the construction of what it terms "the apartheid wall." She lives in a house with other activists in the Palestinian village of Haras. She has been in and out of the West Bank and Gaza for more than a year, surviving on the meager funds from the organization.

The activists surround the house when the bulldozer, belching smoke and groaning, lumbers through the yard on the way to grade the track on the hill below. Three activists chain themselves to a shed next to the house when they think the bulldozer might turn to attack. The shed next to the house, the family has been told, is about to be destroyed. When Maria speaks of the bulldozer, it is as if it is a living object, some Leviathan rising out of the bowels of the earth to swallow up Palestine.

"When we do an action it is beautiful," she says. "It is what life is about, living together, not fighting simply for our own happiness. The real pursuit of happiness is not about making me happy. It is about living together and sharing."

There is something wistful in this, as if she knows much of human sadness, which I later find out she does. Activists, like aid workers and foreign correspondents and soldiers, are often orphans running away from home. I was one. They seek new families and new reasons to live, often messianic reasons intense enough to blot out the past and keep the darker clouds of memory at bay.

She wears a piece of silver jewelry around her neck. It comes from India.

"I put my fingers around it and hold it when I am scared," she says, wrapping her fingers over it. "I have grown superstitious. I risked my life more than once last year. I understand why Palestinians believe in God. When you feel your own impotence in the face of [then-prime minister of Israel Ariel] Sharon and the United States, you have to believe in something bigger. It is the only way to survive. I don't believe in God. I believe in this."

There is the sudden roar and screech of army jeeps. A dozen Israeli soldiers pile out of the vehicles in helmets and flak jackets. They spread out along the road, facing the activists, who now are rousted from their mattresses. Three men grab the chains and run for the shed. The soldiers cradle black M16 assault rifles.

"Oh, hell," she says quickly, pushing the start button on her camera and pointing down at the scene below us, "and another jeep is coming. I have to call the media office and alert them."

The ragged band of forty-five activists spread out in the yard. The soldiers watch, silent, bemused, the way a child watches a line of ants he is about to crush. In a few moments the soldiers depart.

The activists wait in the sun for a few minutes and then go back under the tarps. Maria joins them from the roof. They begin to discuss tactics. Someone proposes singing "Give Peace a Chance" if the soldiers come again. Another suggests building a small model of a Palestinian village in the path of the bulldozer. They begin a heated discussion over what to write on their banners. When people agree, rather than clap, they raise their arms and flutter their fingers. A member of the group suggests they write condemnations of the wall uttered by world leaders including President Bush. The mention of the American president raises the temperature of the debate.

"I don't agree that we put phrases by George Bush on our banners," says a woman with an Israeli accent. "George Bush don't fucking care about this, about anything. I really hate this man. I don't want any fucking thing he said on any action I participate in."

There is a sea of fluttering fingers. I admire their commitment but find them too sanctimonious, infected with the fanatic's zeal that they know what is good for you, good for everyone. Their anger springs, in part, from the fact that no one will listen, as well as the damage, the damage many I suspect nurse internally and wish to heal.

I go into the house and sit with the family. The family lives surrounded by the madness. The bulldozer severed the water pipe to the house. They have spent the last few weeks carrying water into the house in plastic buckets. The children have turned one side of the house into an outdoor toilet. It sinks of human feces.

Munira Ibrahim Amer and her husband, Hani, have four boys and two girls. They scamper around the room, often shouting to be heard above the noise of the heavy machinery busily tearing up the earth outside. I feel I am in an Ionesco play.

"I spent ten years working in Saudi Arabia to buy this land and start our nursery," says Hani. "In a few hours the Israelis bulldozed my greenhouses and my plants into the ground."

The family moved into the house in 1981. They made a decent living. They had many Israeli customers. They grew things.

"A year ago army jeeps appeared in the village and scattered leaflets around the mosque," he says. "Soldiers came to our house. They told us our house was in the way of the fence and would be demolished. They said they would compensate us." But he does not believe them. He says the Israelis determine the worth of the land and property, and he says other Palestinians tell him the Israelis usually never pay: "They will build their wall," he says, "and they will take revenge on me and my family for allowing these internationals to protect us. They will demolish my home."

It is dusk. I leave. The activists, fearing a demolition, sleep under the tarps.

I speak with Maria the next morning by phone. She tells me her real name. It is Maren Karlitzky. She is German. She reveals her name because she is sitting with the other activists in a police station in the Jewish settlement of Ariel. The Israelis have taken her passport. She is under arrest.

She tells me that at 7 A.M. about a hundred soldiers surrounded the house. They pushed the activists onto buses. The activists watched the bulldozer demolish the shed. The group was kept awake all night. Everyone was questioned.

"When I was called in for questioning they told me I could stay [in Israel] if I collaborated with them," she says. "I refused."

At four in the morning the police presented the group with typed Hebrew statements and told the activists to sign them. The statements said that none of them would again enter the West Bank or attempt to renew their visas. They signed the papers.

"It was a mistake," Maren said. "We were tired."

I ask her what she will do next.

"Guess," she says.

I often have to leave my car behind and walk to villages, villages that have not had access to roads for two or three years. Crude barriers of dirt, trenches or torn-up strips of asphalt make the roads impassible. Weeds grow up on either side of the roads. The crude barriers will be replaced soon by walls and fences and ditches and wire.

I am walking down an empty dirt road. It is covered with stones. I am walking to the farming hamlet of al-Nu'man. The farmers have been legally dispossessed, ethnic cleansing by administrative fiat. It was a specialty of the Bosnian Muslims, who did not want the ethnic Croats and Serbs to go back to their old apartments in Sarajevo. So they used the courts to strip them of their property.

There are tens of thousands of Palestinians whom Israeli courts have declared squatters in their own homes, homes they were born and raised in, homes that have been in the family for generations.

The cicadas sing out in a cacophonous chorus. The heat feels like the blast from a furnace. Olive groves, with rows of thick, gnarled trees, line the slope to the valley below me. The hilltops are rocky and gray. There are a few patches of light green.

The road to the hamlet was closed in 1995 by the Israelis. The bulldozers blocked it with dirt and scooped out a huge trench at the edge of the village, tossing the chunks of black asphalt to the side. The Israelis changed the name of the hamlet to Mazmouria, although no Israelis live here. I see the hamlet ahead of me. It is tiny, with twenty-six modest homes, all with flat roofs and stucco exteriors.

I walk down into the trench. Youssif Dara'wi, a large man with a heavy girth, is standing on the other side looking down at me. He helps me up. He is wearing sandals. He clutches a cell phone. There is a large ring of keys on a silver clasp fastened to his belt. I get into his car and we drive to his house. He has set out a dozen white plastic chairs under the one tree in his front yard. Older men, when they see us, come to introduce themselves and take a seat.

Youssif was born in the hamlet. As far as he can tell, his family has been here for 180 years, but probably longer. He owns about one hundred acres of olive groves, making him one of the largest landowners here. The farmers in the village together have one thousand acres. When they were occupied by Israeli troops in 1967, they were given Israeli identification cards. The cards said they were residents of the West Bank. They were incorporated into the Bethlehem municipality.

"It all began to change after the start of the first Palestinian uprising in 1987," Youssif says.

Israeli officials forbade any new construction. When anyone tried to build a house or expand existing ones, Israeli bulldozers tore the structures down. After the Oslo peace agreement the pressure eased, only to come back in greater force with the latest uprising. The road was closed. The children in the village, who formerly had gone to Jerusalem for their schooling, were barred from the city. The Israelis expanded the boundaries of the Jerusalem municipality. The farmers have become West Bank squatters, illegally encamped inside Israel. It is a neat little legal trick.

Members of the community pooled their money to hire an Israeli lawyer. But even when they get to the Supreme Court, even when they result in a decision in favor of the Palestinians, cases can be immediately overruled by the state on grounds of national security. National security, as in my own country, is the god destroying us all.

"I am not allowed to be here or to meet you according to Israeli law," Youssif says. "I am not allowed to be on my own land."

The water to the hamlet was cut three years ago. Water comes now from wells and water trucks.

Youssif pulls out a topographical map. It is marked with colored zones and lines to indicate settlements, the barrier under construction around Jerusalem, the land that has been confiscated, the land that will be confiscated, and the new demarcation lines for the hamlet. The blue line, he explains, is the new boundary for Jerusalem. The hamlet is within the boundary. The yellow line is the barrier, which, when we look up, we can see being built down the hill in front of a new hilltop settlement with several hundred concrete apartment blocks. He traces his thick finger around the roads, the settlements, and the barrier to show how the hamlet will be encircled, how he and his neighbors will soon lose nearly all their land and live illegally in a ghetto with no running water. I have seen this now many times.

Most Palestinians carry maps. They keep them tucked into their shirt pockets and pull them out at the slightest provocation. They spread them on the ground and chart for you the course of their own demise. It happens so often it gets boring, but I always listen and nod and pretend the information is new. The ritual is repeated over and over and seems to be part of the struggle to cope with the scale and horror of what is happening.

A group of Israeli soldiers appeared in the hamlet four months ago. They said Israel was willing to compensate farmers whose homes had been built before 1992. They told the farmers to submit compensation forms. The army would determine the price to be paid. The other homes, they said, would be demolished. If any home was built after 1992, the family would receive nothing. None of the farmers filed for compensation.

Then the physical harassment began. Soldiers arrived early one morning in July, roused six farmers from their beds, and drove them to a nearby military outpost. They were told they would be released when they signed papers saying they would not enter Israeli territory. The farmers signed the papers. They spent the rest of the night walking home.

"I signed," Abid Ataya, 55, tells me as we sit in a half-circle of chairs under a pine tree. "I didn't realize that according to them I live in an Israeli area."

Soldiers come frequently to demand other signatures. They were there the night before, their jeeps roaring into the hamlet at 2:30 A.M. The soldiers handcuffed twenty farmers and took them to the military outpost. All refused to sign. In the morning, after squatting all night outside the compound, they were released.

"The soldiers laughed at us," Mahmoud Ali Hussein, 43, says. "They told us when the wall was finished we would not be able to enter Israel or the West Bank. They told us we would have no land. They sent us home and told us to wait. They said our time is almost up."

The farmers sit, bewildered, trying to comprehend it all, the ability to declare reality to be one way when it is another, the ability to swiftly and irrevocably destroy their life, the only life they have known. I say nothing, so we sit like this for a long time.

"Does a condemned prisoner sign an agreement authorizing his own execution?" asks Mahmoud suddenly.

A boy with a tray holding glasses of lukewarm soda moves between us, handing out drinks. We sip the soda. The farmers light cigarettes.

Ribbons of thin, bluish smoke waft toward the pine branches over our heads. Again we are silent, thinking about it all.

"Too much pressure makes explosions," my host says.

"When you deny us education, medical care, and work, what do you think we will do? When you take our homes and our land from us, when we cannot feed our families, when you strip us of our dignity, how do you think we will behave? How can you ask us to be neighbors after this? What chance do you think there will be for peace?"

The men nod.

"We are going to change the name of our village," he says. "We are going to call it Transfer 2004."

No one laughs.

And what of the good Israelis? Where are they? What are they doing?

I found Allegra Pacheco mopping the floors of her small second-story apartment in Bethlehem. Her infant son is asleep. The furniture is upended in the corner of the living room. She is scrubbing away. The scent of ammonia from the tiled floor fills the room, even with the windows open.

"We will have to go outside," she says.

We sit on her balcony. We look out over the cramped and squalid hovels of the Dheisheh refugee camp. The camp cascades, one hovel nearly on top of the next, down a slope. Pope John Paul II used the camp as a backdrop in 2000, when he visited. He was there long enough for the media to get images and cover his kind beneficence. The camp exploded into rioting five minutes after the pope departed. The local police station was badly vandalized. There was never a coherent explanation for the rioting, other than the obvious: the frustration and rage of a people used once again as a stage prop and then forgotten.

Allegra is a Jew. She grew up in Long Island, where she was a member of a "Zionist-oriented family." She visited Israel as a teenager on one of the tours designed to get Americans to bond with the Jewish state. She went to Barnard and to Columbia Law School. She began to ask questions, questions many around her refused to ask.

She read about the Middle East. The story of the Palestinians began to unsettle her. She began to see another side of Israel. She moved to Israel after a few years as a lawyer in New York. She studied for the Is-

raeli bar. She looked to Lea Tsmel, the Israeli lawyer who has often de-
fended Palestinians, as a mentor.

She opened a law office in Bethlehem. She was the only Israeli ever
to open a law office in Palestinian territory. She handled cases involving
house demolitions, land confiscations, torture, and prisoners who had
been incarcerated without ever being charged. She documented some
torture practices, at first denied by Israel, and took the case to the
Supreme Court. Most of the practices were outlawed.

The second Palestinian uprising began as she had taken a break and
was writing a book as a Peace Fellow at Harvard University. She
dropped the manuscript and came back. The restrictions, however, were
so draconian she often could not get through the checkpoints to her office. It was hard to see clients or make court appearances. She took over
the case of a Palestinian human-rights activist, Abed al-Rahman al-
Ahmar, being held without charge in administrative detention.

"I met my husband Abed in 1996, when he was under interrogation
and being tortured," she says. "He was then sent to two and a half
years of administrative detention, and I continued to represent him.
When he was released, he helped me set up my law office and worked
with me. That's how we fell in love."

They married. They spent their honeymoon trapped in their apartment under almost continuous curfew.

She was eight months pregnant when Abed was arrested for the thir-
teenth time. He was sent to a prison at Ofra. The prisoners live twenty
to a tent in the desert. They sleep on wooden pallets. The tents are swel-
tering in the summer and cold in the winter.

"Abed sleeps under ten blankets in the winter," she said. "There is
no heat."

There is an open sewer nearby and swarms of mosquitoes. He is
being held on "secret evidence," which means he has not been told the
charges against him. Abed has never been sentenced. His six-month military detention order had been extended for another six months in June.
It, too, was done in secret. It can be renewed indefinitely. Amnesty International has adopted him as a prisoner of conscience.

His health is precarious. When he was sixteen, he was arrested for
throwing stones at Israeli soldiers. He was tied to a chair in contorted

positions. His back and stomach were under tremendous pressure. He was in great pain. His head was covered with a bag soaked in urine. Allegra has sued the army for the torture he underwent in 1996. He was also tortured on three other occasions while in detention.

"They have told him he will be released if [we] drop the lawsuit," she says. "He will not."

She gave birth to their first child, Quds, the Arabic name for Jerusalem, this spring. Abed has never seen his son. When Allegra asked for the address of the prison, to mail her husband pictures of their child, she was told there was no address.

"My husband has been banned from Jerusalem for twenty years, so we brought Jerusalem to us," she says.

She is an Israeli citizen, but because her husband is Palestinian, because of his ethnicity, he is refused citizenship. She was born in Long Island. He was born here. This is how it works in Israel. Israel is a democracy only for Jews. If she had married a Jew he would have a passport and citizenship.

"What democratic state builds its laws based on a person's ethnicity?" she asks. "The goal of the South African apartheid regime was to separate whites and blacks to preserve white privilege. How is this different from what is being done to the Palestinians?

"Who is really being shut out by this wall?" she adds. "Who is being shut in? Israel will be a closed society when the wall is finished. It will even further shun reality."

Her son wakes up and begins to cry. She gets up and walks to his room. She comes back with the infant in her arms. She begins to breastfeed him.

As she coos over her son she lets me read a notebook smuggled out of the prison. It has drawings by one of the prisoners for her child Quds with stories by her husband. On the cover of the ruled school notebook are the words "Quds Smart Notebook."

In one picture a small boy is feeding a bird.

"This is Quds's bird," it says. "Quds feeds the bird. The bird loves Quds. The birds are playing in Quds' beautiful garden. They know Quds. They love him very much."

She slips her wedding ring off her finger so I can read the inscription on the band inside. It has two letter *A*'s with a heart between them. The word *forever* is etched into the band. She cradles the child in her arms and whispers words of comfort to him.

She looks up, weary and sad.

"In Israel, I'm considered radical because I advocate equal rights for all persons residing between the Jordan River and the Mediterranean Sea," she says.

It does not matter where I turn. I see the noose tightening. There is no escape. The barrier is closing in from every side, grinding and crushing everything in its path. I begin to feel the claustrophobia, the sense of inevitable doom, the awful fatalness of it all.

Palestinians cling to what they have like shipwrecked sailors clinging to the hull of a sinking boat. There is a mass migration. They are being forced from their homes. Some have moved into their fields. They have set up squalid little encampments in vegetable patches. It is their last stand.

I walk over the heavy earth on the Israeli side of the fence from the village of Jayyous. The village has some 2,200 acres, along with six wells and pumping stations. The fence has separated the farmers in the village from seventy-three percent of its irrigated farmland. About three hundred families are losing their only source of income.

My feet are covered with dirt. I see across the fields the sparks shooting up from numerous campfires. I hear voices, the idle chatter of children, women, and men.

Suffian Youssef, 30, stands beside an old blue truck. His two brothers, his mother, and his father are with him. It is nearly dark. They have set up a small tarp and a crude shack. It is where they sleep. There is a brass coffee pot on the brazier over the fire. I smell wood smoke.

"We began to sleep in our fields a month ago," he said:

We fear that if they close the gate we will not be able to get to our crop. We are having trouble getting our crop to market. We took the crates of potatoes up to the gate in the truck a few days ago. The

Border Police told us to take the crates off the truck and load them back on the truck four times. When we took them off for the fourth time, they dumped the potatoes on the ground and crushed them with their boots. They beat us with their rifle butts.

Crickets chirp softly. I see a half-moon poking through the haze in the sky.

The roadblocks and checkpoints mean that farmers cannot get their produce to urban areas in the West Bank. Israeli suppliers, who can use the settler roads, have now taken over these markets. Because vegetables are bottled up in agricultural areas, prices have plummeted.

"We may not have enough money next year to plant a crop," Youssef says.

When I leave it is night. I stumble out of the fields. I know they will not be here next year.

It is late afternoon at Gate Number 542 in the farming village of Zeita, north of Tulkarm. A sign on the electric fence that runs along the dirt track for as far as the eye can see reads: "Danger. Military Area. Anyone crossing or touching the fence does so at his own risk." It is in Hebrew, Arabic, and English.

The iron gates are painted yellow. Motion sensors and television cameras are mounted along the fence. There is a smooth strip of sand to detect unauthorized footprints. There is a dirt service road. There is a trench about seven feet deep to stop vehicles from crashing through the barrier. There is a paved road for the army jeeps. There are coils of razor wire. The land on either side of the barrier, about 100 feet wide, is desolate. Blackened stumps from uprooted olive trees poke up from the dirt. All living things on or near the barrier have been killed. It tastes of death. This is what the barrier will look like in most places on the West Bank.

Poles are mounted with powerful floodlights along the barrier to turn night into day. The farmers who live on the edge of the wasteland, often once their farmland, cannot sleep because of the glare of the lights.

A dozen poor farmers and shepherds are clustered on the other side of the barrier. They have grazed their flocks or tended their plants on their land, land Israel has swallowed up. They have been there for an hour. The gate is supposed to be opened at 6 P.M. On some nights the Border Police come early. Other nights they come late. There are times they do not come at all. When they do not come the farmers and shepherds sleep on the ground near the gate until morning.

Jamal Hassouna, 43, a farmer, is standing with me. We are standing on land that once belonged to him but was taken without compensation to build the barrier.

"If anyone touches the fence, even a child, they are not allowed to pass," he says. "Every soldier is a little Ariel Sharon."

Two green armored jeeps from the Border Police roar down the asphalt strip enclosed by the two electric fences. They halt and five policemen climb out. They hold their M16s at an angle. They are wearing helmets. One soldier, watched by two others, goes to open the padlock on the gate on the other side. He swings the gate open and the motley crowd walks out into the empty space, across the tarred road and the dirt road to the yellow gate on my side. They show the police their special permits before they are allowed through the yellow gate.

The police are silent. Jamal says it is because I am present. On many nights, he says, farmers are insulted, cursed, made to lift their shirts, or humiliated by being told they have to crawl through the gates. To spare themselves the harassment, wives and children no longer cross. There are many farmers who, although they are never told why, are no longer allowed to pass. Their fields are dying.

I walk to tomato fields covered by gauzy brown netting. Iyad Abu Hamdi, 27, is seated alone on the lip of a small drainage ditch next to the field of tomatoes. His land is on the other side of the barrier.

He was tending his crop of peppers a few days ago when a patrol of the Border Police arrived at his field. The two policemen began to make lewd remarks to his wife, who was working with him. They ordered her to make them coffee. She obeyed. They ordered her sister to bring them water. She refused. They threw their thermos at his brother and told him to fill it with water. He also refused.

"They began to beat my brother," Hamdi says. "They tossed the coffee in our faces. They cursed us. They shouted at us. They confiscated our identification cards. The soldiers told my wife to accept their advances or they would ruin her reputation."

When he says, "accept their advances," his voice quivers with emotion and he turns his head away to avoid my eyes.

The sun is dipping below the earth. There is a dim yellow glow across the fields. His voice is shaking. He bows his head between his knees and looks at the ground.

"This happened on August 3," he begins again. "I have not been allowed to cross since. They slam the gate shut in my face. My crop is dying."

The tears roll down his cheeks. They, too, are serpent's teeth.

Coveting the Holocaust

OCTOBER 23, 2006

I sent my New York University journalism students out to write stories based on any one of the themes in the Ten Commandments. A woman of Armenian descent came back with an article about how Armenians she had interviewed were covetous of the Jewish Holocaust. The idea that one people who suffered near-decimation could be covetous of another that also suffered near-decimation was, to say the least, different. And when the National Assembly, the lower house of the French Parliament, approved a bill earlier this month making it a crime to deny the Armenian genocide, I began to wonder what it was she, and those she had interviewed, actually coveted.

She was writing not about the Holocaust itself—no one covets the suffering of another—but about how it has become a potent political and ideological weapon in the hands of the Israeli government and many in the American Jewish community. While Armenians are still fighting to have the genocide of some 1.5 million Armenians by the Ottoman Turks accepted as historical fact, many Jews have found in the Nazi Holocaust a useful instrument with which to deflect criticism of Israel and the dubious actions of the pro-Israeli lobby and many Jewish groups in the United States.

Norman Finkelstein, who for his writings has been virtually blacklisted in some political and intellectual circles, noted in his book *The Holocaust Industry* that the Jewish Holocaust has allowed Israel to cast itself and "the most successful ethnic group in the United States" as eternal victims. Finkelstein, son of Jewish survivors of the Nazi Holocaust, goes on to argue that this status has enabled Israel, which has "a horrendous human rights record," to play the victim as it oppresses

Palestinians or destroys Lebanon. This victim status has permitted U.S. Jewish organizations (the American Jewish Committee, the American Jewish Congress, and others) to get their hands on billions of dollars in reparations, much of which never finds its way to the dwindling number of Holocaust survivors. Finkelstein's mother, who was in the Warsaw ghetto, received $3,500, while the World Jewish Congress walked away with roughly $7 billion in compensation. The organization pays lavish salaries to its employees and uses the funds to fuel its own empire. For many the Nazi Holocaust is used not to understand and deal with the past, and, more important, the universal human capacity for evil, but to manipulate the present. Finkelstein correctly writes that the fictitious notion of "unique suffering leads to feelings of unique entitlement."[1]

And so what this student, and those she had interviewed, coveted was not the actual experience of the Holocaust, not the suffering of Jews in the death camps, but the political capital that Israel and many of its supporters have successfully gleaned from the Holocaust. And while I sympathize with the Armenians, while I understand their rage toward Turkey, I do not wish to see them, or anyone else, wield their own genocide as a political weapon.

There is a fine and dangerous line between the need for historical truth and public apology, in this case by the Turks, and the gross misuse of human tragedy. French president Jacques Chirac and his interior minister, Nicolas Sarkozy, said this month that Turkey will have to recognize the genocide before Turkey is allowed to join the European Union. Most European nations turned their backs on the French, with the EU issuing a statement saying that the French bill will "prohibit dialogue."

But the French move is salutary, not only for the Armenians who have been humiliated and defamed by successive waves of Turkish governments, but also for the Turks. Historical amnesia, as anyone who has lived in the Middle East or the Balkans knows, makes reconciliation and healing impossible. It fosters a dangerous sense of grievance and rage. It makes any real dialogue impossible. Nearly one hundred years after the murderous rampage by the Turks, it can still be a crime to name the Armenian holocaust under Article 301 of the Turkish Penal

Code. Article 301 prohibits anyone from defaming Turkey. One of the most courageous violators of that law is the writer Orhan Pamuk, who has criticized his country's refusal to confront its past, and who won the 2006 Nobel Prize in Literature. But he is a solitary figure in Turkey.

Historical black holes also empower those who insist the Nazi Holocaust is unique, that it is somehow beyond human comprehension and stands apart from other human activity. These silences make it easier to minimize, misunderstand, and ignore the reality of other genocides, how they work, and how they are carried out. They make it easier to turn tragedy into myth. They make it easier to misread the real lesson of the Holocaust, which, as Christopher Browning illustrated in his book *Ordinary Men: Reserve Police Battalion 101 and the Final Solution in Poland*, is that the line between the victim and the victimizer is razor-thin. Most of us, as Browning correctly argues, can be seduced and manipulated into killing our neighbors.[2] Few are immune.

The communists, not the Jews, were the Nazis' first victims, and the handicapped were the first to be gassed in the German death factories. This is not to minimize the suffering of the Jews, but these victims, too, deserve attention. And what about Roma, homosexuals, prisoners of war, and German political dissidents? What, on a wider scale, about the Cambodians, the Rwandans, and the millions more who have been slaughtered by utopian idealists who believe the eradication of other human beings will cleanse the world?

When I visited the Holocaust Museum in Washington, I looked in vain for these other victims. I did not see explained in detail the awful reality that Jewish officials in the ghettos—the *Judenräte*—worked closely with the Nazis to herd their own off to the death camps. And was the happy resolution of the Holocaust, as we saw in images at the end of the exhibits, the disembarking of European Jews on the shores of Palestine? What about the Palestinians who lived in Palestine and were soon to be pushed off their land? And, as important, what about African Americans and Native Americans? Why is the Nazi genocide, which we did not perpetrate, displayed on the Mall in Washington and the brutal extermination of Native Americans ignored? Why should billions in reparations be paid to Jewish slave laborers and not a dime to those enslaved by our own country?

These questions circle back to the dangerous sanctification of any genocide, the belief that one ethnic group can represent goodness, solely because its members are the victims, and another evil because from its ranks come the thugs who carry out mass slaughter. Once these demented killing machines begin their work, the only thing unique is the method of murder. The lesson of any genocide is not that one group of human beings is better than another, but that in the intoxication of the moment, gripped by the mass hypnosis of state propaganda and the lust for violence, we can all become killers.

All the victims must be heard. None are unique. And all of us have to be on guard lest we be seduced. We carry within us—German, Jew, Armenian, or Christian—dark and dangerous lusts that must be held in check. I applaud the French. I hope the French action pushes the Turks toward contrition and honesty. But I do not wish for the Armenians to covet the Holocaust, to begin the process of sanctifying their own suffering. When we sanctify ourselves we do so at the expense of others.

Bring Down That Wall

NOVEMBER 20, 2006

The last hope of halting Israel's steady ghettoization of Palestinians in the West Bank and Gaza Strip, and the calculated destruction of the Palestinian economy, is the imposition of sanctions against Israel, especially the revocation of $9 billion in U.S. loan guarantees. If we allow Israel to complete its massive $2 billion project to ring Palestinians in militarized, podlike encampments in Gaza and the West Bank with security barriers, walls, and electric fences, we will condemn Israel and the Palestinians to endless cycles of violence that could ultimately, given the mounting rage and despair that grip the Middle East, doom the Jewish state.

There is little dispute about the illegality of Israel's actions. The International Court of Justice has called on Israel to dismantle the security barrier under construction in the West Bank and asked outside states not to render any aid or assistance to the infrastructure. But this call has been ignored, although even the U.S. State Department has gently admonished Israel for its behavior. The U.S. loans that make the barrier and expansion of Jewish settlements possible were granted with the stipulation that if the Israeli government used the funds to build housing and infrastructure beyond the 1967 border known as the Green Line, these funds would be deducted from the loans. In April 2003, when Congress authorized the $9 billion in loan guarantees for Israel, it said that the loans could be used "only to support activities in the geographic areas which were subject to the administration of the Government of Israel before June 5, 1967." The legislation warned that the loan guarantees would be reduced in the light of "activities which the President determines are inconsistent with the objectives and understandings reached between the United States and Israel regarding the implementation of the loan guarantee program." The State Department, acknowledging the misuse of the money, has made a symbolic deduction in the amount handed to the Israeli government and reduced the loan guarantees by $289.5 million. But unless heavy pressure is brought on Israel soon, the project will be completed, made possible by Washington's complicity and a callous disregard for justice.

Israel is pumping hundreds of millions of dollars—some reports say as much as half a billion yearly—into its colonization of the West Bank. Since 1967, Israel has spent more than $10 billion on its settlements, and the total estimated cost for the snaking security barrier, which slices deep into the West Bank and connects with settlements and security roads to create Palestinian ghettos, is at least $1.5 billion. The barrier is being used not only to annex Palestinian land but also to give Israel control of Palestinian aquifers and at least forty thousand acres of Palestinian farmland. It has devastated Palestinian communities, often cutting them in half or denying farmers access to farmland. Travel, even between communities on the West Bank, has become difficult, especially for men, and many have lost their jobs, plunging with their families into squalor and despair.

The spate of deadly attacks by Palestinian suicide bombers in Israel gave Israel the right to impose draconian measures. A barrier running along the Green Line was Israel's prerogative. But the barrier is being used as an excuse to seize Palestinian land. When it is done, the Palestinians in the West Bank, like those in Gaza, will be caged like animals, with little ability to move, even to neighboring towns, find work, or live beyond subsistence level.

The assault on Palestinian society has been accompanied by an alarming increase in Israeli attacks against Palestinians, including the current Israeli offensive in Gaza. Fifteen tank shells landed this month (November 2006) in the town of Beit Hanoun, killing nineteen people and wounding forty. Four women and nine children were among the dead. Two Palestinians were killed November 18, as Israel continued air strikes and ground operations against suspected militant positions in the Gaza Strip, all coming a day after the U.N. General Assembly urged an end to the escalating violence.

Israeli leaders, angered over Palestinian rocket attacks, have dismissed calls for restraint, with far-right cabinet minister Avigdor Lieberman calling for Palestinian prime minister Ismail Haniya and other militant leaders to be sent to "paradise."

When Yasir Arafat agreed to end his exile to return to Gaza, swallow his pride, and formally recognize Israel's right to exist, when he turned his Fatah fighters into a collaboration police force in the West Bank and Gaza, he was broke. The communist states that had once bankrolled him had collapsed. He was humbled to the Oslo Accords, under which he took the bitter pill of accommodation with his detested Zionist enemy. Unless Israel, too, feels pressure it will never seek accommodation with the Palestinians, relying instead on increasing forms of repression and mounting violence. These measures, depriving Palestinians of hope and dignity, are the fuel of radical movements and ensure not peace but unending war. Israel has ignored the terms stipulated for the U.S. loan guarantees, and so we have a choice: to uphold our own demands and international law, or be a party to Israeli policies that will lead to an unraveling of the region's stability.

Israel's Toy Soldiers

OCTOBER 1, 2007

If you are a young Muslim American and head off to the Middle East for a spell in a fundamentalist *madrassa*, or religious school, Homeland Security will probably greet you at the airport when you return. But if you are an American Jew and you join hundreds of teenagers from Europe and Mexico for an eight-week training course run by the Israel Defense Forces, you can post your picture wearing an Israeli army uniform and holding an automatic weapon on MySpace.

The Marva program, part summer camp part indoctrination, was launched in Israel in 1981. It allows participants, who must be Jewish and between the ages of 18 and 28, to fire weapons, live in military barracks in the Negev desert, and saunter around in an Israeli military uniform saluting and taking long hikes with military packs. The Youth and Education Corps of the Israel Defense Forces run four 120-strong training sessions a year.

"Upon arrival, the participants experience an abrupt change into army life: wearing uniforms, accepting army discipline, and learning the programs and lessons integral to the program," the Let Israelis Show You Israel Web site reads:

> The program includes military content such as: navigation, field training, weapons training, shooting ranges, marches and more, as well as educational content such as: Zionism, Jewish Identity, history and knowledge of the land of Israel. All of this is taught in Hebrew in an intensive eight weeks.

"The participants finish the program after completing a short, intensive, exhilarating military experience that allows them to taste Israel in a way that they never could before—as part of the Israel Defense Forces," the site reads. "They leave the program with a feeling of belonging and a strong connection to Israel, and many return to Israel to continue the connection that was created in the framework of the Marva course."

There are, of course, gushing testimonials about the program:

"I spent the first few days of Marva doubting my decision, wondering why I had come, wondering if there was any way out. With all of the running, yelling orders, discipline and Hebrew, I felt horribly out of place," writes Canadian David Roth of his summer:

> It was a completely different world from the one I was used to. All that changed, though, by the end of the first week. We had our first "Masa" (Hike). It was very hard, but at the end, we all knew, our M16s were waiting for us at the "tekes" (Ceremony). We got through the 8 kilometers and had our "tekes" and got our guns. It felt amazing, and from that point on Marva was incredible.[3]

How have we reacted when we discovered that American Muslims were being taught in a foreign country to fire machine guns at paper figures and simulate military maneuvers? And what about the summer schools in Gaza, organized by Islamic Jihad and designed to train young Palestinians in the basics of military life? These Gaza camps, uncovered in 2001, were widely denounced by Israel as proof that the Palestinians were teaching their children to hate and kill.

The argument in favor of such military programs in Israel, as opposed to the same or similar programs in Pakistan, is that these young men and women are not going to come back and use what they have learned to harm Americans. They are not terrorists. Muslims, however, have not cornered the market on terrorism and violence. Radical Jews have also been involved in terrorist attacks in Israel and the United States.

I discovered an American in Israel in 1989 named Robert Manning. A huge, burly man, Manning was living in the West Bank Jewish settlement of Kiryat Arba. When I found him he was carrying a pistol, a large knife strapped to his leg, and an M16. He was part of a Jewish terrorist group, called Committee for Protection and Safety of the High-ways, that set up ad hoc roadblocks and pulled Palestinians from cars to beat and often shoot them. He was a follower of Meir Kahane, the leader of the Jewish Defense League who was implicated in terrorist at-tacks in the United States and Israel. Manning served as a reservist in the Israel Defense Forces in the West Bank.

Manning was wanted in California for murder. He had been charged in a 1980 mail-bomb killing as part of his involvement in the Jewish Defense League. The bomb was intended for the owner of a local com-puter firm, but the package holding the device was opened by the firm's secretary, Patricia Wilkerson, who was killed instantly by the blast.

Manning, full of bluster and a bitter racism toward Arabs, used as his pseudonym the name of the FBI agent in charge of his case, a bit of humor that backfired on him by confirming my suspicion of his iden-tity. I obtained the picture from his California driver's license and showed it to his neighbors at Kiryat Arba. They identified him from the photo. I wrote an article affirming that Manning, heavily armed and an active member of the Israeli army, was living in a Jewish settlement. The Israeli government, until that moment, said it had no information about his location. He was extradited in 1993 and sentenced the next year to life imprisonment without the possibility of parole for thirty years. He is in a maximum-security prison in Florence, Colorado.

Those who go through the Marva summer program are indoctri-nated as thoroughly as Muslims who go overseas and are told they are part of a greater jihad for Islam. The results, given Israel's close alliance with the United States, may not harm those in power in the United States, but they may well harm Americans defined as the enemy, espe-cially Muslims, should we suffer another 9/11. The program inculcates hatred and a belief in the efficacy of violence to solve the problems in the Middle East. It identifies Israel with militarism. It feeds participants the idea that a Jew born in Brooklyn has a birthright to settle in Israel that is denied to an American of Palestinian descent.

Jerusalem, aside from being one of the most beautiful cities in the world, is also one of the most literate, creative, and intellectual. Do these young men and women really learn the best of Israel when they spend eight weeks playing soldier and glorifying the military? Is the cause of Israel advanced by mirroring the twisted militarism of Islamic fundamentalists?

Terrorists arise in all cultures, all nations, and all religions. We have produced more than our share. Ask the people of Vietnam or Iraq. The danger of military programs such as these is that they solidify an us-and-them mind-set. They romanticize violence. They widen the divide that leads to conflict. They make dialogue impossible. There are great Israeli institutions, from the newspaper *Haaretz* to the courageous Israeli human-rights organization B'Tselem to Peace Now. A summer working for such organizations, rather than wearing an army uniform, unleashing bursts of automatic fire in the desert, and singing Israeli patriotic songs, might actually help.

The World as It Is

MARCH 10, 2008

War creates a world without empathy. Those who have empathy cannot, as did Palestinian gunman Alaa Hisham Abu Dheim, coldly murder students in a Jerusalem library a few days ago. Those who have empathy cannot drop tons of iron fragmentation bombs on crowded Palestinian refugee camps in Gaza, killing more than 120 Palestinians in a week, of whom one in five were children and more than half were civilians. Those who have empathy do not, as Israeli deputy defense minister Matan Vilnai did two weeks ago, thunder at the Palestinians that they face a *shoah*, meaning catastrophe or holocaust. Those with empathy are unable to rejoice, as many leaders of Hamas did, over slaughter, as if the murder of "our" innocents justifies the murder of "their" innocents.

We live in a world, at home and in the Middle East, hardened and distorted by hate. We communicate in the language of fear and violence. Human beings are no longer viewed as human beings. They are no longer endowed in our eyes, or the eyes of those who oppose us, with human qualities. They do not love, grieve, suffer, laugh, or weep. They represent cold abstractions of evil. The death-for-death ethic means we communicate only by producing corpses. And we are all guilty, Americans, Palestinians, Iraqis, and Israelis. But we are not all guilty equally.

Israel and the United States bear the responsibility for a world that has unleashed twisted killers such as Abu Dheim. Decades of repression in Gaza, as well as the callous occupation in Iraq, have bequeathed to us a new generation of jihadists and gunmen who walk into yeshivas and spray automatic fire at students bent over books. For as W. H. Auden pointed out:

I and the public know
What all schoolchildren learn,
Those to whom evil is done
Do evil in return

The long, slow drip of collective humiliation and abuse, along with the tiny and large indignities that go into transforming human beings into fanatics, is rarely understood by those on the outside. It ticks away like a clock until it suddenly explodes in our face. Because we do not know where it came from, it strikes us as incomprehensible, irrational, the product of a demented form of humanity. These killers, however, are not formed by the Koran or Islam or a culture that is morally inferior to our own. They are formed by a forty-year occupation, by the continued expansion of Jewish settlements, by the refusal to allow the return of expelled refugees, by the use of fighter jets to bomb squalid refugee camps, and by an Israeli siege of Gaza that has blocked fuel, electricity, and essential supplies and created a humanitarian crisis for 1.5 million Palestinians. It is what the Israelis have done to the Palestinians, what we have done to the Iraqis, that has brought us to this impasse. We unleashed this violence and only we can end it.

Hamas was a nonentity, a tiny group of radicals who wielded no influence and had little following, when in 1988 I first reported from Gaza. But the steady drumbeat of Israeli repression and violence, aided by the corruption and incompetence of Yasir Arafat, led to Hamas' slow rise to supplant Arafat's Fatah party. By 2006 Hamas was elected to power. This election, by all accounts free and fair, saw Jerusalem and Washington begin a covert effort to overthrow Hamas, according to documents obtained by *Vanity Fair* and the *Guardian*. The Fatah leader Muhammad Dahlan was, according to these documents, given cash, weapons, and assistance through Egypt and Jordan to start a Palestinian civil war. Hamas stepped in to thwart the attempted coup. It drove Dahlan and Fatah out of Gaza. The current bifurcation of Palestinian territories, with Hamas in control of Gaza and Fatah in control of the West Bank, began.

Israeli prime minister Ehud Olmert, unable to break Hamas with the siege that began in May 2007, and frustrated by the Palestinians' spontaneous rupture of the barricades that separate the Gaza Strip from Egypt, is trying to pound Gaza into submission. During the past three months of unrelenting Israeli strikes, more than three hundred Palestinians, most of them civilians, have died. The strikes have done nothing, however, to halt the rocket attacks on Israeli towns or end Hamas rule.

In a report last week, Amnesty International, CARE International, Oxfam Great Britain, and other humanitarian aid groups said that living conditions in Gaza are at their worst since Israel occupied the Strip in 1967. The report estimated that eighty percent of Gaza residents are now dependent on food aid, compared with sixty-three percent two years ago. It noted that unemployment is about forty percent among the general population and seventy percent in the private sector. The aid groups document power cuts to hospitals of as long as twelve hours a day, fifty million liters of sewage pouring into the sea daily, and water and sewage systems on the brink of collapse. The groups have called on the European Union and the U.K government to pressure Israel to open border crossings and begin negotiations with Hamas.

Washington and Jerusalem have little interest in a peaceful settlement. They are blinded by their own military prowess. They do not grasp that continuing the violence and tightening the siege will spur more desperate and embittered young men and women to acts of vengeance. The only route left is to hear the cries of all the victims, Israeli and Palestinian, to recapture empathy. Hamas' offer to negotiate a truce, an offer backed by sixty-four percent of Israelis, is the only escape route. There is no option other than finally to give the Palestinians control over their lives and land. It is the only option that will, as well, save us in Iraq. The occupation of Palestinian territory, like the occupation of Iraq, is illegal, increasingly violent, and counterproductive.

I was in Gaza in 1993 after the Oslo Accords were signed. It was as if, after years of suffocation, Palestinians and Israelis could breathe. But Oslo, in the hands of former Israeli prime ministers Benjamin Netanyahu and Ariel Sharon, was strangled and thwarted. Peace eludes us in Palestine, Israel, and Iraq not because people do not want peace but because we are governed by moral and intellectual trolls.

The Palestine Liberation Organization, headed by the Fatah party, was once considered a terrorist organization. It was illegal for an Israeli to have contact with the Palestine Liberation Organization. Israelis who called for negotiations with the PLO were attacked and vilified. The Israeli government, however, under the pragmatism of Yitzhak Rabin, violated its own ban and began secret negotiations. These led to the Oslo peace agreement. Fatah, today, is touted by Jerusalem and Washington as an ally in the war against Hamas and a partner for peace.

The dynamics of power have changed. They will change again. Hamas is a reality that, however distasteful, is not going to go away. Any peace deal reached without Hamas is doomed to fail. The only question left is how many more people are going to die needlessly in Israel, in Palestine, and in Iraq before Israeli and American leaders begin to deal with the world as it is, not as they wish it to be.

Party to Murder

DECEMBER 29, 2008

Can anyone following the Israeli air attacks on Gaza—the buildings blown to rubble, the children killed on their way to school, the long rows of mutilated corpses, the wailing mothers and wives, the crowds of terrified Palestinians not knowing where to flee, the hospitals so overburdened and out of supplies they cannot treat the wounded, and our studied, callous indifference to this widespread human suffering—wonder why we are hated?

Our self-righteous celebration of ourselves and our supposed virtue is as false as that of Israel. We have become monsters, militarized bullies, heartless and savage. We are a party to human slaughter, a flagrant war crime, and do nothing. We forget that the innocents who suffer and die in Gaza are a reflection of ourselves, of how we might have been should fate and time and geography have made the circumstances of our births different. We forget that we are all absurd and vulnerable creatures. We all have the capacity to fear and hate and love. "Expose thyself to feel what wretches feel," King Lear said, entering the mud and straw hovel of Poor Tom, " . . . and show the heavens more just."[4]

Privilege and power, especially military power, is a dangerous narcotic. Violence destroys those who bear the brunt of its force, but also those who try to use it to become gods. More than three hundred and fifty Palestinians have been killed, many of them civilians, and more than a thousand have been wounded since the air attacks began on Saturday. Ehud Barak, Israel's defense minister, said Israel is engaged in a "war to the bitter end" against Hamas in Gaza. A war? Israel uses sophisticated attack jets and naval vessels to bomb densely crowded refugee camps and slums, to attack a population that has no air force, no air defense, no navy, no heavy weapons, no artillery units, no mechanized armor, no command and control, no army, and calls it a war. It is not a war. It is murder.

The U.N. special rapporteur for human rights in the occupied Palestinian territory, former Princeton University law professor Richard Falk, has labeled what Israel is doing to the Palestinians in Gaza "a crime against humanity." Falk, who is Jewish, has condemned the collective punishment of the Palestinians in Gaza as "a flagrant and massive violation of international humanitarian law as laid down in Article 33 of the Fourth Geneva Convention." He has asked the International Criminal Court to "investigate the situation, and determine whether the Israeli civilian leaders and military commanders responsible for the Gaza siege should be indicted and prosecuted for violations of international criminal law."

Falk's unflinching honesty has enraged Israel. He was banned from entering the country on December 14, 2008, during his attempt to visit Gaza and the West Bank.

"After being denied entry I was put in a holding room with about twenty others experiencing entry problems," he said:

At this point I was treated not as a U.N. representative, but as some sort of security threat, subjected to an inch-by-inch body search, and the most meticulous luggage inspection I have ever witnessed. I was separated from my two U.N. companions, who were allowed to enter Israel. At this point I was taken to the airport detention facility a mile or so away, required to put all my bags and cell phone in a room, taken to a locked, tiny room that had five other detainees, smelled of urine and filth, and was an unwelcome invitation to claustrophobia. I spent the next fifteen hours so confined, which amounted to a cram course on the miseries of prison life, including dirty sheets, inedible food, and either lights that were too bright or darkness controlled from the guard office.

The foreign media have been, like Falk, barred by Israel from entering Gaza to report on the destruction.

Israel's stated aim of halting homemade rockets fired from Gaza into Israel remains unfulfilled. Gaza militants have fired more than one hundred rockets and mortars into Israel, killing four people and wounding nearly two dozen more, since Israel unleashed its air assault. Israel has threatened to launch a ground assault and has called up 6,500 army reservists. It has massed tanks on the Gaza border and declared the area a closed military zone.

The rocket attacks by Hamas are, as Falk points out, also criminal violations of international law. But as Falk notes, "Such Palestinian behavior does not legalize Israel's imposition of a collective punishment of a life- and health-threatening character on the people of Gaza, and should not distract the U.N. or international society from discharging their fundamental moral and legal duty to render protection to the Palestinian people."

"It is an unfolding humanitarian catastrophe that each day poses the entire 1.5 million Gazans to an unspeakable ordeal, to a struggle to survive in terms of their health," Falk has said of the ongoing Israeli blockade of Gaza:

This is an increasingly precarious condition. A recent study reports that forty-six percent of all Gazan children suffer from acute anemia. There are reports that the sonic booms associated with Israeli overflights have caused widespread deafness, especially among children. Gazan children need thousands of hearing aids. Malnutrition is extremely high in a number of different dimensions and affects seventy-five percent of Gazans. There are widespread mental disorders, especially among young people without the will to live. Over fifty percent of Gazan children under the age of twelve have been found to have no will to live.

Before the air assaults, Gaza spent twelve hours a day without power, which can be a death sentence to the severely ill in hospitals. Most of Gaza is now without power. There are few drugs and little medicine, including no cancer or cystic fibrosis medication. Hospitals have generators but often lack fuel. Medical equipment, including one of Gaza's three CT scanners, has been destroyed by power surges and fluctuations.

Medical staff cannot control the temperature of incubators for newborns. And Israel has revoked most exit visas, meaning some of those who need specialized care, including cancer patients and those in need of kidney dialysis, have died. Of the 230 Gazans estimated to have died last year because they were denied proper medical care, several spent their final hours at Israeli crossing points, where they were refused entry into Israel. The statistics gathered on children—half of Gaza's population is under the age of seventeen—are increasingly grim. About forty-five percent of children in Gaza have iron deficiency from a lack of fruit and vegetables, and eighteen percent have stunted growth.

"It is macabre," Falk said of the blockade. "I don't know of anything that exactly fits this situation. People have been referring to the Warsaw ghetto as the nearest analogue in modern times.

"There is no structure of an occupation that endured for decades and involved this kind of oppressive circumstances," the rapporteur added. "The magnitude, the deliberateness, the violations of international humanitarian law, the impact on the health, lives, and survival, and the overall conditions warrant the characterization of a crime against humanity. This occupation is the direct intention by the Israeli military and civilian authorities. They are responsible and should be held accountable."

The point of the Israeli attack, ostensibly, is to break Hamas, the radical Islamic group elected to power in 2007. But Hamas has repeatedly proposed long-term truces with Israel and offered to negotiate a permanent truce. During the last cease-fire, established through Egyptian intermediaries in July, Hamas upheld the truce although Israel refused to ease the blockade. It was Israel that, on November 4, 2008, initiated an armed attack that violated the truce and killed six Palestinians. It was only then that Hamas resumed firing rockets at Israel.

"This is a crime of survival," Falk said of the rocket attacks by Palestinians:

Israel has put the Gazans in a set of circumstances where they either have to accept whatever is imposed on them or resist in any way available to them. That is a horrible dilemma to impose upon a people. This does not alleviate the Palestinians, and Gazans in particular, for accountability for doing these acts involving rocket fire, but it also imposes some responsibility on Israel for creating these circumstances.

Israel seeks to break the will of the Palestinians to resist. The Israeli government has demonstrated little interest in diplomacy or a peaceful solution. The rapid expansion of Jewish settlements on the West Bank is an effort to thwart the possibility of a two-state solution by gobbling up vast tracts of Palestinian real estate. Israel also appears to want to thrust the impoverished Gaza Strip onto Egypt. Dozens of tunnels had been the principal means for food and goods, connecting Gaza to Egypt. Israel had permitted the tunnels to operate, most likely as part of an effort to further cut Gaza off from Israel. This ended, however, on December 28, 2008, when Israeli fighter jets bombed more than forty tunnels along Gaza's border with Egypt. The Israeli military said that the tunnels, on the Gaza side of the border, were used for smuggling weapons, explosives, and fugitives. Egypt has sealed its border and refused to let distraught Palestinians enter its territory.

"Israel, all along, has not been prepared to enter into diplomatic process that gives the Palestinians a viable state," Falk said. "They [the Israelis] feel time is on their side. They feel they can create enough facts on the ground so people will come to the conclusion a viable state cannot emerge."

The use of terror and hunger to break a hostile population is one of the oldest forms of warfare. I watched the Bosnian Serbs employ the same tactic in Sarajevo. Those who orchestrate such sieges do not grasp the terrible rage born of long humiliation, indiscriminate violence, and abuse. A father or a mother whose child dies because of a lack of vaccines or proper medical care does not forget. A boy whose ill grandmother dies while detained at an Israel checkpoint does not forget. A family that loses a child in an air strike does not forget. No one who endures humiliation, abuse, and the murder of family members ever forgets. This rage becomes a virus within those who, eventually, stumble out into the daylight. Is it any wonder that seventy-one percent of children interviewed at a school in Gaza recently said they wanted to be a "martyr"?

The Israelis in Gaza, like the American forces in Iraq and Afghanistan, are foolishly breeding the next generation of militants and Islamic radicals. Jihadists, enraged by the injustices done by Israel and the United States, seek to carry out reciprocal acts of savagery, even at the cost of their own lives. The violence unleashed on Palestinian children will, one day, be the violence unleashed on Israeli children. This is the tragedy of Gaza. This is the tragedy of Israel.

Lost in the Rubble

JANUARY 2, 2009

I often visited Nizar Rayan, who was killed January 1 in a targeted assassination by Israel, at his house in the Jabalia refugee camp when I was in Gaza. The house is now rubble. It was hit by two missiles fired by Israeli F-16 fighter jets. Rayan, who would meet me in his book-lined study, was decapitated in the blast. His body was thrown into the street by the explosions. His four wives and eleven children also were killed.

Rayan supported tactics, including suicide bombings, that are morally repugnant. His hatred of Israel ran deep. His fundamentalist brand of Islam was distasteful. But because he and I were students of theology, our discussions frequently veered off into the nature of belief, Islam, the Koran, the Bible, and the religious life. He was a serious, thoughtful man who had suffered deeply under the occupation and dedicated his life to resistance. He could have fled his home and gone underground with other Hamas leaders. Knowing him, I suspect he could not leave his children. Like him or not, one must admit he had tremendous courage.

Hamas, he constantly reminded me, began to target Israeli civilians in 1994 only after Palestinian worshipers were gunned down in a Hebron mosque by a Jewish settler, Baruch Goldstein. Goldstein was a resident of the nearby Kiryat Arba settlement. He entered the mosque dressed in his army uniform, carrying an IMI Galil assault rifle and four magazines of ammunition. He opened fire on those in prayer, killing twenty-nine people and injuring 125. He was rushed and beaten to death by the survivors.

"Before the massacre we targeted only the Israeli military," Rayan said. "We can't sit by and watch Palestinian civilians killed year after year and do nothing. When Israel stops killing our civilians, we will stop killing their civilians."

Rayan was a theology and law professor at Islamic University in Gaza. He was a large man with a thick black beard and the quiet, soft-spoken manner of someone who has spent much of his life reading. On the walls of his office, black-and-white photographs illustrated the history of Palestinians over the last five decades. They showed lines of trucks carrying refugees from their villages in 1948. They showed the hovels of new refugee camps built after the 1967 war. And they showed the gutted and razed remains of Palestinian villages in what is now Israel.

Rayan's grandfather and great-uncle were killed in the 1948 war that led to the establishment of Israel. His grandmother died shortly after she and her son, Rayan's father, were driven from their village by Jewish fighters. His father was passed among relatives and grew up with the bitterness of the dispossessed—a bitterness the father passed on to the son and the son passed on to his own children.

Israeli militias in 1948 drove some 800,000 Palestinians from their homes, farms, towns, and villages into exile in the West Bank, Gaza, and neighboring countries. Israeli historian Ilan Pappe's book *The Ethnic Cleansing of Palestine* details the deliberate Israeli policy of removing Palestinians from their land.

"There was not a single night that we did not think and talk about Palestine," Rayan said the last time I saw him, his eyes growing moist. "We were taught that our lives must be devoted to reclaiming our land."

Rayan spent twelve years in an Israeli jail. His brother-in-law blew himself up in a suicide-bomb attack on an Israeli bus in 1998. One of his brothers had been shot dead by Israelis in street protests five years earlier. Another brother was expelled to Lebanon, and several more were wounded in clashes.

His sons, according to their father, strove to be one thing: martyrs for Palestine.

"I pray only that God will choose them," he said.

Hamas, which assumed power in free and fair elections, insists that the real goal of Israel is to break the will of the Palestinians in Gaza and destroy Hamas as an organization. Since Israel unleashed its air and sea campaign, at least 430 Palestinians have been killed, including sixty-five children, and 2,250 others have been wounded, according to Gaza medics. The bombardment has demolished dozens of houses and raised fears of severe food shortages and disease in the enclave, where most Gazans depend on foreign aid.

"The protection of civilians, the fabric of life, the future of the peace talks and of the regional peace process has been trapped between the irresponsibility of the Hamas attacks and the excessiveness of the Israeli response," Robert Serry, the U.N. envoy for the Middle East, told reporters in Jerusalem.

The Israeli assault began on November 4, when Israel broke the truce Hamas had observed for several months. Israel then blocked food supplies delivered by the U. N. Relief and Works Agency for Palestine Refugees in the Near East and the U.N. World Food Program. It cut off diesel fuel used to run Gaza's power station. It banned journalists and aid workers from entering Gaza. The U.N. World Food Program called the situation in Gaza appalling and said that "many basic food items are no longer available on the market."

All this is being carried out by a modern military against a population with no capacity to resist.

The Israeli leadership has warned that this will be a long campaign and hinted that it may be followed by a ground invasion. Israeli tanks are massed on Gaza's border. The continued pounding of Gaza and the rising death toll are sure to ignite the rage of Palestinians outside Gaza. Israeli police forces are already positioning themselves to deal with what they euphemistically have labeled "spontaneous terrorism," meaning public outbursts of support for Gaza that could turn violent. On January 2, Israeli police used tear gas to quell demonstrations by Palestinians in annexed East Jerusalem. Four Israelis have been killed by Palestinian rockets since the latest resumption of violence.

Barack Obama's only comment on the one-sided slaughter under way in Gaza was: "If my daughters were living in a house that was being threatened by rocket attacks, I would do whatever it takes to end that situation." He repeated word for word the Israeli cliché used to justify an Israeli policy that U.N. Special Rapporteur Richard Falk has labeled "a crime against humanity." If self-defense applies to Israel as a justification of violence, why doesn't it apply to the Rayan family? Why doesn't it apply to the Palestinians? It is Israel, not the Palestinians, which defies U.N. resolutions and international law by occupying and seizing ever-larger chunks of Palestinian land.

The walls of Gaza are plastered with poster-sized photographs of "martyrs" shot by the Israelis. Many are pictured holding a weapon in front of the gold-topped al-Aqsa Mosque in Jerusalem. These are studio photos taken long before their deaths. The gun was a prop and the glittering mosque a carefully chosen backdrop. All that was real in these photos was the yearning of these young men to fight against Israel and for a Palestinian state—and to die. And for a moment, at least until the pictures fade or peel away, the slain youths will have their brief lives and heroism recognized.

Gaza, like Kosovo's capital Pristina, is a derelict, concrete slum where car exhaust mingles with the stench of raw sewage. There are 1.5 million Palestinians—seventy percent of whom are either refugees from what is now Israel or the descendants of refugees. They live crammed into a dusty, flat, coastal area twice the size of Washington, D.C. Most are stateless and have never left the Palestinian territories and Israel. Families are piled in boxy, concrete rooms capped with corrugated tin roofs weighed down by rocks. They have little furniture. Water and electricity service work only sporadically. The population growth rate is one of the highest on the planet: a 3.7 percent annual birthrate, compared with 1.7 percent in Israel. Donkey carts crowd the streets, and orange garbage bins, donated by the European Union, overflow with putrid heaps of refuse.

The only route left for most young men in Gaza to affirm themselves is through death. I have attended countless funerals there. The decision of the young men, sometimes boys, to die is usually a conscious one. It is born of despair and rage. It is born of a sense of impotence and humiliation. It is born of a belief that to forgo sacrifice, even death, is to dishonor those who have gone before, to neglect family members, relatives, and friends who lost their land, endured the decades-long humiliation and abuse of occupation, and suffered or died resisting.

The young in Gaza have nothing to do. There are no jobs. They have nowhere to escape to. They cannot marry because they cannot afford housing. They cannot leave Gaza, even for Israel. They sleep, sometimes ten to a room, and live on less than $2 a day, surviving on U.N. or Hamas charities and food donations. Martyrdom is the only route offered to those who want to achieve a measure, however brief, of recognition and glory.

Palestinians have been nurtured on accounts of abuse, despair, and injustice. Families tell and retell stories of being thrown off their land and of relatives killed or exiled. All can tick off the names of martyrs within their own clan who died for the elusive Palestinian state. The only framed paper in many Palestinians' homes is a sepia land deed from the time of the British mandate. Some elderly men still keep the keys to houses that have long since vanished. From infancy, Palestinians are inculcated with the virus of nationalism and the burden of revenge. And, as in Bosnia, such resentment seeps into the roots of society for generations until it resurfaces or is finally rectified, often after much bloodletting.

"Tell the man what you want to be," one of Rayan's wives, Hyam Temraz, said to her two-year-old son, Abed, as she peeped out of the slit of a black veil the last time I was in their home.

"A martyr," the child timidly answered.

"We were in Jordan when my son Baraa was four," she said. "He saw a Jordanian soldier and ran and hugged him. He asked him if it was he who would liberate Palestine. He has always told me that he would be a martyr and that one day I would dig his grave."

I was caught in a gun battle at the start of the second intifada at the Nazarim junction in Gaza. A few feet away, Marwan Shamalekh, nineteen, was fatally shot through the back by Israeli soldiers. He was tossing homemade Molotov cocktails at an army outpost, the flaming bottles landing harmlessly against the concrete wall of the compound, when he died. He had no firearms. I ran with Marwan's companions as they carried his limp body down the road. We were fired on by Israeli soldiers as we fled.

I stopped shaving and grew a beard as a sign of respect and mourning for the boy. I visited his parents. They pulled up a chair on the cement patio outside their tiny house. They served me plates of dates and demitasse cups of bitter coffee. Mrs. Shamalekh was unable to speak. She sobbed softly into a kerchief.

Abdel Razaq Shamalekh, Marwan's father, clutched his nine-year-old son, Bilal. The boy stared at me vacantly.

"I had to carry Bilal to his bed after I told him his brother had been killed," the father said. "He collapsed. Later I found him leaving the house with a knife he had taken from the kitchen. He told me he was going to Nazarim to kill Israelis."

Israel Crackdown Puts
Liberal Jews on the Spot

MARCH 15, 2010

The Israeli government, its brutal war crimes in Gaza exposed in detail in the U.N. report by Justice Richard Goldstone, has implemented a series of draconian measures to silence and discredit dissidents, leading intellectuals, and human-rights organizations inside and outside Israel that are accused—often falsely—of assisting Goldstone's U.N. investigators. The government of Benjamin Netanyahu is attempting to shut down Israel's premier human-rights organizations, including B'Tselem, the New Israel Fund (NIF), and the Association for Civil Rights in Israel. It is busy expelling or excluding peace activists and foreign nationals from the Palestinian territories. The campaign, if left unchecked, will be as catastrophic for Palestinians as it will be for Israel.

The Goldstone report, which is more than five hundred pages, investigated Israel's twenty-two-day air and ground assault on Gaza from December 27, 2008, to January 18, 2009. The United Nations and the European Parliament have endorsed the report. The report found that Israel used disproportionate military force against Hamas militants in the Gaza Strip while failing to take adequate precautions to protect the civilian population against the military assault. The Israeli attack killed 1,434 people, including 960 civilians, according to the Palestinian Center for Human Rights. More than six thousand homes were destroyed or damaged, leaving behind some $3 billion in destruction in one of the poorest areas on Earth. No Israelis were killed by Hamas rockets fired into Israel during the assault. The report did not limit itself to the twenty-two-day attack; rather, it went on to indict the occupation itself. It examines the beginning of the occupation and condemns Israel for the border closures, the blockade, and for the wall or security barrier in the West Bank. It has two references to the right of return, investigates Israeli use of torture, and criticizes the willful destruction of the Palestinian economy.

"The impact of the Goldstone report is tremendous," Norman Finkelstein said when I reached him in New York:

> It marks and catalyzes the breakup of the Diaspora Jewish support for Israel because Goldstone is the classical Diaspora Jew. He is a lawyer and upholder of human rights and a liberal. He has distinguished himself in the field of law, and he is also a lover of Zion. He calls himself a Zionist. His mother was an activist in the Zionist movement. His daughter did *aliyah*. He sits on the board of governors of the Hebrew University in Jerusalem. He has an honorary degree from the Hebrew University in Jerusalem. He has said over and over again that he is a Zionist. He believes Jews have a right to a state in Palestine. His is a mostly emblematic profile of the classically liberal Jew.

"*Liberal* has a distinct connotation," Finkelstein went on:

> It means to believe in the rule of law. It means to believe in international institutions. It means to believe in human rights. Amnesty International and Human Rights Watch are liberal organizations. What the Goldstone phenomenon registers and catalyzes is the fact that it is impossible to reconcile liberal convictions with Israel's conduct; too much is now known about the history of the conflict and the human rights record and the so-called peace process. It is impossible to be both liberal and defend Israeli policy. That was the conflict that confronted Goldstone. I very much doubt he wanted to condemn Israel.

"Israeli liberalism always had a function in Israeli society," said Finkelstein, whose book *This Time We Went Too Far* examines the Israeli attack a year ago on Gaza:

When I talk about liberals I mean people like A.B. Yehoshua, David Grossman, and Amos Oz. Their function was to issue these anguished criticisms of Israel which not only extenuated Israeli crimes but exalted Israeli crimes. "Isn't it beautiful, the Israeli soul, how it is anguished over what it has done?" It is the classic case of having your cake and eating it. Not only were any crimes being committed extenuated, but they were beautiful. And now something strange happened. Along comes a Jewish liberal and he says, "Spare me your tears. I am only interested in the law."

"Goldstone did not perform the role of the Jewish liberal," Finkelstein said, "which is to be anguished, but no consequences. And all of a sudden Israeli liberal Jews are discovering, hey, there are consequences for committing war crimes. You don't just get to walk into the sunset and look beautiful. They can't believe it. They are genuinely shocked. 'Aren't our tears consequences enough? Aren't our long eyes and broken hearts consequences enough?' 'No,' he said, 'you have to go to the criminal court.'"

The campaign against Israeli dissidents has taken the form of venomous denunciations of activists and jurists, including Justice Goldstone. It includes a bill before the Israeli parliament, the Knesset, which will make it possible to imprison the leaders of Israeli human-rights groups if they fail to comply with crippling new registration conditions. Human-rights activists from outside Israel who work in the Palestinian territories are being rounded up and deported. The government is refusing to issue work visas to employees of 150 nongovernmental organizations (NGOs) operating in the West Bank and East Jerusalem, including Oxfam, Save the Children, and Médecins Sans Frontières (Doctors Without Borders). The new tourist visas effectively bar these employees from Palestinian territory under Israeli occupation. Professor Naomi Chazan, the Israeli head of the NIF, which has donors in the United States, is being publicly vilified by ultranationalist groups such as Im Tirtzu. Foreign donors to the NIF, as well as other human-rights groups, are being pressured by Israeli officials to halt contributions. Billboards have sprouted up around Tel Aviv and Jerusalem with a grotesque caricature of Chazan, who has been branded by Im Tirtzu and other groups as an agent for Hamas and Iran, with a horn growing from her forehead. "Naomi-Goldstone-Chazan," the caption on the billboard reads. Im Tirtzu, the front organization behind many of the attacks, includes among its financial backers the John Hagee Ministries and the New York Central Fund, which also support extremist settler organizations.

The purge is under way because of the belief within the Netanyahu government that these groups and activists provided evidence of Israeli war crimes in Gaza to Justice Goldstone. Israel has no intention of lifting the blockade on Gaza, halting settlement expansion, including the 1,600 new homes to be built in East Jerusalem, or reversing its division of the West Bank into impoverished ghettos of Palestinians. The growing brutality and violence of the occupation, no longer easy to deny or hide, coupled with Israel's increasingly isolated international status, have unleashed a crackdown against all those within the Jewish state who are blamed for the bad publicity. Yuli Edelstein, the Diaspora affairs minister, summed up the witch hunt when he announced that the Cabinet had been "concerned for a time with a number of groups under the guise of NGOs that are funded by foreign agents."

The Knesset bill, if passed, will force human-rights groups to register as political bodies and turn over identification numbers and addresses of all members to the government. These groups will lose their tax-exempt status. Most governmental organizations, such as the European Union, which is a large donor to Israeli human-rights organizations, cannot legally pay taxes to another government, and so the new law will effectively end European Union and other outside funding. The groups will be mandated to provide the government with the records of all foreign donations and account for how these donations were spent. Any public statement, event, or speech by these groups, even if it lasts half a minute, must include a declaration that they are being supported and funded by a foreign power. Those who fail to follow these guidelines, including local volunteers, can face a year in jail.

"This is the first time the human-rights dimension of the Israel Palestine conflict has moved center stage," Finkelstein said:

It has temporarily displaced the fatuous peace process. It is the first time that human-rights reports have counted. There are literally, because I have read them, tens if not hundreds of thousands of pages of accumulation of human-rights reports condemning Israel going back roughly to the first intifada to the present. The human-rights organizations since the 1990s have been quite sharp in their criticism of Israel human-rights policy, but nobody ever reads the reports. They are never reported on, with maybe a couple of exceptions, in the mainstream media. The Goldstone report was the first time the findings of these human-rights organizations moved center stage. People stopped talking about the peace process and started talking about Israel's human-rights record.

There is a growing disenchantment among Israelis with the endless occupation of Gaza and the West Bank as well as endemic government corruption. Major General Avi Zamir, the head of the Israeli military's Personnel Directorate, admitted recently to United Press International that increasing numbers of Israelis are refusing to serve in the occupied territories. "Taking into consideration Israeli Arab youth, we're facing a situation in which seventy percent of youths will not enlist in the military," the general told the news agency.[5] The discontent, along with the international condemnation, is inhibiting Israel's ability to muster international support for further attacks.

"Israel attacked Gaza to restore what it called its deterrence capacity, its ability to terrorize the Arab world into submission," Finkelstein said, "but it actually diminished its deterrence capacity because it can't attack. If they were to attack now, anywhere, all hell would break loose and they wouldn't get sympathy."

The numbers of so-called refuseniks are proliferating with groups such as the Courage to Refuse, Shministim, and New Profile supporting those who will not serve in the Israeli Defense Forces. It is not that many Israelis lack a conscience, it is not that many cannot delineate right from wrong; it is that the Netanyahu government is determined to see that these courageous voices within Israel will be silenced along with those of the Palestinians.

Israel's Racist-in-Chief

APRIL 13, 2009

It was unthinkable, when I was based as a correspondent in Jerusalem two decades ago, that an Israeli politician who openly advocated ethnically cleansing the Palestinians from Israeli-controlled territory, as well as forcing Arabs in Israel to take loyalty oaths or be forcibly relocated to the West Bank, could sit on the Cabinet. The racist tirades of Jewish protofascists such as Meir Kahane stood outside the law, were vigorously condemned by most Israelis, and were prosecuted accordingly. Kahane's repugnant Kach Party, labeled by the United States, Canada, and the European Union as a terrorist organization, was outlawed by the Israeli government in 1988 for inciting racism.

Israel has changed. And the racist virus spread by Kahane, whose thugs were charged with the murders and beatings of dozens of unarmed Palestinians and whose members held rallies in Jerusalem where they chanted, "Death to Arabs!" has returned to Israel in the figure of Israel's powerful new foreign minister, Avigdor Lieberman. Lieberman openly calls for an *araberrein* Israel—an Israel free of Arabs.

There has been a steady decline from the days of the socialist Labor Party, which founded Israel in 1948 and held within its ranks many leaders, such as Yitzhak Rabin, who were serious about peaceful coexistence with the Palestinians. The moral squalor of Prime Minister Bibi Netanyahu and Lieberman reflects the country's degeneration. Labor, like Israel, is a shell of its old self. Lieberman's Yisrael Beiteinu Party, with fifteen seats in the Knesset, is likely to bring down the Netanyahu government the moment his power base is robust enough to move him into the prime minister's office. He is the new face of the Jewish state.

Lieberman, a former nightclub bouncer who was a member of the Kach Party, has the personal and political habits of the Islamic goons he opposes. He was found guilty in 2001 of beating a 12-year-old boy and fined by an Israeli court. He is being investigated for multimillion-dollar fraud and money laundering and is rumored to have close ties with the Russian mafia. He lives, in defiance of international law, in the Jewish settlement of Nokdim on occupied Palestinian land.

Lieberman, as did his mentor Kahane, calls for the eradication of Palestinians from Israel and the territories it occupies. During the massive Israeli bombardment of Gaza in December 2008-January 2009, he said that Israel should fight Hamas the way the United States fought the Japanese in World War II. He noted that occupation of Japan was unnecessary to achieve victory, alluding to the dropping of atomic bombs on Nagasaki and Hiroshima. When he assumed his position as foreign minister, he announced that the peace agreement reached at the Annapolis Conference in November 2007 was dead. He said in 2004 that ninety percent of Israel's Palestinian citizens "have no place here. They can take their bundles and get lost." This statement was especially galling since Lieberman, unlike Palestinians who can trace back their ancestry for generations in the area, is a relative newcomer; he immigrated to Israel in 1978 from Moldova and retains a heavy Russian accent.

Lieberman, from the floor of the Knesset, openly fantasized three years ago about executing the handful of Palestinian Knesset members.

"We requested that in the government guidelines it would say explicitly that all the inciters and collaborators with terrorism that sit in this house should bear the brunt of the penalty for those actions," Lieberman said from the Knesset plenum in May of 2006. "All those who continue to meet freely with Hamas and Hezbollah—who go on monthly visits to Lebanon. Those who declared Israel's Independence Day to be *Nakba* [Arabic for *catastrophe*] Day and raised black flags. . . .

"World War II ended with the Nuremberg trials. The heads of the Nazi Party went to be executed—but not just them, also those who collaborated with them. Just like [prime minister of Vichy France during World War II Pierre] Laval was later executed, I hope that this is the fate of the collaborators in this house."

He has suggested bombing Egypt's Aswan Dam, an act that would lead to a massive loss of Egyptian lives. As Ariel Sharon's minister of transportation, he offered to bus several hundred Palestinian prisoners to the sea and drown them. He recently told Hosni Mubarak, president of Egypt, one of Israel's few Arab allies, to "go to hell." And, along with Netanyahu, he advocates massive air strikes on Iran's nuclear facilities.

Hamas, the Iranian government, and the Taliban have been condemned by Washington for advocating policies that mirror the attitudes expressed by Lieberman toward Palestinians. Ahmad Tibi, an Arab deputy in the Knesset, has called on the international community to boycott Israel as it did Austria when far-right leader Jörg Haider joined that country's government. This seems a fair request. But I expect the hypocrisy and double standards that characterize our relations with the Middle East, along with our obsequious catering to the Israel lobby, to prevail. Racism, as long as it is directed toward Arabs, does little to perturb our conscience or hinder our support of Israel.

The Israeli leadership, following the assassination of Rabin by a Jewish extremist with ties to Kach, never again sought a viable settlement with the Palestinians. Successive Israeli prime ministers talked the language of peace and negotiations largely to placate the international community and Washington while they vigorously expanded Jewish settlements on Palestinian land, seized huge tracts of the West Bank, including most of the aquifers, and imposed a brutal collective punishment on the Palestinians in Gaza. Palestinians have become, by Israeli design, impoverished, reduced to a level of bare subsistence, and dependent on the United Nations for food assistance. They live ringed by Israeli troops in ghettos in the West Bank and in Gaza, which is a massive, fetid open-air prison. And when these little Bantustans become restive, Israel swiftly turns off the delivery of basic food and supplies or uses F-16 fighter jets or heavy artillery to bomb the squalid concrete hovels.

The public embrace by a senior Israeli official of a policy of ethnic cleansing, however, is ominous. It signals a further evolution of the Israeli state from one that at least paid lip service to equality to one that increasingly resembles the former apartheid regime in South Africa. Racism, once practiced in private and condemned in public, has become to many Israelis acceptable.

The Tears of Gaza Must Be Our Tears

AUGUST 9, 2010

When I lived in Jerusalem I had a friend who confided in me that as a college student in the United States she attended events like these, wrote up reports and submitted them to the Israel consulate for money. It would be naïve to assume this Israeli practice has ended. So, I want first tonight to address that person, or those persons, who may have come to this event for the purpose of reporting on it to the Israeli government.

I would like to remind them that it is they who hide in darkness. It is we who stand in the light. It is they who deceive. It is we who openly proclaim our compassion and demand justice for those who suffer in Gaza. We are not afraid to name our names. We are not afraid to name our beliefs. And we know something you perhaps sense with a kind of dread. As Martin Luther King Jr. said, "The arc of the moral universe is long but it bends toward justice," and that arc is descending with a righteous fury that is thundering down upon the Israeli government.

You may have the bulldozers, planes, and helicopters that smash houses to rubble, the commandos who descend from ropes on ships and kill unarmed civilians on the high seas as well as in Gaza, the vast power of the state behind you. We have only our hands and our hearts and our voices. But note this. Note this well. It is you who are afraid of us. We are not afraid of you. We will keep working and praying, keep protesting and denouncing, keep pushing up against your navy and your army, with nothing but our bodies, until we prove that the force of morality and justice is greater than hate and violence. And then, when there is freedom in Gaza, we will forgive . . . you. We will ask you to break bread with us. We will bless your children even if you did not find it in your heart to bless the children of those you occupied. And maybe it is this forgiveness, maybe it is the final, insurmountable power of love, which unsettles you the most.

And so tonight, a night when some seek to name names and others seek to hide names, let me do some naming. Let me call things by their proper names. Let me cut through the jargon, the euphemisms we use to mask human suffering and war crimes. "Closures" mean heavily armed soldiers who ring Palestinian ghettos, deny those trapped inside food or basic amenities—including toys, razors, chocolate, fishing rods, and musical instruments—and carry out a brutal policy of collective punishment, which is a crime under international law. "Disputed land" means land stolen from the Palestinians. "Clashes" mean, almost always, the killing or wounding of unarmed Palestinians, including children. "Jewish neighborhoods in the West Bank" mean fortress-like compounds that serve as military outposts in the campaign of ethnic cleansing of the Palestinians. "Targeted assassinations" mean extrajudicial murders. "Air strikes on militant bomb-making posts" mean the dropping of huge iron fragmentation bombs from fighter jets on densely crowded neighborhoods, a practice that always leaves scores of dead and wounded, whose only contact with a bomb was the one manufactured in the United States and given to the Israeli Air Force as part of our complicity in the occupation. "The peace process" means the cynical, one-way route to the crushing of the Palestinians as a people.

These are some names. There are others. Late in the afternoon of January 16, 2009, Izzeldin Abuelaish had a pair of Israeli tank shells rip through a bedroom in his Gaza apartment, killing three of his daughters—Bessan, Mayar, and Aya—along with a niece, Noor.

"I have the right to feel angry," says Abuelaish. "But I ask, 'Is this the right way?' So many people were expecting me to hate. My answer to them is I shall not hate."

"Whom to hate?" asks the fifty-five-year-old gynecologist, who was born a Palestinian refugee and raised in poverty. "My Israeli friends? My Israeli colleagues? The Israeli babies I have delivered?"

The Palestinian poet Taha Muhammad Ali wrote this in his poem "Revenge":

At times . . . I wish
I could meet in a duel
the man who killed my father
and razed our home,
expelling me
into
a narrow country.
And if he killed me,
I'd rest at last,
and if I were ready—
I would take my revenge!
*

But if it came to light,
when my rival appeared,
that he had a mother
waiting for him,
or a father who'd put
his right hand over
the heart's place in his chest
whenever his son was late
even by just a quarter-hour
for a meeting they'd set—
then I would not kill him,
even if I could.
*

Likewise . . . I
would not murder him
if it were soon made clear
that he had a brother or sisters
who loved him and constantly longed to see him.
Or if he had a wife to greet him
and children who
couldn't bear his absence
and whom his gifts would thrill.
Or if he had
friends or companions,

neighbors he knew
or allies from prison
or a hospital room,
or classmates from his school . . .
asking about him
and sending him regards.
*

But if he turned
out to be on his own—
cut off like a branch from a tree—
without a mother or father,
with neither a brother nor sister,
wifeless, without a child,
and without kin or neighbors or friends,
colleagues or companions,
then I'd add not a thing to his pain
within that aloneness—
not the torment of death,
and not the sorrow of passing away.
Instead I'd be content
to ignore him when I passed him by
on the street—as I
convinced myself
that paying him no attention
in itself was a kind of revenge.[6]

And if these words are what it means to be a Muslim, and I believe it does, name me, too, a Muslim, a follower of the Prophet, peace be upon him.

The boat to Gaza will be named *The Audacity of Hope*. But these are not Barack Obama's words. These are the words of my friend, the Reverend Jeremiah Wright. They are borrowed words. And Jerry Wright is not afraid to speak the truth, not afraid to tell us to stop confusing God with America. "We bombed Hiroshima, we bombed Nagasaki, and we nuked far more than the thousands [killed] in New York and the Pentagon, and we never batted an eye," Reverend Wright said.

"We have supported state terrorism against the Palestinians and black South Africans, and now we are indignant because the stuff we have done overseas is now brought right back into our own front yards. America's chickens are coming home to roost."[7]

Or the words of Edward Said:

> Nothing in my view is more reprehensible than those habits of mind in the intellectual that induce avoidance, that characteristic turning away from a difficult and principled position which you know to be the right one, but which you decide not to take. You do not want to appear too political; you are afraid of seeming controversial; you want to keep a reputation for being balanced, objective, moderate; your hope is to be asked back, to consult, to be on a board or prestigious committee, and so to remain within the responsible mainstream; someday you hope to get an honorary degree, a big prize, perhaps even an ambassadorship.[8]

For an intellectual these habits of mind are corrupting *par excellence*. If anything can denature, neutralize, and finally kill a passionate intellectual life it is the internalization of such habits. Personally I have encountered them in one of the toughest of all contemporary issues, Palestine, where fear of speaking out about one of the greatest injustices in modern history has hobbled, blinkered, muzzled many who know the truth and are in a position to serve it. For despite the abuse and vilification that any outspoken supporter of Palestinian rights and self-determination earns for him or herself, the truth deserves to be spoken, represented by an unafraid and compassionate intellectual.

And some of the last words of Rachel Corrie to her mother and father:

> I'm witnessing this chronic, insidious genocide and I'm really scared, and questioning my fundamental belief in the goodness of human nature. This has to stop. I think it is a good idea for us all to drop everything and devote our lives to making this stop. I don't think it's an extremist thing to do anymore. I still really want to dance around to Pat Benatar and have boyfriends and make comics for my coworkers. But I also want this to stop. Disbelief and horror is what I feel. Disap-

pointment. I am disappointed that this is the base reality of our world and that we, in fact, participate in it. This is not at all what I asked for when I came into this world. This is not at all what the people here asked for when they came into this world. This is not the world you and Dad wanted me to come into when you decided to have me. This is not what I meant when I looked at Capital Lake and said: "This is the wide world and I'm coming to it." I did not mean that I was coming into a world where I could live a comfortable life and possibly, with no effort at all, exist in complete unawareness of my participation in genocide. More big explosions somewhere in the distance outside. When I come back from Palestine, I probably will have nightmares and constantly feel guilty for not being here, but I can channel that into more work. Coming here is one of the better things I've ever done. So when I sound crazy, or if the Israeli military should break with their racist tendency not to injure white people, please pin the reason squarely on the fact that I am in the midst of a genocide which I am also indirectly supporting, and for which my government is largely responsible.[9]

And if this is what it means to be a Christian, and I believe it does, to speak in the voice of Jeremiah Wright, Edward Said, or Rachel Corrie, to remember and take upon us the pain and injustice of others, then name me a Christian, a follower of Jesus Christ.

And what of the long line of Jewish prophets that run from Jeremiah, Isaiah, and Amos to Hannah Arendt, who reminded the world when the state of Israel was founded that the injustice meted out to the Jews could not be rectified by an injustice meted out to the Palestinians, what of our own prophets, Noam Chomsky or Norman Finkelstein, outcasts like all prophets, what of Uri Avnery or the Israeli poet Aharon Shabtai, who writes in his poem "Rypin," the Polish town his father fled from in 1925 to escape anti-Semitism, these words?:

These creatures in helmets and khakis,
I say to myself, aren't Jews,

in the truest sense of the word. A Jew
doesn't dress himself up with weapons like jewelry,

doesn't believe in the barrel of a gun aimed at a target,
but in the thumb of the child who was shot at—

in the house through which he comes and goes,
not in the charge that blows it apart.

The coarse soul and iron fist
he scorns by nature.

He lifts his eyes not to the officer, or the soldier
with his finger on the trigger—but to justice,

and he cries out for compassion.
Therefore, he won't steal land from its people

and will not starve them in camps.
The voice calling for expulsion

is heard from the hoarse throat of the oppressor—
a sure sign that the Jew has entered a foreign country

and, like Umberto Saba, gone into hiding within his own city.
Because of voices like these, father,

at age sixteen, with your family, you fled Rypin;
now here in Rypin is your son.[10]

And if to be Jew means this, and I believe it does, name me a Jew.
Name us all Muslims and Christians and Jews. Name us as human beings who believe that when one of us suffers, all of us suffer, that we
never have to ask for whom the bell tolls, it tolls for us all, that the
tears of the mother in Gaza are our tears, that the wails of the bloodied
children in Al Shifa Hospital are the wails of our own children.

Let me close tonight with one last name. Let me name those who
send these tanks and fighter jets to bomb the concrete hovels in Gaza
with families crouching, helpless, inside. Let me name those who deny

children the right to a childhood and the sick a right to care, those who torture, those who carry out assassinations in hotel rooms in Dubai and on the streets of Gaza City, those who deny the hungry food and the oppressed justice, those who foul the truth with official propaganda and state lies. Let me call them, not by their honorific titles and positions of power, but by the name they have earned for themselves by draining the blood of the innocent into the sands of Gaza. Let me name them for who they are: terrorists.

Formalizing Israel's Land Grab

AUGUST 16, 2010

Time is running out for Israel. And the Israeli government knows it. The Jewish Diaspora, especially the young, has a waning emotional and ideological investment in Israel. The demographic boom means that Palestinians in Israel and the occupied territories will soon outnumber Jews. And Israel's increasing status as a pariah nation means that informal and eventually formal state sanctions against the country are probably inevitable.

Desperate Israeli politicians, watching opposition to their apartheid state mount, have proposed a perverted form of what they term "the one-state solution." It is the latest tool to thwart a Palestinian state and allow Israel to retain its huge settlement complexes and land seizures in East Jerusalem and the West Bank. The idea of a single state was backed by Moshe Arens, a former defense minister and foreign minister from the Likud Party, in a column he wrote last month in the newspaper *Haaretz* asking, "Is There Another Option?" Arens has been joined by several other Israeli politicians including Knesset Speaker Reuven Rivlin.

The Israeli vision, however, does not include a state with equal rights for Jewish and Palestinian citizens. The call for a single state appears to include pushing Gaza into the unwilling arms of Egypt and incorporating the West Bank and East Jerusalem into Israel. Palestinians within Israeli-controlled territory, however, will remain burdened with crippling travel, work, and security restrictions already in place. Palestinians in the occupied territories, for example, cannot reclaim lost property or acquire Israeli citizenship, yet watch as Jews born outside of Israel and with no prior tie to the country become Israeli citizens and receive government-subsidized housing. Palestinians in the West Bank live in roughly eight squalid, ringed ghettos and are governed by military courts. Jews living in the West Bank and East Jerusalem, like all full Israeli citizens, are subject to Israeli civilian law and constitutional protection. Palestinians cannot serve in the armed forces or the security services, while Jewish settlers are issued automatic weapons and protected by the Israel Defense Forces.

If Israel sheds Gaza, the Jewish state will be left with 5.8 million Jews and 3.8 million Arabs. And, at least in the near future, Jews will remain the majority. This seems to be the main attraction of the plan.

The physical and political landscape of the West Bank and East Jerusalem, known as "facts on the ground," has altered dramatically since I first went to Jerusalem more than two decades ago. Huge fortress-like apartment complexes ring East Jerusalem and dominate the hillsides in the West Bank. The settler population is now more than 462,000, with 271,400 living in the West Bank and East Jerusalem, and 191,000 living in and around Jerusalem. The settler population has grown at the rate of 4.6 percent per year since 1990, while Israeli society as a whole has grown at 1.5 percent.

The net effect of the Israeli seizure of land in East Jerusalem, which includes recent approval for an additional nine thousand housing units, and the West Bank is to promulgate a form of administrative ethnic cleansing. Palestinian families are being pushed off land they have owned for generations and evicted from their homes by Israeli authorities. Dozens of families, tossed out of dwellings they have occupied in East Jerusalem for decades, have been forced onto the streets. Groups such as Ateret Cohanim, an ultra-Orthodox Jewish private organization that collects funds from abroad, purchase Palestinian properties and pursue legal strategies to evict families that have long resided in East Jerusalem. Israel's judicial system and police, in violation of international law, facilitate and enforce these evictions and land seizures.

Heavily armed settlers carry out frequent unprovoked attacks, ad hoc raids, and house evictions to supplement the terror imposed by the police and military. They are the civilian arm of the occupation.

"This acquiescence in settler violence is particularly objectionable from the perspective of international humanitarian law because the settlers are already unlawfully present in occupied territory, making it perverse to victimize those who should be protected—the Palestinians— and offer protection to those who are lawbreakers—the settlers," said U.N. Special Rapporteur Richard Falk when we spoke a few days ago.

Falk said that incorporating Palestinians in East Jerusalem and the West Bank into a single Israeli state would see Israel impose gradations of citizenship.

"If the Palestinians in pre-'67 Israel enjoy second-class citizenship, those in the West Bank and East Jerusalem will be given a third-class citizenship," Falk said:

> The real proposal, the envisioned outcome of this kind of proposal, is an extension of Israeli control over the occupied territory as a permanent reality. It is presently a de facto annexation. The creation of a single state would give the arrangement a more legalistic cover. It would seek to resolve the issue of occupied territory without the bother of international negotiations.

"The effect is to fragment the Palestinian people in such defining ways as to make it almost impossible to envision the emergence of a viable Palestinian sovereign state," said Falk. "The longer it continues, the more difficult it is to overcome, and the more serious are the abridgements of fundamental Palestinian rights."

Falk, who taught international law at Princeton University, issued a report to the United Nations in September 2010 in which he asserted that the Israeli process of colonialism and apartheid has accelerated over the past three years. He called for the U.N. to consider unilaterally declaring Palestine an independent state, as it did with Kosovo. Falk cited as examples of Israeli colonialism the 121 official Jewish settlements, as well as roughly one hundred "illegal outposts" in the West Bank, and the extensive network of roads reserved exclusively for Jews that connects the settlements to one another and to Israel behind the Green Line. He estimated that when "all restrictions on Palestinian control and development are taken into account," that Israel has effectively seized thirty-eight to forty percent of the West Bank.

The punishing conditions imposed by the Israeli blockade of the Palestinians in Gaza have been replicated for the roughly forty thousand Palestinians who live in "Area C," the sixty percent of the West Bank that remains under complete Israeli military control. In a recent report called "Life on the Edge," Save the Children UK (STCUK) argues that Israeli policies of land confiscation, expanding settlements, and lack of basic services such as food, water, shelter, and medical clinics are at "a crisis point." The report concludes that food security problems in Area C are even *worse* than in Gaza. According to the report, "Seventy-nine percent of communities surveyed recently don't have enough nutritious food; this is higher than in blockaded Gaza where the rate is 61 percent." Palestinian children growing up in Area C experience, according to the report, malnutrition and stunted growth at double the level of children in Gaza. Forty-four percent of these children were found to suffer from diarrhea, often with lethal effects. STCUK writes that "Israel's restrictions on Palestinian access to and development of agricultural land—in an area where almost all families are herders—mean that thousands of children are going hungry and are vulnerable to killer illnesses like diarrhea and pneumonia."[11]

Jihad al-Shommali of the Defense for Children International Palestine Section said of the problems of Area C children: "Children are being forced to cross settlement areas and risk beatings and harassment by settlers, or walk for hours, just to get to school . . . many children are losing hope in the future."[12]

Falk said, "This overall pattern suggests systematic violations by Israel of Article 55 of Geneva IV and Article 69 of the First Geneva Protocol of 1977 that delimits Israel's obligations to ensure adequate provision of the basic needs of people living under its occupation, especially in Area C, where it exercises undivided control."

The annexation of Palestinian territory has been reinforced by the construction of eighty-five percent of the separation wall—256 of a planned 435 miles have been completed—on occupied Palestinian territory. The barrier cuts the West Bank off from Israel and has been built in a configuration which plunges deep into the West Bank. The settlements and the land to the west of the wall, which makes up 9.4 percent of the West Bank, have already been absorbed into Israel. The seizure of nearly forty percent of the West Bank includes Israeli control of most of the Palestinians' water supply. The Jewish settlers in the West Bank are allotted per capita four to five times the amount of water allotted to Palestinians by the Israeli government.

The settlements in East Jerusalem and the West Bank violate part 6 of Article 49 of the Fourth Geneva Convention, which prohibits the transfer of the population of an occupying power to the territory temporarily occupied. Israel's stubborn rejection of the demand of Security Council Resolution 242 that it withdraw from Palestinian territories it occupied in 1967 creates, as Falk said, "a background that resembles, and in some dimensions exceeds, in important respects the situation confronting the government of Kosovo."

"Lengthy negotiations have not resolved the issue of the status of Palestine, nor do they give any reasonable prospect that any resolution by negotiation or unilateral withdrawal will soon occur," he said:

> Under these circumstances, it would seem that one option available to the Palestine Liberation Organization [the Oslo Agreement empowered the PLO to negotiate international status issues] acting on its own or by way of the Palestinian Authority under international law would be to issue a unilateral declaration of status, seeking independence, diplomatic recognition and membership in the United Nations. The recent Kosovo advisory opinion of the World Court in The Hague provides a well-reasoned legal precedent for such an option.

THE MIDDLE EAST

Inside Egypt

OCTOBER 19, 2006

Qus, Egypt—A line of eighty buses and vans idles as black-uniformed police move with clipboards and snub-nosed machine guns from driver to driver collecting information. Tourists, their faces beet-colored, peer from the aquarium-like windows of the buses above at the teeming world of the street. The high-pitched whine of motorcycles, the honking and squeal of car horns, and the rumble of decrepit blue and white taxis unite in a strident chorus. Bicyclists in long, flowing gray and white galabiyas and turbans weave deftly in and out of the traffic. On the banks of the river, flat-roofed tour boats and floating hotels with names like Cheops III or Hamees are berthed three to a pier. Couples in bathing suits sit on the roofs, next to the pools, shaded by the awning stretched over the boats.

The buses, given a signal at the front of the line, begin to move forward. The convoy rumbles toward the resorts on the Red Sea, escorted by police in pickup trucks. The mud-walled villages, the irrigation ditches, the dirt yards with chickens and donkeys and cattle, the barefoot children, the fields of sugarcane, the whitewashed, domed tombs of local sheiks, the spindly blue and white minarets, the donkey carts with old car tires, the overcrowded passenger buses belching diesel smoke and tilting under the weight of the human cargo, and the dilapidated cars and tractors held up at intersections so the convoy can pass rapidly become a blur, an indistinct and faintly remembered reminder of another Egypt.

There are two Egypts. One is crushed by poverty and groaning under the weight of an autocratic regime in place for nearly three decades. This Egypt is increasingly desperate, as the country's population growth soars, and its economy, burdened by corruption and a stifling state bureaucracy, stagnates. Out of the bowels of this Egypt have come mounting antigovernment street demonstrations, anger, frustration, and renewed terrorist violence by Islamic militants. The second Egypt, the one on view to foreign visitors, bears little in common with the first Egypt. It is a manicured and heavily guarded Egypt of air-conditioned hotels, Nile cruises, majestic archeological sites, afternoons by swimming pools, evenings in disco clubs, posh restaurants, and shops crammed with copies of statues of Horus and Nefertiti and glass jewelry cases filled with silver and gold hieroglyphic pendants.

But the clash between these two Egypts is mounting. It has left tourists, confined to these islands of privilege, caught in the middle, seen as symbols of all that is denied to most Egyptians. And once again, as they were a decade ago, foreigners are being targeted and killed by armed militants as the government of President Hosni Mubarak promises reforms, including presidential and parliamentary election reform that Mubarak's critics dismiss as cosmetic.

My van, after about twenty minutes, pulls off the road at a police checkpoint. An arrow on the sign in front of us points left to the city of Qus. The police, who check the passports, match the names to the list they hold in front of them. The convoy, speeding along the road, disappears ahead of us. All foreigners are required by Egyptian authorities to travel on the roads in the south with armed escorts. They are banned from wandering into the impoverished villages outside of Luxor or Aswan. I am permitted to depart from the city only with the convoy and have been required to pick up a policeman to travel to Qus.

A uniformed officer with an AK-47 and the handle of a pistol poking out from the back of his pants climbs into the van. We turn off the pavement along a rutted road. For the next ten days I will live in the village of Gazira in a mud-brick house with an Egyptian family. It will be a rare look at the Egypt few are allowed to examine, one that has been beyond the reach of most of the outside world since November 1997, when Islamic militants armed with guns and swords killed fifty-eight tourists and four Egyptians in the Temple of Hatshepsut outside Luxor. The six assailants and three police also died in the attack. The terrorist attack was followed by a severe, nationwide crackdown that largely broke the armed Islamic militant cells. That effort without doubt was aided by the widespread revulsion many Egyptians felt toward the murderous rampage. But Islamic radicalism has ebbed and flowed in Egypt for a century. It follows a pattern: Severe state repression cripples the movement for about ten years, and militant campaigns then reappear, with each successive incarnation spawning more radical and deadlier tactics.

This war has ebbed and flowed since 1928, when the homegrown fundamentalist movement known as the Muslim Brotherhood was organized. Advocating a return to the "pure" Islam of the Prophet, the brotherhood grew during the 1940s into a radical political movement prone to antigovernment violence. It helped topple Egypt's monarchy in 1952 and almost succeeded in assassinating Egyptian president Gamal Abdel Nasser in 1954. One of the extremist groups that grew out of the Brotherhood, Islamic Jihad, did succeed in killing President Anwar Sadat in 1981. Sadat's successor, Hosni Mubarak, immediately declared a national state of emergency, suspending civil liberties and other freedoms that have never been restored. Despite these crackdowns, Egypt, the intellectual capital of the Arab world, has continued to produce ideas and political figures with influence far beyond its borders. Most notorious of these is Ayman al-Zawahiri. A leader of Islamic Jihad, he helped organize al-Qaida and serves as Osama bin Laden's chief adviser.

The van turns down a dirt road when we reach the village, dropping down a small rise so that we travel along the border of wheat fields that throw off a dark, luxurious green. The house lies at the end of the road. Facing the two-story house are the fields and rows of palm trees, their tops crowned with delicate leaves bowing over the serrated, brown trunks. The palms cast a delicate, lacy shadow on the dirt. On the far side of the fields is an irrigation canal and, beyond, the whitewashed tomb of a local sheikh. Birds chatter. The Nile, which we cannot see, is close. The river seems to have calmed the village, given it another pace, its wide, stately majesty decreeing that all movement, even human movements, should be slowed.

We carry our bags into the house down a dirt path. We step over a small drainage ditch. The house has a blue wooden front door. In the sky we see the faint half-crescent of the moon. For water, there is a green metal hand pump a few feet from the front door. The pump empties into a small concrete trough. Ahmed, a minor official in the government information office, invites us to sit in his front room. His wife brings us glasses of tea. We are soon joined by two "state security" officials. The police officer who rode with us, wearing a green sweater with red bars for epaulets and beige slacks, is tall and lanky and towers over his two colleagues. One of the new arrivals wears a long-sleeved beige shirt with a blue pen poking out of his pocket and has closely cropped hair. The other is wearing a gray galabiya and worn plastic sandals.

"This gentleman is from the general police," Ahmed says, turning to the uniformed officer. "This gentleman is from state security," he says, turning to the man with the shirt. "And this gentleman . . ." and here Ahmed stumbles, not sure what to say, until he hastily adds, "is also from the police."

The mud-brick walls of the room are whitewashed. The rafters, as in all the houses in the village, are made of palm wood. There is a ceiling fan. There are three couches, where we sit with our interrogators. We lean back on hard red pillows. On the floor is a straw mat with a red, yellow, and white design of small diamonds. The one window in the room is closed by blue wooden shutters. It has iron bars and no glass. The sun slants into the room through the cracks in the shutters, the dust dancing in the narrow rays of light. Black-and-white family pictures are framed on the wall.

The police look closely at my Swiss passport. They hand the documents to each other for inspection. They examine my press card. They look at the letter given to Ahmed that says I have permission to visit Qus and the village. The officer with the blue pen laboriously writes down my name and the information from my passport in a notebook.

"You will write and photograph the life of the villagers, how they live and work, and go to school," he says slowly as he spells out each word in Arabic.

The three police officers shift uneasily. They rise to depart and motion for Ahmed to follow them outside. They speak in hushed tones for several minutes. Reza, my photographer, and I take our bags upstairs to our room. We greet Ahmed's wife and two children.

Ahmed is a warm, gentle man who spends his week in Aswan, where he works, and on weekends returns to his village, where his wife and children live. His dark hair is tinged on the sides with gray, and he has a moustache. He speaks French and some English. French and Arabic become the languages we use to communicate. We often slip from one to the other in mid-sentence.

Ahmed's departures for Aswan on Sunday nights are painful.

"My son cries and cries," he says. "He asks me not to leave. And when I walk out the door I cry in my heart."

Ahmed's cell phone has been ringing constantly since we left Luxor. It rings again and, as usual, he begins to speak in a low voice as he walks away from us. This time the phone call is from Kena, the seat of the governorate. He has been taking calls, almost nonstop, from security officials in Luxor, Aswan, Qus, and Cairo.

"I need to go to buy more phone cards," he says in exasperation. "Can I get some money to pay for them? I need to make a lot of calls."

So my first foray into this Egypt is to buy phone cards so my host can report on my movements, my conversations, and my plans for the day. He has been told to relay this information to a variety of state security officials from Qus to Cairo. His confrontation with the layers of state security that we, and probably he as well, did not know existed in President Mubarak's Egypt is leaving him nervous and jumpy.

We head to Qus. No one in the village sells phone cards.

The road to Qus, about five miles long, cuts through cane fields. Twenty-four villages ring Qus. It is harvesting time, and the cane fields have green stalks shooting up in long, crazy rows snaking through the middle of the fields waiting for the workers with machetes to finish their job. Tractors, pulling metal carts with rubber wheels, are piled with yellowed stalks of cane and rumble down the road to deliver their product to the Quena Newsprint Paper Co. on the edge of Qus.

Qus is an ugly city. What charm it may have once held has been sucked out of it by cement, diesel fumes, piles of rotting garbage, looping telephone and electrical wires, dust, noise, horn blasts, overcrowding, and the ubiquitous four- and five-story apartment houses that give most Egyptian cities the same boxy appearance. When we enter the city we stop in front of the railroad tracks. A whitewashed villa with balconies and French windows is on our left. It was, in the days of the monarchy, one of the palaces of aristocracy, but its care has been neglected and the Nile, domesticated by the high dam, is no longer within sight of its high double doors. The socialist revolution led by Nasser turned the villa into a school. Girls with head scarves are gathered on the porch.

We are behind a pickup with metal benches in the back where paying passengers are seated facing each other. The buses, trucks, and cars wait in three lines. The train that eventually rumbles past is third-class. Its carriages, packed with peasants in long galabiyas, have no glass panes, only metal bars, in the windows. There are few seats. The human cargo is forced to sit or stand in the carriages, which rock slightly as they move along the track. Carriages designed to hold fifty passengers routinely hold two hundred. A few young men, "fare dodgers," are on the tops of some carriages as the ancient locomotive, belching black smoke, squeals and huffs its way into the station and lurches to a high-pitched stop.

The third-class train is how most of the country's 2.8 million train passengers travel, moving from city to city and village to village along the 4,900 kilometers of track that run like a ribbon along the Nile. President Mubarak, when he boards a train, takes the opulent carriages that once made up the personal train of King Farouk, who was overthrown in 1952. Tourists are required to travel in special tourist trains that have no third-class carriages. Reza and I, although we entered Qus in a van with an armed escort, have asked to depart on the third-class train to Cairo, although the safety record of the third-class trains is dismal. Dozens of Egyptians over the past decade have died on the rails in head-on collisions, as well as in accidents with vehicles at railroad crossings. But for most Egyptians, who do not own cars, this is the only way to travel. And it is most Egyptians who interest us.

Qus has been settled for thousands of years. The local folklore holds that it was the place where the ancient Egyptians embalmed and mummified the dead. This messy and foul-smelling work was usually done, Egyptologists believe, in tents set up around burial places. The remains of what must have been an imposing temple are tucked down an alley in the heart of the city. It has never been excavated, in large part because the owners of the houses that ring it know they are perched on top of an archeological site and are hostile to all outsiders poking around the ruins. It is, once the phone cards are purchased, the first place we visit.

The heavy blocks that once composed the top of the building bear carvings of the falcon-headed god Horus, god of the sky, and numerous hieroglyphs. The blocks are in a sandy courtyard flanked by mud and concrete hovels that reach three or four stories in the air. Goats next to the granite blocks root around in piles of garbage. Laundry hangs from the windows. Ahmed told us, before we got there, that local legend says that if anyone digs beneath the monument, out of the depths underneath will come jets of fire, water, or gold. The possibility of catastrophe has kept the monument underneath the sand and the houses above it intact.

As we stand looking at the blocks of stone, a government health worker, Mahmoud Sayed, followed by a young woman wearing a red head scarf and carrying a small cooler filled with oral polio vaccine, makes his way down one of the alleys. He holds a piece of chalk. I look down the narrow alley behind him and see that he has marked the doors of houses to show that the children inside have taken the vaccine. He has a pen tucked behind his ear. He sees us peering at the monument.

"If you dig there it will see Qus consumed by fire, water, or gold," he tells us. "This is the reason we do not touch it. I believe this."

As we talk, an older woman dressed in black opens her door and casually empties a bowl of orange peels onto her doorstep.

I move slowly around the monument, and only after close examination do I make out the figure of a hunter who holds in his left hand an ibex, the animal's feet crossed and tied together. The hunter has taken a knife in his right hand and plunged it through the neck of the animal. He is offering it up to the royal personage in front of him. The monument is only a hundred feet away from a church and a mosque. This small patch of Qus has been, for several thousand years, sacred space.

The poverty of Egypt has left the country of sixty million with a strange mixture of the modern and the ancient, often coexisting in ways that befuddle the outsider. We can hear the chatter from television sets pumping popular and slightly racy soap operas from Cairo into the small hovels. Workers in Qus covet secure jobs in the sugar and paper mills. The belief in folklore, ingrained xenophobia, and superstition, however, coexist with modern medicine, factories, and cell phones. This tension, as it does in much of the Middle East, spawns confusion and alienation, especially for those who leave the vital and close kinship ties of the village and seek work in the urban slums of Cairo.

There are in Qus several small shops where herbs and potions are sold for ailments, real and imagined. Small glass bottles with oddly colored liquids promise to replace hair and increase fertility, sexual prowess, and intelligence. It is one of these shops we decide to visit. We wait while Ahmed calls to report our movements and find, when we arrive, two uniformed police.

The shop is hidden in a narrow alley, too small for cars but wide enough for donkey carts. It is dingy and has the sour smells of herbs and spices that lie in burlap sacks on the dirt floor. In the center of the shop is a massive granite wheel. The wheel, which is upright, has a beam, worn to a shiny smoothness over the years, poking out of its center. It resembles a huge Tinkertoy that has lost one of its wheels. The end of the beam has a harness. When the harness is hitched to the cow currently resting out back, it is pushed slowly around the bowl-shaped stone below. The granite wheel grinds the herbs and spices into a mush that is distilled by a press into liquid and sold in small vials.

"It is all medicine," one of the owners says. "We use onion oil for sexual enhancement. The man takes the onion oil and the man becomes very strong and virile. It is good for the whole body."

On shelves in the front room are very small glass bottles of oils made from carrots, white radishes, watercress, parsley, bitter almond, eucalyptus, anise, coriander, and lettuce. A twenty-four-year-old customer, Ahmed Mohammed, comes into the shop.

"If you have a chest cough, take this," the owner says, offering something called Baraka Nagila and clutching his cell phone. "It costs four pounds."

As we walk out of the shop, we see a wooden lintel over the opposite door. Into it is carved ornate verses from the Koran, and in the middle of the board there is a Star of David, left as a calling card by a Jewish carpenter who long ago departed Qus, perhaps during the great Jewish exodus of 1956, when Israel and Egypt went to war. His name is forgotten, but the emblem of his faith remains, and there are mosques throughout the Middle East where, if you look closely, his brother carpenters also left behind Jewish stars in the ornate woodwork.

Gazira, perched on the rich agricultural land along the Nile, is one of the local centers for the manufacture of mud bricks. We arrive early in the morning at the home of Abdel Azim, forty-six, who has made mud bricks for the past decade, a trade he was taught by his father. He wears a dirty black galabiya and has a white cloth wound tight into a turban on his head. He is barefoot and the bottom of his galabiya is rolled up to protect it from the mud. He works six hours a day making the bricks, leaving them to dry in the sun or firing them at night by burning straw over them, a practice banned by the government authorities. But the village is known for its night fires, with local family brickyards sending flames up toward the starlit dome. He and his children can make up to ten thousand bricks by hand a month, with an average of six hundred to nine hundred a day. The state security has preceded our visit apparently, since the brick maker, when asked about firing his bricks, answers: "We are not allowed to tell you we fire our bricks."

The mud bricks, composed of straw and sheep or cattle manure, have changed little through the centuries. The mud, taken out of a watery hole, is deftly mixed by hand with the organic materials, kept in neat mounds on the ground, and then placed in wooden rectangular molds. The bricks are set out in rows to dry.

Abdel Azim has ten children, ranging in age from five to twenty years old. His oldest, Mohammed, is in the army, but his other sons are working with him. The family makes about two dollars a day selling the bricks. They make the bricks when a builder places an order.

"I don't want to do this," one of the sons, Hassan, says flatly, dun-colored mud caked on his arms and legs.

"First, I will look for another job," he says, "but if I don't find one I will work with my father. This is hard work. I will look in Qus, but if I do not find a job there I may go to Cairo. I will look for a job at the paper and sugarcane factories. These are the best jobs, the ones where you work in a factory. If I want any kind of other job, I need an advanced diploma."

Hassan loads the mud, scooped out of the hole where he stands with his pants rolled up, into a wheelbarrow. He lifts himself out of the hole and wheels the mixture over to his father, squatting on the ground. Hassan stands and squeezes the mud from his fingers and flings it aside. He dips a white plastic pail on the end of a rope into the canal, draws up some water, and dumps it into his mud hole. He climbs into the hole and stomps the mixture with his bare feet. We talk about his life in the village, where he says he would like to remain and raise a family. For lunch he eats white cheese, bread, and tea; at night the family cooks fava beans known as *foul*. He has one pair of shoes. He has never been to Luxor or Cairo. He has never visited the ancient pharaonic monuments because "I don't have enough money."

"When the day is done I feel pain in my hand," he says. "My skin is dry. Sometimes I get cuts. The work hurts your back."

As the men work making bricks, the mother, Suad al-Sayyah, who says she is about forty, washes the laundry in a small enclosure bordered by a fence. She wears hoop earrings, a long gray robe, and a blue, red, and green head scarf. She said the family is saving to pay for electrical service. She, too, has never visited Luxor, a luxury she said she could not afford since the money had to be spent "for useful things." On the mud wall of her small hut are posters of Egyptian film stars and prominent clerics.

The dearth of jobs thrusts young Egyptians back onto their families, who will at least make sure they remain housed and fed. Those that head to the teaming slums that have made Cairo one of the most densely populated and impoverished cities in the world leave behind this safety net. It is the disintegration of these kinship ties—a disintegration directly related to the faltering economy—that has proved to be the powerful wedge used by militant Islam to reach young, dislocated Egyptians. No longer able to depend on family for support, they find in militant Islam a kind of traditional, cultural, and emotional reassurance that holds out the promise of something better and a replacement community. Traditional Islam, a powerful force in village life, mutates in the slums into something deadly.

Qus and the surrounding villages are "dry," something that would have dismayed the builders of the buried temple, who consumed beer and wine. There were, after all, thirty-six wine jars in Tutankhamen's tomb, each with a docket in hieratic script, giving the date, place, and vintage. But Islamic culture remains powerful. Women in Qus do not congregate in the male domain of coffee shops or go out without head coverings. The mosques, neglected and filled mostly with the elderly a couple of decades ago, are filled with young men and women. It is a creeping Islamic revolution.

The center of life is the mosque. The imams, appointed and paid by the government, are careful about what they say. But the mosques have swelled with young people seeking another way of life. The large al-Amri mosque in Qus, built at the time of the Ottoman Empire, is the biggest in upper Egypt. It is an open space, the roof held up by pillars, with a green carpet. Its ornate wooden pulpit, made from teak imported from India, is one of the most intricate in the Islamic world with its twelve carved wooden steps. But the recent government renovation of the mosque has turned it into a soulless, concrete monstrosity, the old beams and marble pillars, many of them Roman in origin, incorporated at random into the design. The walls are a pale yellow. Fans are suspended from the ceiling.

I sit in the sea of worshippers and listen to the sermon. The imam speaks of feeding the poor and how most of our problems are caused by human selfishness.

"Allah calls on us to cooperate to promote goodness and not to cooperate to promote evil," he says.

I meet with the imam after the service in his small office, the shelves filled with theological works. He wears a red turban, a white collarless shirt buttoned up to his chin, a pressed gray galabiya, and a neatly trimmed salt-and-pepper beard. He is a large man with beefy hands and an easy smile. He is careful when asked questions that skirt into politics, keeping things vague enough to make a point yet keep him out of trouble.

"There is no cooperation between the rich and the poor in this country," he says. "The rich should help the poor."

He tells me that a proper Muslim woman must cover her head, and when I ask him about the singers and actresses in Cairo, and the wives of high officials, including the wife of President Mubarak, who appear uncovered, he picks his words with care.

"These singers spread corruption in society," he says. "This leads to illegal relationships between men and women, which is not allowed in Islam. It leads people away from religious principles, away from the true Islam, and finally angers Allah."

Late that night we sit in the small coffee shop in Gazira. A television on a table in the corner transmits a soccer game.

"Nurses will go to your homes to give vaccines," a commercial informs viewers.

The mud-brick buildings are three and four stories high, the arched doors and window frames neatly painted with white trim. They remind me of the towering mud buildings in Yemen. The windows on the bottom floors are closed off with wooden shutters. Two young men work over a small stove with jets of blue gas. On the wall, in red letters, is a sign that reads: "Remember the Prophet."

But there is despair in the coffee shop. Few of the men have jobs.

Moustafa Abdel Safat, in a brown galabiya and with a yellow scarf draped around his neck, helps his father grow wheat and vegetables. He lives with his mother, father, and eight brothers and sisters. He moonlights hooking the houses in the village up to the electrical grid, setting up a ladder, hammering holes in the walls, and stringing the wire out to the poles. I have a hard time determining whether, as I suspect, he is pirating the current.

"The bad part is that I get electrocuted," he says.

"If I grip the wire like this," he adds, folding the palm of his left hand around his right index finger, "I die. A lot of people have died doing this work."

"I will leave soon for another country to find work," he says. "I have a bachelor's degree in social work from Aswan University. I graduated three years ago. I can't find a job. I do not want to work in the fields with my family. I want to find another kind of work."

He has applied for a work visa to Saudi Arabia and has been waiting for two months for a response. He hopes to work as an electrician.

The television is broadcasting a popular soap opera called *I Do Not Love My Father's Galabiya*, about a younger generation that does not subscribe to the old ways of life. The girls do not cover their heads. The boy wants to go to college rather than work with his father. The first commercial is for Tide.

The two boys behind the counter are busy packing tobacco in round metal cylinders for the water pipes. The hiss of the gas competes with the radio above the counter playing a folk song by Rabia al-Baraka.

"A plant grows then I cry for it when it dies," the words go. "This happened to me."

Alla Adel is sixteen, with a thin moustache and sideburns. He works for about a dollar a day and gives the money to his father when he comes home at night. He has four brothers and three sisters. The other waiter, Ahmed Nour, who is fifteen, also uses the money for his family. The two boys say they dream of something else, especially Ahmed, who wants to be a professional soccer player. Alla points to a spot on the wall where he scratched his name. "It was when I started work," he says.

The owner, Said Bishair, sits out with the patrons, leaning forward on his bamboo cane. He wears a white turban and a brown scarf. He has had the coffee shop for thirty years. Before that he was a farmer.

Those who seek work can go at this time of the year to the sugarcane fields, where they can cut cane for less than a dollar a day. It is brutal work, especially in the heat, one of the reasons the harvesters begin work before dawn. We arrive in a field not far from the paper and cane factory. The men in galabiyas and sandals cut the green stalks with machetes and strip them of the leaves before tossing them in a pile. Donkeys, tethered in the field, bray.

Mohamed Kamal, forty-five, the owner, stands next to a wooden cart and watches about twenty workers fill it with stalks. He allows them to take the leaves home to feed their animals. Several of the donkeys are already eating their fill of leaves.

One of the workers is a young man clearly unused to hard labor. He gives me his name and tells me he graduated from the university with a degree in social work. He is cutting stalks in exchange for leaves for his animals. He is also angry, and as we speak, Ahmed, who accompanies us everywhere, begins to inch closer to us.

"I searched for a job," he says, "but there are no jobs. I am angry. A job is very important."

He tells me he has never been to Cairo, but he may have to go there to seek work. He began to attend the mosque and do his five daily prayers about six years ago. And then he lays out a new vision for Egypt, one that lurks not far beneath the surface of the secular Mubarak regime.

"When there are Islamic laws governing our lives, things will be better," he says. "There will be more work. Everyone will fear Allah. This will make a change. If you fear Allah there is no corruption. This will make it better for us."

He watches as I write down his words.

"Please omit my name," he says softly, glancing at Ahmed, who stands a few feet away with his back to us. I cross his name out in my notebook. He looks at the black lines through his name and asks me to continue to blot out his name.

As we get in the van Ahmed asks if he can go to Qus and find a phone so he can report on our conversations over the past two hours without using his cell phone. Cellular service is down today and he has lost contact with state security. We suspect the comments of the cane cutter mean trouble for him. We head to the central phone exchange, and Ahmed disappears into a cabin for nearly an hour.

We retreat to the Nile, sure now that Ahmed and our state security minders will exert even greater control over our activities. Ahmed refuses to let us leave for the river, an enforced delay that will color the rest of our visit, and when we arrive there are several large men in galabiyas, all wearing expensive watches and with the well-fed jowls of men who do not eke out a living in the fields. Girls are washing laundry in the river, laughing gaily in the water. The banks of the river are sandy, and wind whips down the broad expanse of water. Women in black robes, with straw mats or baskets of clothes balanced on their heads, move toward the river's edge. A boy swims naked alone in the shallow water.

Faiza Hussein, twelve, is washing with her cousin. She wears a blue dress and stands knee-deep with laundry floating around her.

"Afaf," she shouts to her cousin, "where is the brush?"

She takes the brush and begins to work on a curtain in the water, soapsuds rising from the material as she scrubs. Two of the large men stand a few feet away, watching me.

As I chat with the girls, who banter and giggle with teenage enthusiasm, a young man pushes a friend who is a paraplegic down through the sand to the water. The paraplegic sits on the seat of a crude, large tricycle he can peddle by turning cranks at chest level. His withered legs contrast with his upper build.

He is Ahmed Fahty, twenty-five. He had polio when he was a child. The young man pushing him, Ramadan Sayyed, is a mute. They are neighbors.

"I spend most of my time with Ramadan," Fahty tells me. "We go everywhere with each other. We have a lot in common. We are more than brothers. We need to help each other."

The two men look out at the water. A pair of crutches are strapped to the back of the tricycle.

"We just come to look," he says. "In the summer I will go in the water, but Ramadan will not go in. He is afraid. When Ramadan wants something I can understand his gestures. We give each other help. We share our food."

He says he lives at home with his parents, a life that is hard and often lonely.

"The hardest thing is mental," he says. "Sometimes I get angry with my mother or sister at home. Sometimes my chest hurts me, and when my chest hurts me I do not want anyone to speak with me. If someone speaks with me I get angry. Ramadan stays with me when I have this pain. He will tell me we should go down to the Nile and look at the water. Ramadan and I understand each other."

One of the large men comes to stand next to me. He is clutching a cell phone. The two young men nervously glance at him. When I ask Fahty what he does when people make fun of Sayyed, it is the stranger at our side who answers.

"This kind of thing never happens," the man says briskly.

On the way home we are told that our request to visit the elementary school where Ahmed's small daughter is a student has been denied. We decide to visit the offices of the Ministry of Education in Qus to get them to reconsider the request. When we arrive we find the director, Rushdi Abu el-Safa', behind a large desk. He is smoking, flicking the ash on the floor. He oversees the 180 schools in the district, which has 87,000 students. He promises to pass on our request. Ahmed, who receives a call later that day, is told we will not be allowed in any schools, nor can we visit the local factories. When we get home we find Ahmed's wife nervous and silent. The constant phone calls, the long reports Ahmed has to fax each day on our activities, have cast a pall over the house. The strain of our visit shows in the darting looks, whispers, and uncomfortable gaps in conversation where we had once laughed and joked.

We walk that evening to the tomb of the village sheikh. The blue dome of the tomb, with vermillion and green flags on top, is a local shrine. A sign outside says: "This is the place of Sheikh Abdullah Mohammed Ahmed." About ten children play in the dirt outside the tomb.

"He lived a simple life," says Abdullah Ali, who built the tomb in 1984 for his uncle. "He was a farmer. He was very kind. He did not hurt or annoy his neighbors."

The sheikh, according to the villagers, had supernatural powers. He knew what people were carrying in their pockets. He could predict the future. He could take a pot of boiling liquid and drink it. In his final days, when he was sick and bedridden, villagers claimed to have seen him visit their houses. When he spat at a water pump it exploded. When thieves descended on the village they fled, believing they were chased by the sheikh for fifty kilometers.

"He could go forty-five days without food or water," his nephew says. "He did not live in any one place. He wandered. He once jumped from the highest palm tree in the village and was not hurt. He was illiterate."

His nephew did not build the tomb until his two sons suffered accidents, including the collapse of a wall on one of the boys. He saw these as signs of displeasure from his uncle.

"Since I built the tomb nothing has happened," he tells me.

I ask him if all venerated sheikhs have magical powers. He looks at me with disapproval.

"Magic is forbidden in Islam," he says.

We do not eat until late at night. Ahmed spends two hours writing up our day to fax to the state security services. When the photographer traveling with me picks up the report he reminds Ahmed that he has not mentioned the trip to the tomb.

"Oh no," Ahmed says, clearly upset, "I forgot."

The next morning at dawn the photographer asks to take pictures in the cane fields, but Ahmed does not let him leave the house. He calls state security. He waits to be called back. When he finally arrives in the fields, Reza notices several large men with cell phones interspersed among the cane cutters.

We drift at night to the coffee shops, tailed now, as we are during the day, by the heavyset men in the clean, pressed galabiyas and holding the cell phones. They offer no explanation for their intrusiveness.

Our decision to go back to the pharaonic temple, however, the next morning makes us glad to have them. Our return visit is not taken lightly by the neighbors, who believe it is connected with an excavation. Within minutes people start shouting at us in rage, telling us to get out.

A young man had let us into his home during the previous visit, and his father begins to yell and curse him and us.

"Why did you let them into the house?" he shouts at his son. "They will report about the whole temple to the government, and all the houses will be destroyed."

Curse words begin to fly. We back away. Three uniformed police swiftly arrive and hustle us to the van, shouting at the small mob to get back.

It is only at midnight on our last day that we are told we will not be allowed on the third-class train. We will be put, we are told, into a first-class car to Cairo. We will not be allowed to speak to anyone on the train.

We enter the train with escorts, including uniformed police with assault rifles. When we attempt to walk into the second-class car, we are abruptly pushed back by a policeman between the two cars.

"No foreigners," we are told.

When the train pulls into the Shohaj station security men enter our car. They check the documents of the few Egyptians seated in our car and frisk them. The Egyptians are asked to leave our compartment. We become, in a matter of minutes, as hermetically sealed off from the Egypt we sought to reach as the tourists in the lumbering buses whose convoy we had joined a few days before. We sit on the long ride to Cairo and watch the other Egypt glide past us.

A Culture of Atrocity

JUNE 18, 2007

All troops, when they occupy and battle insurgent forces, as in Iraq, or Gaza, or Vietnam, are swiftly placed in what the psychiatrist Robert Jay Lifton terms "atrocity-producing situations." In this environment, surrounded by a hostile population, in simple acts such as going to a store to buy a can of Coke or driving down a street, you can be killed. This constant fear and stress leads troops to view everyone around them as the enemy. The hostility is compounded when the enemy, as in Iraq, is elusive, shadowy, and hard to find. The rage that soldiers feel after a roadside bomb explodes, killing or maiming their comrades, is one that is easily directed eventually to innocent civilians seen as supporting the insurgents. It is a short psychological leap, but a massive moral one. It is a leap from killing—the shooting of someone who has the capacity to do you harm—to murder—the deadly assault against someone who cannot harm you. The war in Iraq is primarily involves murder. There is very little killing. U.S. Marines and soldiers have become, after four years of war, acclimated to atrocity.

The American killing project is not described in these terms to the distant public. The politicians still speak in the abstract of glory, honor, and heroism, of the necessity of improving the world, in lofty phrases of political and spiritual renewal. As in most wars, the media are slavishly compliant. The reality of the war—the fact that the occupation forces have become, along with the rampaging militias, a source of terror to most Iraqis—is not transmitted to the American public. The media chronicle the physical and emotional wounds visited on those who kill in our name. The Iraqis, those we kill, are largely nameless, faceless dead. Those who kill large numbers of people always claim it as a regrettable but necessary virtue.

The reality and the mythic narrative of war collide when embittered combat veterans return home. They find themselves estranged from the world around them, a world that still believes in the myth of war and the virtues of the nation.

In a recent article in the *Los Angeles Times*, Tina Susman gave readers a rare glimpse into this side of the war. She wrote about a seventeen-year-old Iraqi boy killed by the wild, random fire unleashed by American soldiers in a Baghdad neighborhood following a bomb blast. Such killings, which Iraqis say occur daily, are seldom confirmed, but in this case the boy was the son of a local *Los Angeles Times* employee.

Iraqi physicians, overseen by epidemiologists at Johns Hopkins University's Bloomberg School of Public Health, published a study last year in the British medical journal *Lancet*. The study estimated that 655,000 more people than normal have died in Iraq since coalition forces invaded the country in March 2003. This is more than twenty times the estimate of thirty thousand civilian deaths President Bush gave in a speech in December 2006.

Of the total 655,000 estimated "excess deaths," 601,000 resulted from violence. The remaining deaths occurred from disease and other causes, according to the study. This is about five hundred additional violent deaths per day throughout the country.

Lieutenant Colonel Andrew J. Bacevich, a Vietnam veteran who is a professor of international relations at Boston University, estimated last year that U.S. troops had killed "tens of thousands" of innocent Iraqis through accidents or reckless fire.

Official figures have ceased to exist. The Iraqi government no longer releases the number of civilian casualties, and the U.S. military does not usually give reports about civilians killed or wounded by U.S. forces.

"It's a psychological thing. When one U.S. soldier gets killed or injured, they shoot in vengeance," Alaa Safi told the *Los Angeles Times*. He said his brother, Ahmed, was killed April 4 when U.S. troops riddled the streets of their southwestern Baghdad neighborhood with bullets after a sniper attack.

War is the pornography of violence. It has a dark beauty, filled with the monstrous and the grotesque. The Bible calls it "the lust of the eye" and warns believers against it. War allows us to engage in primal impulses we keep hidden in the deepest, most private interiors of our fantasy lives. It allows us to destroy not only things but also human beings. In that moment of wholesale destruction, we wield the power of the divine, the power to give or annihilate life. Armed units become crazed by the frenzy of destruction. All things, including human beings, become objects—objects to gratify, destroy, or both. Almost no one is immune. The contagion of the crowd sees to that.

Human beings are machine-gunned and bombed from the air, automatic grenade launchers pepper hovels and neighborhoods with high-powered explosives, and convoys tear through Iraq, seeding freight trains of death. These soldiers and Marines have at their fingertips the heady ability to call in firepower that obliterates landscapes and villages. The moral universe is turned upside down. No one walks away uninfected. War thrusts us into a vortex of barbarity, pain, and fleeting ecstasy. It thrusts us into a world where law is of little consequence.

It takes little in wartime to turn ordinary men and women into killers. Most give themselves willingly to the seduction of unlimited power to destroy. All feel the peer pressure to conform. Few, once in battle, find the strength to resist gratuitous slaughter. Physical courage is common on a battlefield. Moral courage is not.

Military machines and state bureaucracies, which seek to make us obey, seek also to silence those who return from war and speak the truth. Besides, the public has little desire to puncture the mythic, heroic narrative. The essence of war, which is death, is carefully masked from view. The few journalists who attempt to speak the truth about war, to describe the experience of constantly being on the receiving end of American firepower, soon become pariahs, no longer able to embed with the military, dine out with officials in the Green Zone, or get press credentials. And so the vast majority of the media lie to us, although not overtly; it is the lie of omission, but it is a lie nonetheless.

The veterans who return, even if they do not speak about the atrocities they have committed or witnessed in Iraq, will spend the rest of their lives coping with what they have done. They will suffer delayed reactions to stress. They will endure, as have those who returned from Vietnam, a crisis of faith. The God they knew, or thought they knew, failed them. The high priests of our civic religion, from politicians to preachers to television pundits, who promised them glory and honor through war betrayed them.

War always involves betrayal, betrayal of the young by the old, of idealists by cynics, and of troops by politicians. This bitter knowledge of betrayal is seeping into the ranks of the American military. It is bringing us a new wave of enraged and disenfranchised veterans who will never again trust the country that sent them to war.

We make our heroes out of clay. We laud their gallant deeds. We give them uniforms with colored ribbons for the acts of violence they committed or endured. They are our false repositories of glory and honor, of power, of self-righteousness, of patriotism and self-worship, all that we want to believe about ourselves. They are our plaster saints, the icons we cheer to defend us and make us and our nation great. They are the props of our demented civic religion, our love of power and force, our belief in our right as a chosen nation to wield this force against the weak. This is our nation's idolatry of itself.

Prophets are not those who speak of piety and duty from pulpits—there are few people in pulpits worth listening to. The prophets are the battered wrecks of men and women who return from Iraq and find the courage to speak the halting words we do not want to hear, words we must hear and digest in order to know ourselves. These veterans, the ones who dare to tell the truth, have seen and tasted how war plunges us into barbarity, perversion, pain, and an unchecked orgy of death. And it is their testimonies, if we take the time to listen, which alone can save us.

Becoming What We Seek to Destroy

MAY 11, 2009

The bodies of dozens, perhaps well over a hundred, women, children, and men, their corpses blown into bits of human flesh by iron fragmentation bombs dropped by U.S. warplanes in a village in the western province of Farah, illustrates the futility of the Afghan war. We are not delivering democracy or liberation or development. We are delivering massive, sophisticated forms of industrial slaughter. And because we have employed the blunt and horrible instrument of war in a land we know little about and are incapable of reading, we embody the barbarism we claim to be seeking to defeat.

We are morally no different from the psychopaths within the Taliban, whom Afghans remember we empowered, funded, and armed during the ten-year war with the Soviet Union. Acid thrown into a girl's face or beheadings? Death delivered from the air or fields of shiny cluster bombs? This is the language of war. It is what we speak. It is what those we fight speak.

Afghan survivors carted some two dozen corpses from their villages to the provincial capital in trucks this week to publicly denounce the carnage. Some two thousand angry Afghans in the streets of the capital chanted "Death to America!" But the grief, fear, and finally rage of the bereaved do not touch those who use high-minded virtues to justify slaughter. The death of innocents, they assure us, is the tragic cost of war. It is regrettable, but it happens. It is the price that must be paid. And so, guided by a president who once again has no experience of war and defers to the bull-necked generals and militarists whose careers, power, and profits depend on expanded war, we are transformed into monsters.

There will soon be 21,000 additional U.S. soldiers and Marines in Afghanistan in time for the expected surge in summer fighting. There will be more clashes, more air strikes, more deaths, and more despair and anger from those forced to bury their parents, sisters, brothers, and children. The grim report of the killings in the air strike, issued by the International Committee of the Red Cross, which stated that bombs hit civilian houses and noted that an ICRC counterpart in the Red Crescent was among the dead, will become familiar reading in the weeks and months ahead.

We are the best recruiting weapon the Taliban possesses. We enabled it to rise from the ashes seven years ago to control openly more than half the country and carry out daylight attacks in the capital Kabul. And the war we wage is being exported like a virus to Pakistan in the form of drones that bomb Pakistani villages, and in increased clashes between the inept Pakistani military and a restive internal insurgency.

I spoke in New York City a few days ago with Juliette Fournot, who lived with her parents in Afghanistan as a teenager, speaks Dari, and led teams of French doctors and nurses from Médecins Sans Frontières, or Doctors Without Borders, into Afghanistan during the war with the Soviets. She participated in the opening of clandestine cross-border medical operations missions between 1980 and 1982 and became head of the French humanitarian mission in Afghanistan in 1983. Fournot established logistical bases in Peshawar and Quetta and organized the dozen cross-border and clandestine permanent missions in the resistance-held areas of Herat, Mazar-i-Sharif, Badakhshan, Paktia, Ghazni, and Hazarajat, through which more than five hundred international aid workers rotated.

She is one of the featured characters in a remarkable book called *The Photographer*, produced by photojournalist Didier Lefèvre and graphic novelist Emmanuel Guibert. The book tells the story of a three-month mission in 1986 into Afghanistan led by Fournot. It is an unflinching look at the cost of war, what bombs, shells and bullets do to human souls and bodies. It exposes, in a way the rhetoric of our politicians and generals do not, the blind, destructive fury of war. The French humanitarian group withdrew from Afghanistan in July 2004 after five of its aid workers were assassinated, even though they were riding in a clearly marked vehicle.

"The American ground troops are midterm in a history that started roughly in 1984 and 1985, when the State Department decided to assist the mujahideen, the resistance fighters, through various programs and military aid. USAID [the United States Agency for International Development], the humanitarian arm serving political and military purposes, was the seed for having a different kind of interaction with the Afghans," she told me. "The Afghans were very grateful to receive arms and military equipment from the Americans.

"But the way USAID distributed its humanitarian assistance was very debatable," she went on:

> It still puzzles me. They gave most of it to the Islamic groups such as the Hezb-e Islami of [Gulbuddin] Hekmatyar. And I think it is possibly because they were more interested in the future stability of Pakistan rather than saving Afghanistan. Afghanistan was probably a good ground to hit and drain the blood from the Soviet Union. I did not see a plan to rebuild or bring peace to Afghanistan. It seemed that Afghanistan was a tool to weaken the Soviet Union. It was mostly left to the Pakistani intelligence services to decide what would be best and how to do it, and how by doing so they could strengthen themselves.

The Pakistanis, Fournot said, developed a close relationship with Saudi Arabia. The Saudis, like the Americans, flooded the country with money and also exported conservative and often radical Wahhabi clerics. The Americans, aware of the Pakistan-Saudi Arabia relationship, as well as Pakistan's secret program to build nuclear weapons, looked the other way. Washington sowed, unwittingly, the seeds of destruction in Afghanistan and Pakistan. It trained, armed, and empowered the militants who now kill them.

The relationship, she said, bewildered most Afghans, who did not look favorably on this radical form of Islam. Most Afghans, she said, wondered why American aid went almost exclusively to the Islamic radicals and not to more moderate and secular resistance movements.

"The population wondered why they did not have more credibility with the Americans," she said:

They could not understand why the aid was stopped in Pakistan and distributed to political parties that had limited reach in Afghanistan. These parties stockpiled arms and started fighting each other. What the people got in the provinces was miniscule and irrelevant. And how did the people see all this? They had great hopes in the beginning and gradually became disappointed, bitter, and then felt betrayed. This laid the groundwork for the current suspicion, distrust, and disappointment with the U.S. and NATO.

Fournot sees the American project in Afghanistan as mirroring that of the doomed Soviet occupation that began in December 1979. A beleaguered Afghan population, brutalized by chaos and violence, desperately hoped for stability and peace. The Soviets, like the Americans, spoke of equality, economic prosperity, development, education, women's rights, and political freedom. But within two years, the ugly face of Soviet domination had unmasked the flowery rhetoric. The Afghans launched their insurgency to drive the Soviets out of the country.

Fournot fears that years of war have shattered the concept of nationhood. "There is so much personal and mental destruction," she said. "Over seventy percent of the population has never known anything else but war. Kids do not go to school. War is normality. It gives that adrenaline rush that provides a momentary sense of high, and that is what they live on. And how can you build a nation on that?"

The Pashtuns, she noted, have built an alliance with the Taliban to restore Pashtun power lost in the 2001 invasion. The border between Pakistan and Afghanistan is, to the Pashtuns, a meaningless demarcation drawn by imperial powers through the middle of their tribal lands. There are thirteen million Pashtuns in Afghanistan and another twenty-eight million in Pakistan. The Pashtuns are fighting forces in Islamabad and Kabul they see as seeking to wrest from them their honor and autonomy. They see little difference among the Pakistani military, American troops, and the Afghan army.

Islamabad, while it may battle Taliban forces in Swat or the provinces, does not regard the Taliban as a mortal enemy. The enemy is and has always been India. The balance of power with India requires the Pakistani authorities to ensure that any Afghan government is allied with it. This means it cannot push the Pashtuns in the Northwest Frontier Province or in Afghanistan too far. It must keep its channels open. The cat-and-mouse game between the Pakistani authorities and the Pashtuns, which drives Washington to fury, will never end. Islamabad needs the Pashtuns in Pakistan and Afghanistan more than the Pashtuns need them.

The United States fuels the bonfires of war. The more troops we send to Afghanistan, the more drones we send on bombing runs over Pakistan, the more air strikes we carry out, the worse the unraveling will become. We have killed twice as many civilians as the Taliban have this year, and that number is sure to rise in the coming months.

"I find this term *collateral damage* dehumanizing," Fournot said, "as if it is a necessity. People are sacrificed on the altar of an idea. Air power is blind. I know this from having been caught in numerous bombings."

We are faced with two stark choices. We can withdraw and open negotiations with the Taliban or continue to expand the war until we are driven out. The corrupt and unpopular regimes of Hamid Karzai in Afghanistan and Asif Ali Zardari in Pakistan are impotent allies. The longer they remain tethered to the United States, the weaker they become. And the weaker they become, the louder become the calls for intervention in Pakistan. During the war in Vietnam, we invaded Cambodia to bring stability to the region and cut off rebel sanctuaries and supply routes. This tactic only empowered the Khmer Rouge. We seem poised, in much the same way, to do the same for radical Islamists in Afghanistan and Pakistan.

"If the Americans step up the war in Afghanistan, they will be sucked into Pakistan," Fournot warned. "Pakistan is a time bomb waiting to explode. You have a huge population, 170 million people. There is nuclear power. Pakistan is much more dangerous than Afghanistan. War always has its own logic. Once you set foot in war, you do not control it. It sucks you in."

Iran Had a Democracy Before We Took It Away

JUNE 22, 2009

Iranians do not need or want us to teach them about liberty and representative government. They have long embodied this struggle. It is we who need to be taught. It was Washington that orchestrated the 1953 coup to topple Iran's democratically elected government, the first in the Middle East, and install the compliant Shah Mohammad Reza Pahlavi in power. It was Washington that forced Prime Minister Mohammed Mosaddeq, a man who cared as much for his country as he did for the rule of law and democracy, to spend the rest of his life under house arrest. We gave to the Iranian people the corrupt regime of the Shah and his savage secret police and the primitive clerics that rose out of the swamp of the dictator's Iran. Iranians know they once had a democracy until we took it away.

The fundamental problem in the Middle East is not a degenerate and corrupt Islam. The fundamental problem is a degenerate and corrupt Christendom. We have not brought freedom and democracy and enlightenment to the Muslim world. We have brought the opposite. We have used the iron fist of the American military to implant our oil companies in Iraq, occupy Afghanistan, and ensure that the region is submissive and cowed. We have supported a government in Israel that has carried out egregious war crimes in Lebanon and Gaza and is daily stealing ever-greater portions of Palestinian land. We have established a network of military bases, some the size of small cities, in Iraq, Afghanistan, Saudi Arabia, Turkey, and Kuwait, and we have secured basing rights in the Gulf states of Bahrain, Qatar, Oman, and the United Arab Emirates.

We have expanded our military operations to Uzbekistan, Pakistan, Kyrgyzstan, Tajikistan, Egypt, Algeria, and Yemen. And no one naively believes, except perhaps us, that we have any intention of leaving.

We are the biggest problem in the Middle East. We have through our cruelty and violence created and legitimized the Mahmoud Ahmadinejads and the Osama bin Ladens. The longer we lurch around the region dropping bombs and seizing Muslim land, the more these monsters, reflections of our own distorted image, will proliferate. The theologian Reinhold Niebuhr wrote, "Perhaps the most significant moral characteristic of a nation is its hypocrisy."[1] But our hypocrisy no longer fools anyone but ourselves. It will ensure our imperial and economic collapse.

The history of modern Iran is the history of a people battling tyranny. These tyrants were almost always propped up and funded by foreign powers. This suppression and distortion of legitimate democratic movements over the decades resulted in the 1979 revolution that brought the Iranian clerics to power, unleashing another tragic cycle of Iranian resistance.

"The central story of Iran over the last two hundred years has been national humiliation at the hands of foreign powers who have subjugated and looted the country," Stephen Kinzer, the author of *All the Shah's Men: An American Coup and the Roots of Middle East Terror*, told me: "For a long time the perpetrators were the British and Russians. Beginning in 1953, the United States began taking over that role. In that year, the American and British secret services overthrew an elected government, wiped away Iranian democracy, and set the country on the path to dictatorship.

"Then, in the 1980s, the U.S. sided with Saddam Hussein in the Iran-Iraq war, providing him with military equipment and intelligence that helped make it possible for his army to kill hundreds of thousands of Iranians," Kinzer said:

> Given this history, the moral credibility of the U.S. to pose as a promoter of democracy in Iran is close to nil. Especially ludicrous is the sight of people in Washington calling for intervention on behalf of democracy in Iran when just last year they were calling for the

bombing of Iran. If they had had their way then, many of the brave protesters on the streets of Tehran today—the ones they hold up as heroes of democracy—would be dead now.

Washington has never recovered from the loss of Iran—something our intelligence services never saw coming. The overthrow of the Shah, the humiliation of the embassy hostages, and the laborious piecing together of tiny shreds of paper from classified embassy documents to expose America's venal role in thwarting democratic movements in Iran and the region, allowed the outside world to see the dark heart of the American empire. Washington has demonized Iran ever since, painting it as an irrational and barbaric country filled with primitive, religious zealots. But Iranians, as these street protests illustrate, have proved in recent years far more courageous in the defense of democracy than most Americans.

Where were we when our election was stolen from us in 2000 by Republican operatives and a Supreme Court that overturned all legal precedent to anoint George W. Bush president? Did tens of thousands of us fill the squares of our major cities and denounce the fraud? Did we mobilize day after day to restore transparency and accountability to our election process? Did we fight back with the same courage and tenacity as the citizens of Iran? Did Al Gore defy the power elite and, as opposition candidate Mir-Hossein Mousavi has done, demand a recount at the risk of being killed?

President Obama retreated in his Cairo speech into our spectacular moral nihilism, suggesting that our crimes matched the crimes of Iran, that there is, in his words, "a tumultuous history between us." He went on: "In the middle of the Cold War, the United States played a role in the overthrow of a democratically elected Iranian government. Since the Islamic Revolution, Iran has played a role in acts of hostage-taking and violence against U.S. troops and civilians."[2] It all, he seemed to say, balances out.

I am no friend of the Iranian regime, which helped create and arm Hezbollah; is certainly meddling in Iraq; has persecuted human-rights activists, gays, women, and religious and ethnic minorities; embraces racism and intolerance; and uses its power to deny popular will. But I do not remember Iran orchestrating a coup in the United States to replace an elected government with a brutal dictator who for decades persecuted, assassinated, and imprisoned democracy activists. I do not remember Iran arming and funding a neighboring state to wage war against our country. Iran never shot down one of our passenger jets, as did the USS *Vincennes*—caustically nicknamed "Robocruiser" by the crews of other American vessels—when in June 1988 it fired missiles at an Airbus filled with Iranian civilians, killing everyone on board. Iran is not sponsoring terrorism within the United States, as our intelligence services currently do in Iran. The attacks on Iranian soil include suicide bombings, kidnappings, beheadings, sabotage, and "targeted assassinations" of government officials, scientists, and other Iranian leaders. What would we do if the situation were reversed? How would we react if Iran carried out these policies against us?

We are, and have long been, the primary engine for radicalism in the Middle East. The greatest favor we can do for democracy activists in Iran, as well as in Iraq, Afghanistan, the Persian Gulf, and the dictatorships that dot North Africa is withdraw our troops from the region and begin to speak to Iranians and the rest of the Muslim world in the civilized language of diplomacy, respect, and mutual interests. The longer we cling to the doomed doctrine of permanent war, the more we give credibility to the extremists who need, indeed yearn for, an enemy that speaks in their crude slogans of nationalist cant and violence. The louder the Israelis and their idiot allies in Washington call for the bombing of Iran to thwart its nuclear ambitions, the happier are the bankrupt clerics who are ordering the beating and murder of demonstrators. We may laugh when crowds supporting Ahmadinejad call us "the Great Satan," but there is a very palpable reality that has informed the terrible algebra of their hatred.

Our intoxication with our military prowess blinds us to all possibilities of hope and mutual cooperation. It was Mohammad Khatami, the president of Iran from 1997 to 2005—perhaps the only honorable Middle East leader of our time—whose refusal to countenance violence by his own supporters led to the demise of his lofty "civil society" at the hands of more ruthless, less scrupulous opponents. It was Khatami who proclaimed that "the death of even one Jew is a crime." And we sputtered

back to this great and civilized man the primitive slogans of all deformed militarists. We were captive, as all bigots are, to our demons,
and could not hear any sound but our own shouting. It is time to banish these demons. It is time to stand not with the helmeted goons who
beat protesters, not with those in the Pentagon who make endless wars,
but with the unarmed demonstrators in Iran who daily show us what
we must become.

The fight of the Iranian people is our fight. And, perhaps for the first
time, we can match our actions to our ideals. We have no right under
post-Nuremberg laws to occupy Iraq or Afghanistan. These occupations are defined by these statutes as criminal "wars of aggression."
They are war crimes. We have no right to use force, including the state-
sponsored terrorism we unleash on Iran, to turn the Middle East into a
private gas station for our large oil companies. We have no right to empower Israel's continuing occupation of Palestine, a flagrant violation of
international law. The resistance you see in Iran will not end until Iranians, and all those burdened with repression in the Middle East, free
themselves from the tyranny that comes from within and without. Let
us, for once, be on the side of those who share our democratic ideals.

Opium, Rape, and the American Way

NOVEMBER 2, 2009

The warlords we champion in Afghanistan are as venal, as opposed to the rights of women and basic democratic freedoms, and as heavily involved in opium trafficking as the Taliban. The moral lines we draw between us and our adversaries are fictional. The uplifting narratives used to justify the war in Afghanistan are pathetic attempts to redeem acts of senseless brutality. War cannot be waged to instill any virtue, including democracy or the liberation of women. War always empowers those who have a penchant for violence and access to weapons. War turns the moral order upside down and abolishes all discussions of human rights. War banishes the just and the decent to the margins of society. And the weapons of war do not separate the innocent and the damned. An aerial drone is our version of an improvised explosive device. An iron fragmentation bomb is our answer to a suicide bomb. A burst from a belt-fed machine gun causes the same terror and bloodshed among civilians no matter who pulls the trigger.

"We need to tear the mask off of the fundamentalist warlords who after the tragedy of 9/11 replaced the Taliban," Malalai Joya, who was expelled from the Afghan parliament two years ago for denouncing government corruption and the Western occupation, told me during her visit to New York last week. "They used the mask of democracy to take power," she said. "They continue this deception. These warlords are mentally the same as the Taliban. The only change is physical. These warlords during the civil war in Afghanistan from 1992 to 1996 killed sixty-five thousand innocent people. They have committed human-rights violations, like the Taliban, against women and many others."

"In eight years less than two thousand Talib have been killed and more than eight thousand innocent civilians have been killed," she went on:

> We believe that this is not war on terror. This is war on innocent civilians. Look at the massacres carried out by NATO forces in Afghanistan. Look what they did in May in the Farah province, where more than 150 civilians were killed, most of them women and children. They used white phosphorus and cluster bombs. There were two hundred civilians on 9th of September [2009] killed in the Kunduz province, again most of them women and children. You can see the Web site of professor Marc Herold, this democratic man, to know better the war crimes in Afghanistan imposed on our people. The United States and NATO eight years ago occupied my country under the banner of woman's rights and democracy. But they have only pushed us from the frying pan into the fire. They put into power men who are photocopies of the Taliban.

Afghanistan's boom in the trade in opium, used to produce heroin, over the past eight years of occupation has funneled hundreds of millions of dollars to the Taliban, al-Qaida, local warlords, criminal gangs, kidnappers, private armies, drug traffickers, and many of the senior figures in the government of Hamid Karzai. The *New York Times* reported that the brother of President Karzai, Ahmed Wali Karzai, has been collecting money from the CIA although he is a major player in the illegal opium business. Afghanistan produces ninety-two percent of the world's opium in a trade that is worth some $65 billion, the United Nations estimates. This opium feeds some fifteen million addicts worldwide and kills around 100,000 people annually. These fatalities should be added to the rolls of war dead.

Antonio Maria Costa, executive director of the United Nations Office on Drugs and Crime (UNODC), said that the drug trade has permitted the Taliban to thrive and expand despite the presence of 100,000 NATO troops.

"The Taliban's direct involvement in the opium trade allows them to fund a war machine that is becoming technologically more complex and increasingly widespread," said Costa.[3]

The UNODC estimates the Taliban earned $90 million to $160 million a year from taxing the production and smuggling of opium and heroin between 2005 and 2009, as much as double the amount it earned annually while it was in power nearly a decade ago. And Costa described the Afghan-Pakistani border as "the world's largest free trade zone in anything and everything that is illicit," an area blighted by drugs, weapons, and illegal immigration. The "perfect storm of drugs and terrorism" may be on the move along drug trafficking routes through Central Asia, he warned. Profits made from opium are being pumped into militant groups in Central Asia, and "a big part of the region could be engulfed in large-scale terrorism, endangering its massive energy resources."

"Afghanistan, after eight years of occupation, has become a world center for drugs," Joya told me:

> The drug lords are the only ones with power. How can you expect these people to stop the planting of opium and halt the drug trade? How is it that the Taliban, when they were in power, destroyed the opium production and a superpower not only cannot destroy the opium production but allows it to increase? And while all this goes on, those who support the war talk to you about women's rights. We do not have human rights now in most provinces. It is as easy to kill a woman in my country as it is to kill a bird. In some big cities like Kabul, some women have access to jobs and education, but in most of the country the situation for women is hell. Rape, kidnapping, and domestic violence are increasing. These fundamentalists during the so-called free elections made a misogynist law against Shia women in Afghanistan. This law has even been signed by Hamid Karzai. All these crimes are happening under the name of democracy.

Thousands of Afghan civilians have died from insurgent and foreign military violence. And American and NATO forces are responsible for almost *half* the civilian deaths in Afghanistan. Tens of thousands of Afghan civilians have also died from displacement, starvation, disease, exposure, lack of medical treatment, crime, and lawlessness resulting from the war.

Joya argues that neither Karzai nor his rival Abdullah Abdullah, who withdrew from the November 7 runoff election, will do anything to halt the transformation of Afghanistan into a narco-state. She said that NATO, by choosing sides in a battle between two corrupt and brutal opponents, has lost all its legitimacy in the country.

The recent resignation of a high-level U.S. diplomat in Afghanistan, Matthew Hoh, was in part tied to the drug problem. Hoh wrote in his resignation letter that Karzai's government is filled with "glaring corruption and unabashed graft." Karzai, he wrote, is a president "whose confidants and chief advisers comprise drug lords and war crimes villains who mock our own rule of law and counter-narcotics effort."[4]

"Where do you think the $36 billion of money poured into country by the international community have gone?" Joya asked:

> This money went into the pockets of the drug lords and the warlords. There are 18 million people in Afghanistan who live on less than two dollars a day while these warlords get rich. The Taliban and warlords together contribute to this fascism while the occupation forces are bombing and killing innocent civilians. When we do not have security, how can we even talk about human rights or women's rights?

"This election under the shade of Afghan warlordism, drug-lordism, corruption, and occupation forces has no legitimacy at all," she said:

> The result will be like the same donkey but with new saddles. It is not important who is voting. It is important who is counting. And this is our problem. Many of those who go with the Taliban do not support the Taliban, but they are fed up with these warlords and this injustice, and they go with the Taliban to take revenge. I do not agree with them, but I understand them. Most of my people are against the Taliban and the warlords, which is why millions did not take part in this tragic drama of an election.

"The U.S. wastes taxpayers' money and the blood of their soldiers by supporting such a Mafia corrupt system of Hamid Karzai," said

Joya, who changes houses in Kabul frequently because of the numerous death threats made against her.

Eight years is long enough to learn about Karzai and Abdullah. They chained my country to the center of drugs. If Obama was really honest he would support the democratic-minded people of my country. We have a lot [of those people]. But he does not support the democratic-minded people of my country. He is going to start war in Pakistan by attacking in the border area of Pakistan. More civilians have been killed in the Obama period than even during the criminal Bush.

"My people are sandwiched between two powerful enemies," she lamented:

The occupation forces from the sky bomb and kill innocent civilians. On the ground, Taliban and these warlords deliver fascism. As NATO kills more civilians, the resistance to the foreign troops increases. If the U.S. government and NATO do not leave voluntarily, my people will give to them the same lesson they gave to Russia and to the English, who three times tried to occupy Afghanistan. It is easier for us to fight against one enemy rather than two.

Afghanistan's Sham Army

NOVEMBER 9, 2009

Success in Afghanistan is measured in Washington by the ability to create an indigenous army that will battle the Taliban, provide security and stability for Afghan civilians, and remain loyal to the puppet government of Hamid Karzai. A similar set of goals eluded the Red Army, although the Soviets spent a decade attempting to pacify the country. It eluded the British a century earlier. And the United States, too, will fail.

American military advisers who work with the Afghan National Army, or ANA, speak of poorly trained and unmotivated Afghan soldiers who have little stomach for military discipline and even less for fighting. They describe many ANA units as being filled with brigands who terrorize local populations, exacting payments and engaging in intimidation, rape, and theft. They contend that the ANA is riddled with Taliban sympathizers. And when there are combined American and Afghan operations against the Taliban insurgents, ANA soldiers are fickle and unreliable combatants, the U.S. advisers say.

American military commanders in Afghanistan, rather than pump out statistics about enemy body counts, measure progress by the swelling size of the ANA. The bigger the ANA, the better we are supposedly doing. The pressure on trainers to increase the numbers of the ANA means that training and vetting of incoming Afghan recruits is nearly nonexistent.

The process of induction for Afghan soldiers begins at the Kabul Military Training Center. American instructors at the Kabul center routinely complain of shortages of school supplies such as whiteboards, markers, and paper. They often have to go to markets and pay for these supplies on their own or do without them. Instructors are pressured to pass all recruits and graduate many who have been absent for a third to half the training time. Most are inducted into the ANA without having mastered rudimentary military skills.

"I served the first half of my tour at the Kabul Military Training Center, where I was part of a small team working closely with the ANA to set up the country's first officer basic course for newly commissioned Afghan lieutenants," a U.S. Army first lieutenant who was deployed last year, and who asked not to be identified by name, told me. "During the second half of my tour, I left Kabul's military schoolhouse and was reassigned to an embedded tactical training team, or ETT team, to help stand up a new Afghan logistics battalion in Herat."

"Afghan soldiers leave the KMTC grossly unqualified," this lieutenant, who remains on active duty, said. "American mentors do what they can to try and fix these problems, but their efforts are blocked by pressure from higher, both in Afghan and American chains of command, to pump out as many soldiers as fast as possible."

Afghan soldiers are sent from the Kabul Military Training Center directly to active-duty ANA units. The units always have American trainers, known as a "mentoring team," attached to them. The rapid increase in ANA soldiers has outstripped the ability of the American military to provide trained mentoring teams. The teams, normally composed of members of the Army Special Forces, are now formed by plucking American soldiers, more or less at random, from units all over Afghanistan.

"This is how my entire team was selected during the middle of my tour: a random group of people from all over Kabul—Air Force, Navy, Army, active-duty, and National Guard—pulled from their previous assignments, thrown together and expected to do a job that none of us were trained in any meaningful way to do," the officer said. "We are expected, by virtue of time-in-grade and membership in the U.S. military, to be able to train a foreign force in military operations, an extremely irresponsible policy that is ethnocentric at its core and which assumes some sort of natural superiority in which an untrained American soldier has everything to teach the Afghans, but nothing to learn."

"You're lucky enough if you had any mentorship training at all, something the Army provides in a limited capacity at premobilization training at Fort Riley, but having none is the norm," he said. "Soldiers who receive their pre-mobilization training at Fort Bragg learn absolutely nothing about mentoring foreign forces aside from being given a booklet on the subject, and yet soldiers who go through Bragg before being shipped to Afghanistan are just as likely to be assigned to mentoring teams as anyone else."

The differences between the Afghan military structure and the American military structure are substantial. The ANA handles logistics differently. Its rank structure is not the same. Its administration uses different military terms. It rarely works with the aid of computers or basic technology. The cultural divide leaves most trainers, who do not speak Dari, struggling to figure out how things work in the ANA.

"The majority of my time spent as a mentor involved trying to understand what the Afghans were doing and how they were expected to do it, and only then could I even begin to advise anyone on the problems they were facing," this officer said. "In other words, American military advisers aren't immediately helpful to Afghans. There is a major learning curve involved that is sometimes never overcome. Some advisers play a pivotal role, but many have little or no effect as mentors."

The real purpose of American advisers assigned to ANA units, however, is not ultimately to train Afghans but to function as a liaison between Afghan units and American firepower and logistics. The ANA is unable to integrate ground units with artillery and air support. It has no functioning supply system. It depends on the American military to do basic tasks. The United States even pays the bulk of ANA salaries.

"In the unit I was helping to mentor, orders for mission-essential equipment such as five-ton trucks went unfilled for months, and winter clothes came late due to national shortages," the officer told me. "Many soldiers in the unit had to make do for the first few weeks of Afghanistan's winter without jackets or other cold-weather items."

But what disturbs advisers most is the widespread corruption within the ANA that has enraged and alienated local Afghans and proved to be a potent recruiting tool for the Taliban.

"In the Afghan logistics battalion I was embedded with, the commander himself was extorting a local shopkeeper, and his staff routinely stole from the local store," the adviser said:

In Kabul, on one humanitarian aid mission I was on, we handed out school supplies to children, and in an attempt to lend validity to the ANA we had them [ANA members] distribute the supplies. As it turns out, we received intelligence reports that that very same group of ANA had been extorting money from the villagers under threat of violence. In essence, we teamed up with well-known criminals and local thugs to distribute aid in the very village they had been terrorizing, and that was the face of American charity.

We have pumped billions of dollars into Afghanistan and occupied the country for eight years. We currently spend some $4 billion a month on Afghanistan. But we are unable to pay for whiteboards and markers for instructors at the Kabul Military Training Center. Afghan soldiers lack winter jackets. Kabul is still in ruins. Unemployment is estimated at about forty percent. And Afghanistan is one of the most food-insecure countries on the planet.

What are we doing? Where is this money going?

Look to the civilian contractors. These contractors dominate the lucrative jobs in Afghanistan. The American military, along with the ANA, is considered a poor relation.

"When I arrived in theater, one of the things I was shocked to see was how many civilians were there," the U.S. officer said:

Americans and foreign nationals from Eastern Europe and Southeast Asia were holding jobs in great numbers in Kabul. There are a ton of corporations in Afghanistan performing labor that was once exclusively in the realm of the military. If you're a [military] cook, someone from Kellogg Brown & Root has taken your spot. If you're a logistician or military adviser, someone from MPRI, Military Professional Resources Inc., will probably take over your job soon. If you're a technician or a mechanic, there are civilians from Harris Corp. and other companies there who are taking over more and more of your responsibilities.

"I deployed with a small unit of about one hundred or so military advisers and mentors," he went on:

When we arrived in Afghanistan, nearly half our unit had to be reassigned because their jobs had been taken over by civilians from MPRI. It seems that even in a war zone, soldiers are at risk of losing their jobs to outsourcing. And if you're a reservist, the situation is even more unfortunate. You are torn from your life to serve a yearlong tour of duty away from your civilian job, your friends, and family only to end up in Afghanistan with nothing to do because your military duty was passed on to a civilian contractor. Eventually you are thrown onto a mentoring team somewhere, or some [other] responsibility is created for you. It becomes evident that the corporate presence in Afghanistan has a direct effect on combat operations.

The American military has been largely privatized, although General Stanley McChrystal, the commander of U.S. and NATO forces in Afghanistan, has still recommended a 40,000-troop increase. The Army's basic functions have been outsourced to no-bid contractors. What was once done by the military with concern for tactical and strategic advancement is done by war profiteers concerned solely about profit. The aims of the military and the contractors are in conflict. A scaling down of the war or a withdrawal is viewed by these corporations as bad for business. But expansion of the war, as many veterans will attest, is making the situation only more precarious.

"American and Afghan soldiers are putting their lives at risk, Afghan civilians are dying, and yet there's this underlying system in place that gains more from keeping all of them in harm's way rather than taking them out of it," the officer complained. "If we bring peace and stability to Afghanistan, we may profit morally, we might make gains for humanity, but moral profits and human gains do not contribute to the bottom line. Peace and profit are ultimately contradictory forces at work in Afghanistan."

The wells that are dug, the schools that are built, the roads that are paved, and the food distributed in Afghan villages by the occupation forces are used to obscure the huge profits made by contractors. Only an estimated ten percent of the money poured into Afghanistan is used to ameliorate the suffering of Afghan civilians. The remainder is swallowed by contractors who siphon the money out of Afghanistan and into foreign bank accounts. This misguided allocation of funds is compounded in Afghanistan because the highest-paying jobs for Afghans go to those who can act as interpreters for the American military and foreign contractors. The best-educated Afghans are enticed away from Afghan institutions that desperately need their skills and education.

"It is this system that has broken the logistics of Afghanistan," the officer said:

> It is this system of waste and private profit from public funds that keeps Kabul in ruins. It is this system that manages to feed Westerners all across the country steak and lobster once a week while an estimated 8.4 million Afghans—the entire population of New York City, the five boroughs—suffer from chronic food insecurity and starvation every day. When you go to Bagram Air Base, or Camp Phoenix, or Camp Eggers, it's clear to see that the problem does not lie in getting supplies into the country. The question becomes who gets them. And we wonder why there's an insurgency.

The problem in Afghanistan is not ultimately a military problem. It is a political and social problem. The real threat to stability in Afghanistan is not the Taliban, but widespread hunger and food shortages, crippling poverty, rape, corruption, and a staggering rate of unemployment that mounts as foreign companies take jobs away from the local workers and businesses. Corruption and abuse by the Karzai government and the ANA, along with the presence of foreign contractors, are the central impediments to peace. The more we empower these forces, the worse the war will become. The plan to escalate the number of American soldiers and Marines, and to swell the ranks of the Afghan National Army, will not defeat or pacify the Taliban.

"What good are a quarter-million well-trained Afghan troops to a nation slipping into famine?" the officer asked. "What purpose does a strong military serve with a corrupt and inept government in place? What hope do we have for peace if the best jobs for the Afghans involve working for the military? What is the point of getting rid of the

Taliban if it means killing civilians with air strikes and supporting a government of misogynist warlords and criminals?

"We as Americans do not help the Afghans by sending in more troops, by increasing military spending, by adding chaos to disorder," he said. "What little help we do provide is only useful in the short term and is clearly unsustainable in the face of our own economic crisis. In the end, no one benefits from this war, not America, not Afghans. Only the CEOs and executive officers of war-profiteering corporations find satisfactory returns on their investments."

THE DECAY OF EMPIRE

Surviving the Fourth of July

JULY 7, 2008

I survive the degradation that has become America—a land that exalts itself as a bastion of freedom and liberty while it tortures human beings, stripped of their rights, in offshore penal colonies, a land that wages wars defined under international law as criminal wars of aggression, a land that turns its back on its poor, its weak, its mentally ill, in a relentless drive to embrace totalitarian capitalism—because I read books. I have five thousand of them. They line every wall of my house. And I do not own a television.

I survive the gradual, and I now fear inevitable, disintegration of our democracy because great literature and poetry, great philosophy and theology, the great works of history, remind me that there were other ages of collapse and despotism. They remind me that through it all, men and women of conscience endured and communicated, at least with each other, and that it is possible to refuse to participate in the process of self-annihilation, even if this means we are pushed to the margins of society. They remind me, as the poet W. H. Auden wrote in "September 1, 1939," that "ironic points of light / Flash out wherever the Just / Exchange their messages." And if you tire, as all who can think critically must, of the empty cant and hypocrisy of John McCain and Barack Obama, of the simplistic and intellectually deadening epistemology of television and the consumer age, you can retreat to your library. Books were my salvation during the wars and conflicts I covered for two decades as a foreign correspondent in Central America, Africa, the Middle East, and the Balkans. They are my salvation now. The fundamental questions about the meaning, or meaninglessness, of our existence are laid bare when we sink to the lowest depths. And it is those depths that Homer, Euripides, William Shakespeare, Fyodor Dostoyevsky, George Eliot, Joseph Conrad, Marcel Proust, Vasily Grossman, George Orwell, Albert Camus, and Flannery O'Connor understood.

"That's what the practice of any art is. It isn't to make a living," Kurt Vonnegut said. "It's to make your soul grow."[1]

The historian Will Durant calculated that there have been only twenty-nine years in all of human history during which a war was not under way somewhere. Rather than being aberrations, war and tyranny expose a side of human nature masked by the often unacknowledged constraints that glue society together. Our cultivated conventions and little lies of civility lull us into a refined and idealistic view of ourselves. But look at our last two decades: two million dead in the war in Afghanistan, 1.5 million dead in the fighting in Sudan, some 800,000 butchered in the ninety-day slaughter of Tutsis and moderate Hutus by soldiers and militias directed by the Hutu government in Rwanda, a half-million dead in Angola, a quarter of a million dead in Bosnia, 200,000 dead in Guatemala, 150,000 dead in Liberia, a quarter of a million dead in Burundi, 75,000 dead in Algeria, an estimated 600,000 dead in Iraq, and untold tens of thousands lost in the border conflict between Ethiopia and Eritrea, the fighting in Colombia, the Israeli-Palestinian conflict, Chechnya, Sri Lanka, southeastern Turkey, Sierra Leone, Northern Ireland, Kosovo. Civil war, brutality, ideological intolerance, conspiracy, and murderous repression are the daily fare for all but the privileged few in the industrialized world.

"The gallows," the gravediggers in *Hamlet* aptly remind us, "is built stronger than the church."[2]

I have little connection, however, with academics. Most professors of literature, who read the same books I read, who study the same authors, are to literature what forensic medicine is to the human body. These academics seem to spend more time sucking the life out of books than absorbing the profound truths the authors struggle to communicate. Perhaps it is because academics, sheltered in their gardens of privilege, often have hyper-developed intellects and the emotional maturity of twelve-year-olds. Perhaps it is because they fear the awful revelations in front of them, truths that, deeply understood, would demand they fight back. It is easier to eviscerate the form, the style, and the structure with textual analysis and ignore the passionate call for our common humanity.

"As long as reading is for us the instigator whose magic keys have opened the door to those dwelling-places deep within us that we would not have known how to enter, its role in our lives is salutary," Proust wrote. "It becomes dangerous, on the other hand, when, instead of awakening us to the personal life of the mind, reading tends to take its place. . . ."[3]

Although Shakespeare's Jack Falstaff is a coward, a liar, and a cheat, although he embodies all the scourges of human frailty Henry V rejects, I delight more in Falstaff's address to himself in the Boar's Head Tavern, where he at least admits to serving his own hedonism, than I do in Henry's heroic call to arms before Agincourt. Falstaff personifies a lust for life and the mockery of heaven and hell, of the crown and all other instruments of authority. He disdains history, honor, and glory. Falstaff is a much more accurate picture of the common soldier who wants to save his own hide and finds little in the rhetoric of officers who urge him into danger. Prince Hal is a hero and defeats Percy while Falstaff pretends to be a corpse. But Falstaff embodies the basic desires we all have. He is baser than most. He lacks the essential comradeship necessary among soldiers, but he clings to life in a way a soldier under fire can sympathize with. It is to the alehouses and the taverns, not the court, that these soldiers return when the war is done. Jack Falstaff's selfish lust for pleasure hurts few, while Henry's selfish lust for power leaves corpses strewn across muddy battlefields. And while we have been saturated with the rhetoric of *Henry V* this past July 4 holiday, we would be better off listening to the truth spoken by Falstaff.

There is a moment in *1 Henry IV* when Falstaff leads his motley band of followers to the place where the army has assembled. Lined up behind him are cripples and beggars, all in rags, because those with influence and money (shades of George W. Bush) evade military service. Prince Hal looks askance at the pathetic collection before him, but Falstaff says, "Tut, tut, good enough to toss, food for powder, food for powder. They'll fill a pit as well as better. Tush, man, mortal men, mortal men."[4]

I have seen the pits in the torpid heat in El Salvador, the arid valleys in northern Iraq, and the forested slopes in Bosnia. Falstaff is right. Despite the promises never to forget the sacrifices of the dead, of those crippled and maimed by war, the loss and suffering eventually become superfluous. The pain is relegated to the pages of dusty books, the corridors of poorly funded VA hospitals, and sustained by grieving families who still visit the headstones of men or women who died too young. This will be the fate of our dead and wounded from Iraq and Afghanistan. It is the fate of all those who go to war. We honor them only in the abstract. The causes that drove the nation to war, and for which they gave their lives, are soon forgotten, replaced by new ones that are equally absurd.

In his novel *Life in the Tomb*, Stratis Myrivilis makes this point. Myrivilis's speaker is commenting on Greek participation in World War I, in which many Greeks fought with the nationalistic dream of retaking Constantinople:

> A few years from now . . . perhaps others would be killing each other for anti-nationalist ideals. Then they would laugh at our own killings just as we had laughed at those of the Byzantines. These others would indulge in mutual slaughter with the same enthusiasm, though their ideals were new. Warfare under the entirely fresh banners would be just as disgraceful as always. They might even rip out each other's guts then with religious zeal, claiming that they were "fighting to end all fighting." But they too would be followed by still others who would laugh at them with the same gusto.[5]

Patriotic duty and the disease of nationalism lure us to deny our common humanity. Yet to pursue, in the broadest sense, what is human, what is moral, in the midst of conflict or under the heel of the totalitarian state, is often a form of self-destruction. And while Shakespeare, Proust, and Conrad meditate on success, they honor the nobility of failure, knowing more value lies in how a life is lived than in what it achieves. Lear and Richard II gain knowledge only as they are pushed down the ladder, as they are stripped of power and the illusions power makes possible.

Late one night, unable to sleep during the war in El Salvador, I picked up *Macbeth*. It was not a calculated decision. I had come that day from a village where about a dozen people had been murdered by the death squads, their thumbs tied behind their backs with wire and their throats slit.

I had read the play before as a student. Now it took on a new, electric force. Thirst for power at the cost of human life was no longer an abstraction. It had become part of my own experience.

I came upon Lady Macduff's speech, made when the murderers, sent by Macbeth, arrive to kill her and her small children. "Whither should I fly?" she asks:

> *I have done no harm. But I remember now*
> *I am in this earthly world, where to do harm*
> *Is often laudable, to do good sometime*
> *Accounted dangerous folly.*[6]

Those words seized me like Furies and cried out for the dead I had seen lined up that day in a dusty market square, and the dead I would see later: the three thousand children killed in Sarajevo, the dead in unmarked mass graves in Bosnia, Kosovo, Iraq, Sudan, Algeria, El Salvador, the dead who are my own, who carried notebooks, cameras, and a vanquished idealism into war and never returned. Of course resistance is usually folly, of course power exercised with ruthlessness will win, of course force easily snuffs out gentleness, compassion, and decency. In the end, all we can cling to is each other.

Thucydides, knowing that Athens was doomed in the war with Sparta, consoled himself with the belief that his city's artistic and intellectual achievements would in the coming centuries overshadow raw Spartan militarism. Beauty and knowledge could, ultimately, triumph over power. But we may not live to see such a triumph. And on this July Fourth weekend of collective exaltation, I did not attend fireworks or hang a flag outside my house. I did not participate in rituals designed to hide from ourselves who we have become. I read the *Eclogues* by

Virgil. These poems were written during Rome's brutal civil war. They consoled me in their wisdom and despair. Virgil understood that the words of a poet were no match for war. He understood that the chant of the crowd urges nearly all to collective madness, and yet he wrote with the hope that there were some among his readers who might continue, even when faced with defeat, to sing his hymns of compassion.

> . . . *sed carmina tantum*
> *nostra valent, Lycida, tela inter Martia, quantum*
> *Chaonias dicunt aquila veniente columbas.*
> . . . but songs of ours
> Avail among the War-God's weapons, Lycidas,
> As much as Chaonian doves, they say, when the
> eagle comes.[7]

America's Wars of Self-Destruction

NOVEMBER 17, 2008

War is a poison. It is a poison that nations and groups must at times ingest to ensure their survival. But, like any poison, it can kill you just as surely as the disease it is meant to eradicate. The poison of war courses unchecked through the body politic of the United States. We believe that because we have the capacity to wage war we have the right to wage war. We embrace the dangerous self-delusion that we are on a providential mission to save the rest of the world from itself, to implant our virtues—which we see as superior to all other virtues—on others, and that we have a right to do this by force. This belief has corrupted Republicans and Democrats alike. And if Barack Obama drinks, as it appears he will, the dark elixir of war and imperial power offered to him by the national security state, he will accelerate the downward spiral of the American empire.

Obama and those around him embrace the folly of the "war on terror." They may want to shift the emphasis of this war to Afghanistan rather than Iraq, but this is a difference in strategy, not policy. By clinging to Iraq and expanding the war in Afghanistan, we ensure that the poison will continue in deadly doses. These wars of occupation are doomed to failure. We cannot afford them. The rash of home foreclosures, the mounting job losses, the collapse of banks and the financial services industry, the poverty ripping apart the working class, our crumbling infrastructure, and the killing of hapless Afghans in wedding parties and Iraqis by our bombs are neatly interwoven. These events form a perfect circle. The costly forms of death we dispense on one side of the globe are hollowing us out from the inside at home.

The "war on terror" is an absurd war against a tactic. It posits the idea of perpetual, or what is now called "generational," war. It has no discernable end. There is no way to define victory. It is, in metaphysical terms, a war against evil, and evil, as any good seminarian can tell you, will always be with us. The most destructive evils, however, are not those that are externalized. The most destructive are those that are internal. These hidden evils, often defined as virtues, are unleashed by our hubris, self-delusion, and ignorance. Evil masquerading as good is evil in its deadliest form.

The decline of American empire began long before the current economic meltdown or the wars in Afghanistan and Iraq. It began before the first Gulf War or Ronald Reagan. It began when we shifted, in the words of the historian Charles Maier, from an "empire of production" to an "empire of consumption."[8] By the end of the Vietnam War, when the costs of the war ate away at Lyndon Johnson's Great Society and domestic oil production began its steady, inexorable decline, we saw our country transformed from one that primarily produced to one that primarily consumed. We started borrowing to maintain a lifestyle we could no longer afford. We began to use force, especially in the Middle East, to feed our insatiable demand for cheap oil. The years after World War II, when the United States accounted for one-third of world exports and half of the world's manufacturing, gave way to huge trade imbalances, outsourced jobs, rusting hulks of abandoned factories, stagnant wages, and personal and public debts that most of us cannot repay.

The bill is now due. America's most dangerous enemies are not Islamic radicals, but those who promote the perverted ideology of national security that, as Andrew Bacevich writes, is "our surrogate religion." If we continue to believe we can expand our wars and go deeper into debt to maintain an unsustainable level of consumption, we will dynamite the foundations of our society.

"The Big Lies are not the pledge of tax cuts, universal health care, family values restored, or a world rendered peaceful through forceful demonstrations of American leadership," Bacevich writes in *The Limits of Power*:

> The Big Lies are the truths that remain unspoken: that freedom has an underside; that nations, like households, must ultimately live

within their means; that history's purpose, the subject of so many confident pronouncements, remains inscrutable. Above all, there is this: Power is finite. Politicians pass over matters such as these in silence. As a consequence, the absence of self-awareness that forms such an enduring element of the American character persists.[9]

Those clustered around Barack Obama, from Madeleine Albright to Hillary Clinton to Dennis Ross to Colin Powell, have no interest in dismantling the structure of the imperial presidency or the vast national security state. They will keep these institutions intact and seek to increase their power. We have a childish belief that Obama will magically save us from economic free fall, restore our profligate levels of consumption, and resurrect our imperial power. This naïve belief is part of our disconnection from reality. The problems we face are structural. The old America is not coming back.

The corporate forces that control the state will never permit real reform. This is the Faustian bargain made between these corporate forces and the Republican and Democratic parties. We will never, under the current system, achieve energy independence. Energy independence would devastate the profits of the oil and gas industry. It would wipe out tens of billions of dollars in weapons contracts, spoil the financial health of a host of private contractors from Halliburton to Blackwater, and render obsolete the existence of U.S. Central Command.

There are groups and people who seek to do us harm. The attacks of September 11, 2001, will not be the last acts of terrorism on American soil. But the only way to defeat terrorism is to isolate terrorists within their own societies, to mount cultural and propaganda wars, to discredit their ideas, to seek concurrence even with those defined as our enemies. Force, while a part of this battle, is rarely necessary. The 2001 attacks that roused our fury and unleashed the "war on terror" also unleashed a worldwide revulsion against al-Qaida and Islamic terrorism, including throughout the Muslim world, where I was working as a reporter at the time. If we had had the courage to be vulnerable, to build on this empathy rather than drop explosive ordinance all over the Middle East, we would be far safer and more secure today. If we had reached out for allies and partners instead of arrogantly assuming that

American military power would restore our sense of invulnerability and mitigate our collective humiliation, we would have done much to defeat al-Qaida. But we did not. We demanded that all kneel before us. And in our ruthless and indiscriminate use of violence and illegal wars of occupation, we resurrected the very forces that we could, under astute leadership, have marginalized. We forgot that fighting terrorism is a war of shadows, an intelligence war, not a conventional war. We forgot that, as strong as we may be militarily, no nation, including us, can survive isolated and alone.

The American empire, along with our wanton self-indulgence and gluttonous consumption, has come to an end. We are undergoing a period of profound economic, political, and military decline. We can continue to dance to the tunes of self-delusion, circling the fire as we chant ridiculous mantras about our greatness, virtue, and power, or we can face the painful reality that has engulfed us. We cannot reverse this decline. It will happen no matter what we do. But we can, if we break free from our self-delusion, dismantle our crumbling empire and the national security state with a minimum of damage to ourselves and others. If we refuse to accept our limitations, if we do not face the changes forced upon us by a bankrupt elite that has grossly mismanaged our economy, our military, and our government, we will barrel toward internal and external collapse. Our self-delusion constitutes our greatest danger. We will either confront reality or plunge headlong into the minefields that lie before us.

Confronting the Terrorist Within

DECEMBER 1, 2008

The Hindu-Muslim communal violence that led to the attacks in Mumbai, as well as the warnings that the New York City transit system may have been targeted by al-Qaida, are one form of terrorism. There are other forms.

The wars in Iraq and Afghanistan, when viewed from the receiving end, are state-sponsored acts of terrorism. These wars defy every ethical and legal code that seek to determine when a nation can wage war, from Just War Theory to the statutes of international law largely put into place by the United States after World War II. These wars are criminal wars of aggression. They have left hundreds of thousands of people, who never took up arms against us, dead and seen millions driven from their homes. We have no right as a nation to debate the terms of these occupations. And an Afghan villager, burying members of his family's wedding party after an American air strike, understands in a way we often do not that terrorist attacks can also be unleashed from the arsenals of an imperial power.

Barack Obama's decision to increase troop levels in Afghanistan and leave behind tens of thousands of soldiers and Marines in Iraq—he promises only to withdraw combat brigades—is a failure to rescue us from the status of a rogue nation. It codifies Bush's "war on terror." And the continuation of these wars will corrupt and degrade our nation just as the long and brutal occupation of Gaza and the West Bank has corrupted and degraded Israel. George W. Bush has handed Barack Obama a poisoned apple. Obama has bitten it.

The invasions and occupations of Afghanistan and Iraq were our response to feelings of vulnerability and collective humiliation after the attacks of September 11, 2001. They were a way to exorcise through re-ciprocal violence what had been done to us.

Collective humiliation is also the driving force behind al-Qaida and most terrorist groups. Osama bin Laden cites the Sykes-Picot Agree-ment, which led to the carving up of the Ottoman Empire, as the be-ginning of Arab humiliation. He attacks the agreement for dividing the Muslim world into "fragments." He rails against the presence of Amer-ican troops on the soil of his native Saudi Arabia. The dark motiva-tions of Islamic extremists mirror our own.

In *Dying to Win: The Strategic Logic of Suicide Terrorism*, Robert Pape found that most suicide bombers are members of communities that feel humiliated by genuine or perceived occupation. Almost every major suicide-terrorism campaign—more than ninety-five percent—carried out attacks to drive out an occupying power. This was true in Lebanon, Sri Lanka, Chechnya, and Kashmir, as well as Israel and the Palestinian territories. The large number of Saudis among the 9/11 hi-jackers appears to support this finding.

A militant who phoned an Indian TV station from the Jewish center in Mumbai during the recent siege offered to talk with the government con-cerning the release of hostages. He complained about army abuses in Kashmir, where ruthless violence has been used to crush a Muslim insur-gency. "Ask the government to talk to us and we will release the hostages," he said, speaking in Urdu with what sounded like a Kashmiri accent.

"Are you aware how many people have been killed in Kashmir? Are you aware how your army has killed Muslims? Are you aware how many of them have been killed in Kashmir this week?" he asked.

Terrorists, many of whom come from the middle class, support acts of indiscriminate violence not because of direct, personal affronts to their dignity, but more often for lofty, abstract ideas of national, ethnic, or religious pride and the establishment of a utopian, harmonious world purged of evil. The longer the United States occupies Afghanistan and Iraq, the more these feelings of collective humiliation are aggravated and the greater the number of jihadists willing to attack American targets.

We have had tens of thousands of troops stationed in the Middle East since 1990, when Saddam Hussein invaded Kuwait. The presence of these troops is the main appeal, along with the abuse meted out to the Palestinians by Israel, of bin Laden and al-Qaida. Terrorism, as Pape wrote, "is not a supply-limited phenomenon where there are just a few hundred around the world willing to do it because they are religious fanatics. It is a demand-driven phenomenon. That is, it is driven by the presence of foreign forces on the territory that the terrorists view as their homeland. The operation in Iraq has stimulated suicide terrorism and has given suicide terrorism a new lease on life."[10]

The decision by the incoming Obama administration to embrace an undefined, amorphous "war on terror" will keep us locked in a war without end. This war has no clear definition of victory, unless victory means the death or capture of every terrorist on earth—an impossibility. It is a frightening death spiral. It feeds on itself. The concept of a "war on terror" is no less apocalyptic or world-purifying than the dreams and fantasies of terrorist groups like al-Qaida.

The vain effort to purify the world through force is always self-defeating. Those who insist that the world can be molded into their vision are the most susceptible to violence as antidote. The more uncertainty, fear, and reality impinge on this utopian vision, the more strident, absolutist and aggressive are those who call for the eradication of "the enemy." Immanuel Kant called absolute moral imperatives that are used to carry out immoral acts "a radical evil." He wrote that this kind of evil was always a form of unadulterated self-love. It was the worst type of self-deception. It provided a moral façade for terror and murder. The wars in Iraq and Afghanistan are a "radical evil."[11]

The tactic of suicide bombing, equated by many in the United States with Islam, did not arise from the Muslim world. It had its roots in radical Western ideologies, especially Leninism, not religion. And it was the Tamil Tigers, a Marxist group that drew its support from the Hindu families of the Tamil regions of Sri Lanka, who invented the suicide vest for their May 1991 suicide assassination of Rajiv Gandhi.

Suicide bombing is what you do when you do not have artillery or planes or missiles and you want to create maximum terror for an occupying power. It was used by secular anarchists in the nineteenth and early twentieth centuries, who bequeathed to us the first version of the car bomb—a horse-drawn wagon laden with explosives that was ig-nited on September 16, 1920, on Wall Street. The attack was carried out by an Italian immigrant named Mario Buda in protest over the ar-rest of the anarchists Sacco and Vanzetti. It left forty people dead and wounded more than two hundred.

Suicide bombing was adopted later by Hezbollah, al-Qaida, and Hamas. But even in the Middle East, suicide bombing is not restricted to Muslims. In Lebanon, during the attacks in the 1980s against French, American, and Israeli targets, only eight suicide bombings were carried out by Islamic fundamentalists. Twenty-seven were the work of communists and socialists. Christians were responsible for three.

The dehumanization of Muslims in U.S. social culture and the will-ful ignorance of the traditions and culture of the Islamic world reflect our nation's disdain for self-reflection and self-examination. They allow us to exult in the illusion of our own moral and cultural superiority. The world is far more complex than our childish vision of good and evil. We as a nation and a culture have no monopoly on virtue. We carry within us the same propensities for terror as those we oppose.

At the end of the sixteenth century, the Muslim Indian emperor Akbar the Great filled his court with philosophers, mystics, and reli-gious scholars, including Sunni, Sufi, and Shiite Muslims, Hindu fol-lowers of Shiva and Vishnu, as well as atheists, Christians, Jains, Jews, Buddhists, and Zoroastrians. They debated ethics and belief. Akbar was one of the great champions of religious dialogue and tolerance. He for-bade any person to be discriminated against on the basis of belief. He declared that everyone was free to follow any religion. His enlightened rule took place as the Inquisition was at its height in Spain and Portu-gal, and in Rome the philosopher Giordano Bruno was being burnt at the stake in Campo dei Fiori for heresy.

Tolerance, as well as religious and political plurality, is not exclusive to Western culture. The Judeo-Christian tradition was born and came to life in the Middle East. Its intellectual and religious beliefs were cul-tivated and formed in cities such as Jerusalem, Antioch, Alexandria, and Constantinople. Many of the greatest tenets of Western civiliza-tion, as is true with Islam and Buddhism, are Eastern in origin. Our concept of the rule of law and freedom of expression, the invention of printing, paper, the book, as well as the translation and dissemination of the classical Greek philosophers, algebra, geometry, and universities were given to us by the Islamic world. The first law code was invented by the ancient Iraqi ruler Hammurabi. One of the first known legal protections of basic freedoms and equality was promulgated in India, in the third century B.C. by the Buddhist emperor Ashoka. And, unlike Aristotle, he insisted on equal rights for women and slaves.

The East and the West do not have separate, competing value systems. We do not treat life with greater sanctity than those we belittle. There are aged survivors in Hiroshima and Nagasaki who can tell us something about our high moral values and passionate concern for innocent human life, about our own acts of terrorism. Eastern and Western traditions have within them varied ethical systems, some of which are repugnant and some of which are worth emulating. To hold up the highest ideals of our own culture and our denial that these great ideals exist in other cultures, especially Eastern cultures, is driven by our historical and cultural illiteracy.

The civilization we champion and promote as superior is, in fact, a product of the fusion of traditions and beliefs of the Orient and the Occident. We advance morally and intellectually when we cross these cultural lines, when we use the lens of other cultures to examine our own. The remains of villages destroyed by our bombs, the dead killed from our munitions, leave us, too, with bloody hands. We can build a new ethic only when we face our complicity in the cycle of violence and terror.

The fantasy of an enlightened West that spreads civilization to a savage world of religious fanatics is not supported by history. The worst genocides and slaughters of the last century were perpetrated by highly industrialized nations. Muslims, including those of Saddam Hussein's brutal regime, have a long way to go before they reach the body count of the secular regimes of the Nazis, the Soviet Union, or the Chinese communists. It was, in fact, the Muslim-led government in Bosnia that protected minorities during the war while the Serbian Orthodox Christians carried out mass executions, campaigns of genocide, and ethnic cleansing that left 250,000 dead.

Those who externalize evil and seek to eradicate that evil through violence lose touch with their own humanity and the humanity of others. They cannot make moral distinctions. They are blind to their own moral corruption. In the name of civilization and high ideals, in the name of reason and science, they become monsters. We will never free ourselves from the self-delusion of the "war on terror" until we first vanquish the terrorist within.

Man Is a Cruel Animal

It was Joseph Conrad I thought of when I read an article in the *Nation* magazine this month about white vigilante groups that rose up out of the chaos of Hurricane Katrina in New Orleans to terrorize and murder blacks. It was Conrad I thought of when I saw the ominous statements by authorities, such as International Monetary Fund Managing Director Dominique Strauss-Kahn, warning of potential civil unrest in the United States as we funnel staggering sums of public funds upward to our bankrupt elites and leave our poor and working class destitute, hungry, without health care, and locked out of their foreclosed homes. We fool ourselves into believing we are immune to the savagery and chaos of failed states. Take away the rigid social structure, let society continue to break down, and we become, like anyone else, brutes.

Conrad saw enough of the world as a sea captain to know the irredeemable corruption of humanity. The noble virtues that drove characters like Kurtz in *Heart of Darkness* into the jungle veiled abject self-interest, unchecked greed, and murder. Conrad was in the Congo in the late nineteenth century when the Belgian monarch King Leopold, in the name of Western civilization and antislavery, was plundering the country. The Belgian occupation resulted in the death by disease, starvation, and murder of some 10 million Congolese. Conrad understood what we did to others in the name of civilization and progress. And it is Conrad, as our society unravels internally and plows ahead in the costly, morally repugnant, and self-defeating wars in Afghanistan and Iraq, whom we do well to heed.

This theme of our corruptibility is central to Conrad. In his short story "An Outpost of Progress," he writes of two white traders, Carlier and Kayerts, who are sent to a remote trading station in the Congo. The mission is endowed with a great moral purpose—to export European "civilization" to Africa. But the boredom and lack of constraints swiftly turn the two men, like our mercenaries and soldiers and Marines in Iraq and Afghanistan, into savages. They trade slaves for ivory. They get into a feud over dwindling food supplies, and Kayerts shoots and kills his unarmed companion Carlier.

"They were two perfectly insignificant and incapable individuals," Conrad wrote of Kayerts and Carlier:

> whose existence is only rendered possible through the high organi-zation of civilized crowds. Few men realize that their life, the very essence of their character, their capabilities and their audacities, are only the expression of their belief in the safety of their surroundings. The courage, the composure, the confidence; the emotions and prin-ciples; every great and every insignificant thought belongs not to the individual but to the crowd; to the crowd that believes blindly in the irresistible force of its institutions and its morals, in the power of its police and of its opinion. But the contact with pure unmitigated sav-agery, with primitive nature and primitive man, brings sudden and profound trouble into the heart. To the sentiment of being alone of one's kind, to the clear perception of the loneliness of one's thoughts, of one's sensations—to the negation of the habitual, which is safe, there is added the affirmation of the unusual, which is dangerous; a suggestion of things vague, uncontrollable, and repulsive, whose dis-composing intrusion excites the imagination and tries the civilized nerves of the foolish and the wise alike.[12]

The Managing Director of the Great Civilizing Company—for, as Conrad notes, "civilization" follows trade—arrives by steamer at the end of the story. He is not met at the dock by his two agents. He climbs the steep bank to the trading station with the captain and engine driver be-hind him. The director finds Kayerts, who, after the murder, committed suicide by hanging himself by a leather strap from a cross that marked the grave of the previous station chief. Kayerts's toes are a couple of inches above the ground. His arms hang stiffly down "and, irreverently, he was putting out a swollen tongue at his Managing Director."[13]

Conrad saw cruelty as an integral part of human nature. This cruelty arrives, however, in different forms. Stable, industrialized societies, awash in wealth and privilege, can construct internal systems that mask this cruelty, although it is nakedly displayed in their imperial outposts. We are lulled into the illusion in these zones of safety that human beings can be rational. The "war on terror," the virtuous rhetoric about saving the women in Afghanistan from the Taliban or the Iraqis from tyranny, are two more in a series of long and sordid human campaigns of violence carried out in the name of a moral good.

Those who attempt to mend the flaws in the human species through force embrace a perverted idealism. Those who believe that history is a progressive march toward human perfectibility, and that they have the moral right to force this progress on others, no longer know what it is to be human. In the name of the noblest virtues they sink to the depths of criminality and moral depravity. This self-delusion comes to us in many forms. It can be wrapped in the language of Western civilization, democracy, religion, the master race, *Liberté, égalité, fraternité*, the worker's paradise, the idyllic agrarian society, the new man, or scientific rationalism. The jargon is varied. The dark sentiment is the same.

Conrad understood how Western civilization and technology lend themselves to inhuman exploitation. He had seen in the Congo the barbarity and disdain for human life that resulted from a belief in moral advancement. He knew humankind's violent, primeval lusts. He knew how easily we can all slip into states of extreme depravity.

"Man is a cruel animal," he wrote to a friend. "His cruelty must be organized. Society is essentially criminal—or it wouldn't exist. It is selfishness that saves everything—absolutely everything—everything that we abhor, everything that we love."[14]

Conrad rejected all formulas or schemes for the moral improvement of the human condition. Political institutions, he said, "whether contrived by the wisdom of the few or the ignorance of the many, are incapable of securing the happiness of mankind."[15]

He wrote that "international fraternity may be an object to strive for . . . but that illusion imposes by its size alone. *Franchement*, what would you think of an attempt to promote fraternity amongst people living in the same street, I don't even mention two neighboring streets?"[16] He bluntly told the pacifist Bertrand Russell, who saw humankind's future in the rise of international socialism, that it was "the sort of thing to which I cannot attach any definite meaning. I have never been able to find in any man's book or any man's talk anything convincing enough to stand up for a moment against my deep-seated sense of fatality governing this man-inhabited world."[17]

Russell said of Conrad: "I felt, though I do not know whether he would have accepted such an image, that he thought of civilized and morally tolerable human life as a dangerous walk on a thin crust of barely cooled lava which at any moment might break and let the unwary sink into fiery depths."[18]

Conrad's novel *Heart of Darkness* ripped open the callous heart of civilized Europe. The great institutions of European imperial powers and noble ideals of European enlightenment, as Conrad saw in the Congo, were covers for rapacious greed, exploitation, and barbarity. Kurtz is the self-deluded megalomaniac ivory trader in *Heart of Darkness* who ends by planting the shriveled heads of murdered Congolese on pikes outside his remote trading station. But Kurtz is also highly educated and refined. Conrad describes him as an orator, writer, poet, musician, and the respected chief agent of the ivory company's Inner Station. He is "an emissary of pity, and science, and progress." Kurtz was a "universal genius" and "a very remarkable person." He is a prodigy, at once gifted and multitalented. He went to Africa fired by noble ideals and virtues. He ended his life as a self-deluded tyrant who thought he was a god.

"His mother was half-English, his father was half-French," Conrad writes of Kurtz:

All Europe contributed to the making of Kurtz; and by-the-by I learned that, most appropriately, the International Society for the Suppression of Savage Customs had entrusted him with the making of a report, for its future guidance. . . . He began with the argument that we whites, from the point of development we had arrived at, "must necessarily appear to them [savages] in the nature of supernatural beings—we approach them with the might as of a deity," and so on, and so on. "By the simple exercise of our will we can exert a power for good practically unbounded," etc., etc. From that point he soared and took me with him. The peroration was magnificent, though difficult to remember, you know. It gave me the notion of an exotic Immensity ruled by an august Benevolence. It made me tingle with enthusiasm. This was the unbounded power of eloquence—of words—of burning noble words. There were no practical hints to interrupt the magic current of phrases, unless a kind of note at the foot of the last page, scrawled evidently much later, in an unsteady hand, may be regarded as the exposition of a method. It was very simple, and at the end of that moving appeal to every altruistic sentiment it blazed at you, luminous and terrifying, like a flash of lightning in a serene sky: "Exterminate all the brutes!"[19]

We Are Breeding Ourselves
to Extinction

MARCH 9, 2009

All measures to thwart the degradation and destruction of our ecosystem will be useless if we do not cut population growth. By 2050, if we continue to reproduce at the current rate, the planet will have between eight billion and ten billion people, according to a recent U.N. forecast. This is an approximate doubling since 1980. And yet government-commissioned reviews, such as the Stern report in Britain, do not mention the word *population*. Books and documentaries that deal with the climate crisis, including Al Gore's *An Inconvenient Truth*, fail to discuss the danger of population growth. This omission is odd, given that such a growth in population, even if we cut back on the use of fossil fuels, shut down all our coal-burning power plants, and build seas of wind turbines, will plunge us into an age of extinction and desolation unseen since the end of the Mesozoic era, sixty-five million years ago, when the dinosaurs disappeared.

We are experiencing an accelerated obliteration of the planet's life-forms—an estimated 8,760 species die off per year—because, simply put, there are too many people. Most of these extinctions are the direct result of the expanding need for energy, housing, food, and other resources. The Yangtze River dolphin, Atlantic gray whale, West African black rhino, Merriam's elk, California grizzly bear, silver trout, blue pike, and dusky seaside sparrow are all victims of human overpopulation. Population growth, as E. O. Wilson says, is "the monster on the land."[20] Species are vanishing at a rate of a hundred to a thousand times faster than they did before the arrival of humans. If the current rate of extinction continues, *Homo sapiens* will be one of the few life-forms left on the planet, its members scrambling violently among themselves for water, food, fossil fuels, and perhaps air, until they too disappear. Humanity, Wilson says, is leaving the Cenozoic, the age of mammals, and entering the Eremozoic—the era of solitude. As long as the Earth is viewed as the personal property of the human race, a belief embraced by everyone from born-again Christians to Marxists to free-market economists, we are destined soon to inhabit a biological wasteland.

The populations in industrialized nations maintain their lifestyles because they have the military and economic power to consume a disproportionate share of the world's resources. The United States alone gobbles up about twenty-five percent of the oil produced in the world each year. These nations view their stable or even zero-growth birthrates as sufficient. It has been left to developing countries to cope with the emergent population crisis. India, Egypt, South Africa, Iran, Indonesia, Cuba, and China, whose one-child policy has prevented the addition of 400 million people, have all tried to institute population control measures. But on most of the planet, population growth is exploding. The United Nations estimates that 200 million women worldwide do not have access to contraception. The population of the Persian Gulf states, along with the Israeli-occupied territories, will double in two decades, a rise that will ominously coincide with precipitous peak oil declines.

In the overpopulated regions of the globe, human beings will ravage their local environments, cutting down rainforests and the few remaining wilderness areas in a desperate bid to grow food. And the depletion and destruction of resources will eventually create an overpopulation problem in industrialized nations as well. The resources industrialized nations consider their birthright will become harder and more expensive to obtain. The rise of water levels along coastlines, which may submerge coastal nations such as Bangladesh, will disrupt agriculture and displace millions, who will attempt to flee to areas on the planet where life is still possible. Rising temperatures and droughts have already begun to destroy croplands in Africa, Australia, Texas and California. As mentioned, the effects of this devastation will first be felt in places like Bangladesh, but will soon spread within our borders. Footprint data suggests that, based on current lifestyles, the sustainable population of the United Kingdom—the number of people the country, with an estimated population by 2010 of about 62 million, could feed, fuel, and support from its own biological capacity—is about 18 million. This means that in an age of extreme scarcity, some 44 million people in Great Britain would not be able to survive. Overpopulation will become a serious threat to the viability of many industrialized states the instant the cheap consumption of the world's resources can no longer be maintained. This moment may be closer than we think.

A world in which eight billion to ten billion people are competing for diminishing resources will not be peaceful. The industrialized nations will, as we have done in Iraq, turn to their militaries to ensure a steady supply of fossil fuels, minerals, and other nonrenewable resources in the vain effort to sustain a lifestyle that will, in the end, be unsustainable. The collapse of industrial farming, possible only with cheap oil, will lead to an increase in famine, disease, and starvation. And the reaction of those on the bottom will be the low-tech tactics of terrorism and war. Perhaps the chaos and bloodshed will be so massive that the problem of overpopulation will be solved through violence, but this is hardly a comfort.

James Lovelock, an independent British scientist who has spent most of his career locked out of the mainstream, warned several decades ago that disrupting the delicate balance of the Earth, which he refers to as a living body, would be a form of collective suicide. The atmosphere on Earth—twenty-one percent oxygen and seventy-nine percent nitrogen—is not common among planets, he notes. These gases are generated and maintained at an equable level for life's processes by living organisms themselves. Oxygen and nitrogen would disappear if the biosphere were destroyed. The result would be a greenhouse atmosphere similar to that of Venus, a planet consequently hundreds of degrees hotter than Earth. As part of a theory that has been named the Gaia hypothesis, Lovelock argues that the atmosphere, oceans, rocks, and soil are living entities. They constitute, he says, a self-regulating system. In support of this thesis, Lovelock studied the cycle in which algae in the oceans produce volatile sulfur compounds. These compounds act as seeds to form oceanic clouds. Without these dimethyl sulfide "seeds," the cooling oceanic clouds would be lost. This self-regulating system is remarkable because it maintains favorable conditions for human life. Its destruction would not mean the death of the planet. It would not mean the death of life-forms. But it would mean the death of *Homo sapiens*.

Lovelock advocates nuclear power and thermal solar power; the latter, he says, can be produced by huge mirrors mounted in deserts such as those in Arizona and the Sahara. He proposes reducing atmospheric carbon dioxide with large plastic cylinders thrust vertically into the ocean. These, he says, could bring nutrient-rich lower waters to the surface, producing an algal bloom that would increase the cloud cover. But he warns that these steps will be ineffective if we do not first control population growth. He believes the Earth is overpopulated by a factor of about seven. As the planet overheats—and he believes we can do nothing to halt this process—overpopulation will make all efforts to save the ecosystem futile.

In his book *The Revenge of Gaia*, said that if we do not radically and immediately cut greenhouse gas emissions, the human race might not die out but it would be reduced to "a few breeding pairs." *The Vanishing Face of Gaia*, his latest book, which has for its subtitle *The Final Warning*, paints an even grimmer picture. Lovelock says a continued population boom will make the reduction of fossil fuel use impossible. If we do not reduce our emissions by sixty percent, something that can be achieved only by walking away from fossil fuels, the human race is doomed, he argues. Time is running out. This reduction will never take place, he says, unless we can dramatically reduce our birthrate.

No effort to stanch the effects of climate change will work unless we practice vigorous population control. Overpopulation, in times of hardship, will create as much havoc in industrialized nations as in the impoverished slums around the globe. Population growth is often overlooked, or at best considered a secondary issue, by many environmentalists, but it is as fundamental a consideration in our survival as reducing the emissions melting the polar ice caps.

War Is Sin

JUNE 1, 2009

The crisis faced by combat veterans returning from war is not simply a profound struggle with trauma and alienation. It is often, for those who can slice through the suffering to self-awareness, an existential crisis. War exposes the lies we tell ourselves about ourselves. It rips open the hypocrisy of our religions and secular institutions. Those who return from war have learned something often incomprehensible to those who have stayed home. We are not a virtuous nation. God and fate have not blessed us above others. Victory is not assured. War is neither glorious nor noble. And we carry within us the capacity for evil we ascribe to those we fight.

Those who return to speak this truth, such as members of Iraq Veterans Against the War, are our contemporary prophets. But like all prophets they are condemned and ignored for their courage. They struggle, in a culture awash in lies, to tell what few have the fortitude to digest. They know that what we are taught in school, in worship, by the media, by the entertainment industry, and at home, that the melding of the state's rhetoric with the rhetoric of religion is empty and false.

The words these prophets speak are painful. We, as a nation, prefer to listen to those who speak from the patriotic script. We prefer to hear ourselves exalted. If veterans speak of terrible wounds visible and invisible, of lies told to make them kill, of evil committed in our name, we fill our ears with wax. Not our boys, we say, not them, bred in our homes, endowed with goodness and decency. For if it is easy for them to murder, what about us? And so it is simpler and more comfortable not to hear. We do not listen to the angry words that cascade from their lips, wishing only that they would calm down, be reasonable, get some help, and go away. We, the deformed, brand our prophets as madmen. We cast them into the desert. And this is why so many veterans are estranged and enraged. This is why so many succumb to suicide or addictions.

War comes wrapped in patriotic slogans, calls for sacrifice, honor, and heroism, and promises of glory. It comes wrapped in the claim of privilege under divine providence. It is what a grateful nation asks of its children. It is what is right and just. It is waged to make the nation and the world a better place, to cleanse evil. War is touted as the ultimate test of manhood, where the young can find out what they are made of. War, from a distance, seems noble. It gives us comrades and power and a chance to play a small bit in the great drama of history. It promises to give us an identity as warriors, patriots, as long as we go along with the myth, the one the war-makers need to wage wars and the defense contractors need to increase their profits.

But up close, war is a soulless void. War is barbarity, perversion, and pain. Human decency and tenderness are crushed. Those who make war work overtime to reduce love to smut, and all human beings become objects, pawns to use or kill. The noise, the stench, the fear, the scenes of eviscerated bodies and bloated corpses, the cries of the wounded, all combine to spin those in combat into another universe. In this moral void, naively blessed by secular and religious institutions at home, the hypocrisy of our social conventions, our strict adherence to moral precepts, come unglued. War, for all its horror, has the power to strip away the trivial and the banal, the empty chatter and foolish obsessions that fill our days. It lets us see, although the cost is tremendous.

In his book *Out of the Night: The Spiritual Journey of Vietnam Vets*, the Reverend William P. Mahedy, who was a Catholic chaplain in Vietnam, tells of a soldier, a former altar boy, who says to him: "Hey, Chaplain . . . how come it's a sin to hop into bed with a mama-san but it's okay to blow away gooks out in the bush?"

"Consider the question that he and I were forced to confront on that day in a jungle clearing," Mahedy writes:

> How is it that a Christian can, with a clear conscience, spend a year in a war zone killing people and yet place his soul in jeopardy by spending a few minutes with a prostitute? If the New Testament prohibitions of sexual misconduct are to be stringently interpreted, why,

then, are Jesus' injunctions against violence not binding in the same way? In other words, what does the commandment "Thou shalt not kill" really mean?[21]

Military chaplains, a majority of whom are evangelical Christians, defend the life of the unborn, tout America as a Christian nation, and eagerly bless the wars in Iraq and Afghanistan as holy crusades. The hollowness of their morality, the staggering disconnect between reality and the values they claim to promote, is ripped open in war.

In the wars in Iraq and Afghanistan, where the enemy is elusive and rarely seen, murder occurs far more often than killing. Families are massacred in air strikes. Children are gunned down in blistering suppressing fire laid down in neighborhoods after an improvised explosive device goes off near a convoy. Artillery shells obliterate homes. And no one stops to look. The dead and maimed are left behind.

The utter failure of nearly all our religious institutions—whose texts are unequivocal about murder—to address the essence of war has rendered them useless. These institutions have little or nothing to say in wartime because the god they worship is a false god, one that promises victory to those who obey the law and believe in the manifest destiny of the nation.

We all have the capacity to commit evil. It takes little to unleash it. For those of us who have been to war, this awful knowledge is the hardest to digest, the knowledge that the line between the victims and the victimizers is razor-thin, that human beings find a perverse delight in destruction and death, and that few can resist the pull. At best, most of us become silent accomplices.

Wars may have to be fought to ensure survival, but they are always tragic. They always bring to the surface the worst elements of any society, those who have a penchant for violence and a lust for absolute power. They turn the moral order upside down. It was the criminal class that first organized the defense of Sarajevo. When these goons were not manning roadblocks to hold off the besieging Bosnian Serb army, they were looting, raping, and killing the Serb residents in the city. And politicians who speak of war as an instrument of power, those who wage war but do not know its reality, those powerful statesmen—the

Henry Kissingers, Robert McNamaras, Donald Rumsfelds, the Dick Cheneys—who treat war as part of the great game of nations, are as amoral as the religious stooges who assist them. And when the wars are over, what they have to say to us in their thick memoirs about war is also hollow, vacant, and useless.

"In theological terms, war is sin," writes Mahedy: "This has nothing to do with whether a particular war is justified or whether isolated incidents in a soldier's war were right or wrong. The point is that war as a human enterprise is a matter of sin. It is a form of hatred for one's fellow human beings. It produces alienation from others and nihilism, and it ultimately represents a turning away from God."[22]

Young soldiers and Marines do not plan or organize the war. They do not seek to justify it or explain its causes. They are taught to believe. The symbols of the nation and religion are interwoven. The will of God becomes the will of the nation. This trust is forever shattered for many in war. Soldiers in combat see the myth used to send them to war implode. They see that war is not clean or neat or noble, but venal and frightening. They see into war's essence, which is death.

In war, society's institutions, including our religious institutions, which mold us into compliant citizens, are unmasked. This betrayal is so deep that many veterans never find their way back to faith in the nation or in any god. They nurse a self-destructive anger and resentment, understandable and justified, but also crippling. Ask a combat veteran struggling to piece his or her life together about God and watch the raw vitriol and pain pour out. They have seen into the corrupt heart of America, into the emptiness of its most sacred institutions, into our staggering hypocrisy, and those of us who refuse to heed their words become complicit in the evil they denounce.

The American Empire Is Bankrupt

JUNE 15, 2009

This week marks the end of the dollar's reign as the world's reserve currency. It marks the start of a terrible period of economic and political decline in the United States. And it signals the last gasp of the American imperium. That's over. It is not coming back. And what is to come will be very, very painful.

Barack Obama, and the criminal class on Wall Street, aided by corporate media that continue to peddle fatuous gossip and trash talk as news while we endure the greatest economic crisis in our history, may have fooled us, but the rest of the world knows we are bankrupt. And these nations are damned if they are going to continue to prop up an inflated dollar and sustain the massive federal budget deficits, swollen to more than $2 trillion, that fund America's imperial expansion in Eurasia and our system of casino capitalism. They have us by the throat. They are about to squeeze.

Meetings are being held Monday and Tuesday in Yekaterinburg, Russia, (formerly Sverdlovsk) among Chinese president Hu Jintao, Russian president Dmitry Medvedev and other top officials of the six-nation Shanghai Cooperation Organization. The United States, which asked to attend, was denied admittance. Watch what happens there carefully. The gathering is, in the words of economist Michael Hudson, "the most important meeting of the twenty-first century so far."

It is the first formal step by our major trading partners to replace the dollar as the world's reserve currency. If they succeed, the dollar will dramatically plummet in value, the cost of imports, including oil, will skyrocket, interest rates will climb, and jobs will hemorrhage at a rate that will make the last few months look like boom times. State and federal services will be reduced or shut down for lack of funds. The United States will begin to resemble the Weimar Republic or Zimbabwe. Obama, endowed by many with the qualities of a savior, will suddenly look pitiful, inept, and weak. And the rage that has kindled a handful of shootings and hate crimes in the past few weeks will engulf vast segments of a disenfranchised and bewildered working and middle class. The people of this class will demand vengeance, radical change, order, and moral renewal, which an array of protofascists, from the Christian Right to the goons who disseminate hate talk on Fox News, will assure the country they will impose.

I called Hudson, who had an article in a recent edition of *Global Research* called "The Yekaterinburg Turning Point: De-Dollarization and the Ending of America's Financial-Military Hegemony." "Yekaterinburg," Hudson writes, "may become known not only as the death place of the czars but of the American empire as well."[23] His article is worth reading, along with John Lanchester's disturbing exposé of the world's banking system, titled "It's Finished," which appeared in the May 28, 2009, issue of the *London Review of Books*.

"This means the end of the dollar," Hudson told me:

> It means China, Russia, India, Pakistan, Iran are forming an official financial and military area to get America out of Eurasia. The balance-of-payments deficit is mainly military in nature. Half of America's discretionary spending is military. The deficit ends up in the hands of foreign banks, central banks. They don't have any choice but to recycle the money to buy U.S. government debt. The Asian countries have been financing their own military encirclement. They have been forced to accept dollars that have no chance of being repaid. They are paying for America's military aggression against them. They want to get rid of this.

China, as Hudson points out, has already struck bilateral trade deals with Brazil and Malaysia to denominate their trade in China's yuan rather than the dollar, pound, or euro. Russia promises to begin trading in the ruble and local currencies. The governor of China's central bank has openly called for the abandonment of the dollar as reserve currency, suggesting in its place the use of the International Monetary Fund's Special Drawing Rights. What the new system will be remains unclear, but the flight from the dollar has clearly begun. The goal, in the words of the Russian president, is to build a "multipolar world order" that will break the economic and, by extension, military domination by the United States. China is frantically spending its dollar reserves to buy factories and property around the globe so it can unload its U.S. currency. This is why Aluminum Corporation of China made so many major concessions in the failed attempt to salvage its $19.5 billion alliance with the Rio Tinto mining concern in Australia. It desperately needs to shed its dollars.

"China is trying to get rid of all the dollars they can in a trash-for-resource deal," Hudson said. "They will give the dollars to countries willing to sell off their resources since America refuses to sell any of its high-tech industries, even Unocal, to the yellow peril. It realizes these dollars are going to be worthless pretty quickly."

The architects of this new global exchange realize that if they break the dollar they also break America's military domination. Our military spending cannot be sustained without this cycle of heavy borrowing. The official U.S. defense budget for fiscal year 2008 is $623 billion, even before we add on things like nuclear research. The next closest national military budget is China's, at $65 billion, according to the Central Intelligence Agency.

There are three categories of the balance-of-payment deficits. America imports more than it exports. This is trade. Wall Street and American corporations buy up foreign companies. This is capital movement. The third and most important balance-of-payment deficit for the past fifty years has been Pentagon spending abroad. It is primarily military spending that has been responsible for the balance-of-payments deficit for the last five decades. Look at table five in the Balance of Payments Report, published in the Survey of Current Business quarterly, and check under *military spending*. There you can see the deficit.

To fund our permanent war economy, we have been flooding the world with dollars. The foreign recipients turn the dollars over to their central banks for local currency. The central banks then have a problem. If a central bank does not spend the money in the United States, the exchange rate against the dollar will go up. This will penalize exporters. This has allowed America to print money without restraint to buy imports and foreign companies, fund our military expansion, and ensure that foreign nations like China continue to buy our Treasury Bonds. This cycle appears now to be over. Once the dollar cannot flood central banks and no one buys our Treasury Bonds, our empire collapses. The profligate spending on the military, some $1 trillion when everything is counted, will be unsustainable.

"We will have to finance our own military spending," Hudson warned, "and the only way to do this will be to sharply cut back wage rates. The class war is back in business. Wall Street understands that. This is why it had Bush and Obama give it $10 trillion in a huge rip-off so it can have enough money to survive."

The desperate effort to borrow our way out of financial collapse has promoted a level of state intervention unseen since World War I. It has also led us into uncharted territory.

"We have in effect had to declare war to get us out of the hole created by our economic system," John Lanchester wrote in the *London Review of Books*. "There is no model or precedent for this, and no way to argue that it's all right really, because under such-and-such a model of capitalism . . . there is no such model. It isn't supposed to work like this, and there is no road map for what's happened."[24]

As the dollar plunges, the cost of daily living, from buying food to getting medical care, will become difficult for all but a few. States and cities will see their pension funds drained and finally shut down. The government will be forced to sell off infrastructure, including roads and transport, to private corporations. We will be increasingly charged by privatized utilities—think Enron—for what was once regulated and subsidized. Commercial and private real estate will be worth less than half its current value. The negative equity that already plagues twenty-five percent of American homes will expand to include nearly all property owners. It will be difficult to borrow and impossible to sell real estate unless we accept massive losses. There will be block after block of empty stores and boarded-up houses. Foreclosures will be epidemic. There will be long lines at soup kitchens and many, many homeless.

Our corporate-controlled media, already banal and trivial, will work overtime to anesthetize us with useless gossip, spectacles, sex, gratuitous violence, fear, and tawdry junk politics. America will be composed of a large dispossessed underclass and a tiny empowered oligarchy that will run a ruthless and brutal system of neofeudalism from secure compounds. Those who resist will be silenced, many by force. We will pay a terrible price, and we will pay this price soon, for the gross malfeasance of our power elite.

Globalization Goes Bankrupt

SEPTEMBER 20, 2009

The rage of the disposed is fracturing the country, dividing it into camps that are unmoored from the political mainstream. Movements are building on the ends of the political spectrum that have lost faith in the mechanisms of democratic change. You can't blame them. But unless we on the Left move quickly, this rage will be captured by a virulent and racist right wing, one that seeks a disturbing protofascism.

Every day counts. Every deferral of protest hurts. We should, if we have the time and the ability, make our way to Pittsburgh for the meeting of the G-20 this week rather than do what the power elite is hoping we will do—stay home. Complacency comes at a horrible price.

"The leaders of the G-20 are meeting to try and salvage their power and money after everything that has gone wrong," said Benedicto Martínez Orozco, co-president of the Mexican Frente Auténtico del Trabajo, who is in Pittsburgh for the protests. "This is what this meeting is about."[25]

The draconian security measures put in place to silence dissent in Pittsburgh are disproportionate to any actual security concern. They are a response not to a real threat, but to the fear gripping the established centers of power. The power elite grasps, even if we do not, the massive fraud and theft being undertaken to save a criminal class on Wall Street and international speculators of the kinds who were executed in other periods of human history. They know the awful cost this plundering of state treasuries will impose on workers, who will become a permanent underclass. And they also know that once this is clear to the rest of us, rebellion will no longer be a foreign concept.

The delegates to the G-20, the gathering of the world's wealthiest nations, will consequently be protected by a National Guard combat battalion, recently returned from Iraq. The battalion will shut down the area around the city center, man checkpoints, and patrol the streets in combat gear. Pittsburgh has augmented the city's police force of 1,000 with an additional 3,000 officers. Helicopters have begun to buzz gatherings in city parks, buses driven to Pittsburgh to provide food to protesters have been impounded, activists have been detained, and permits to camp in the city parks have been denied. Web sites belonging to resistance groups have been hacked and trashed, and many groups suspect that they have been infiltrated and that their phones and e-mail accounts are being monitored.

Larry Holmes, an organizer from New York City, stood outside a tent encampment on land owned by the Monumental Baptist Church in the city's Hill District. He is one of the leaders of the Bail Out the People Movement. Holmes, a longtime labor activist, on Sunday led a march on the David L. Lawrence Convention Center, site of the G-20 meeting, by unemployed people calling for jobs. He will coordinate more protests during the week.

"It is de facto martial law," he said, "and the real effort to subvert the work of those protesting has yet to begin. But voting only gets you so far. There are often not many choices in an election. When you build democratic movements around the war or unemployment, you get a more authentic expression of democracy. It is more organic. It makes a difference. History has taught us this."[26]

Our global economy, like our political system, has been hijacked by a tiny oligarchy, composed mostly of wealthy white men who serve corporations. They have pledged or raised a staggering $18 trillion, looted largely from state treasuries, to prop up banks and other financial institutions that engaged in suicidal acts of speculation and ruined the world economy. They have formulated trade deals so corporations can speculate across borders with currency, food, and natural resources even as, according to the Food and Agriculture Organization of the United Nations, 1.02 billion people on the planet struggle with hunger. Globalization has obliterated the ability of many poor countries to protect food staples such as corn, rice, beans, and wheat with subsidies or taxes on imported staples. The abolishment of these protections has permitted the giant mechanized farms to wipe out tens of millions of small farmers—two million in Mexico alone—bankrupting many and driving them off their land. Those who could once feed themselves can no longer find enough food, and the wealthiest governments use institutions such as the International Monetary Fund, the World Bank, and the World Trade Organization like pit bulls to establish economic supremacy. There is little that most governments seem able to do to fight back.

But the game is up. The utopian dreams of globalization have been exposed as a sham. Force is all the elite have left. We are living through one of civilization's great seismic reversals. The ideology of globalization, like all utopias sold as inevitable and irreversible, has become a farce. The power elite, perplexed and confused, cling to the disastrous principles of globalization and its outdated language to mask the political and economic vacuum before us. The absurd idea that the marketplace alone should determine economic and political constructs caused the crisis. It led the G-20 to sacrifice other areas of human importance—from working conditions, to taxation, to child labor, to hunger, to health and pollution—on the altar of free trade. It left the world's poor worse off and the United States with the largest deficits in human history. Globalization has become an excuse to ignore the mess. It has left a mediocre elite desperately trying to save a system that cannot be saved and, more important, trying to save itself. "Speculation," then-President Jacques Chirac of France once warned, "is the AIDS of our economies."[27] We have reached the terminal stage.

"Each of Globalization's strengths has somehow turned out to have an opposing meaning," John Ralston Saul wrote in *The Collapse of Globalism*:

> The lowering of national residency requirements for corporations has morphed into a tool for massive tax evasion. The idea of a global economic system mysteriously made local poverty seem unreal, even normal. The decline of the middle class—the very basis of democracy—seemed to be just one of those things that happen, unfortunate but inevitable. That the working class and the lower

middle class, even parts of the middle class, could only survive with more than one job per person seemed to be expected punishment for not keeping up. The contrast between unprecedented bonuses for mere managers at the top and the four-job families below them seemed inevitable in a globalized world. For two decades an elite consensus insisted that unsustainable third-world debts could not be put aside in a sort of bad debt reserve without betraying Globalism's essential principles and moral obligations, which included an unwavering respect for the sanctity of international contracts. It took the same people about two weeks to abandon sanctity and propose bad debt banks for their own far larger debts in 2009.[28]

The institutions that once provided alternative sources of power, including the media, government, agencies of religion, universities, and labor unions, have proved morally bankrupt. They no longer provide a space for voices of moral autonomy. No one will save us now but ourselves.

"The best thing that happened to the establishment is the election of a black president," Holmes said. "It will contain people for a given period of time, but time is running out. Suppose something else happens? Suppose another straw breaks? What happens when there is a credit card crisis or a collapse in commercial real estate? The financial system is very, very fragile. The legs are being kicked out from underneath it.

"Obama is in trouble," Holmes went on:

The economic crisis is a structural crisis. The recovery is only a recovery for Wall Street. It can't be sustained, and Obama will be blamed for it. He is doing everything Wall Street demands. But this will be a dead end. It is a prescription for disaster, not only for Obama but the Democratic Party. It is only groups like ours that provide hope. If labor unions will get off their ass and stop focusing on narrow legislation for their members, if they will go back to being social unions that embrace broad causes, we have a chance of effecting change. If this does not happen it will be a right-wing disaster.[29]

Celebrating Slaughter:
War and Collective Amnesia

OCTOBER 5, 2009

War memorials and museums are temples to the god of war. The hushed voices, the well-tended grass, the flapping of the flags allow us to ignore how and why our young died. They hide the futility and waste of war. They sanitize the savage instruments of death that turn young soldiers and Marines into killers, and small villages in Vietnam or Afghanistan or Iraq into hellish bonfires. There are no images in these memorials of men or women with their guts hanging out of their bellies, screaming pathetically for their mothers. We do not see mangled corpses being shoved in body bags. There are no sights of children burned beyond recognition or moaning in horrible pain. There are no blind and deformed wrecks of human beings limping through life. War, by the time it is collectively remembered, is glorified and heavily censored.

I blame our war memorials and museums, our popular war films and books, for the wars in Iraq and Afghanistan as much as George W. Bush. They provide the mental images and historical references to justify new conflicts. We equate Saddam Hussein with Adolf Hitler. We see al-Qaida as a representation of Nazi evil. We view ourselves as eternal liberators. These plastic representations of war reconfigure the past in light of the present. War memorials and romantic depictions of war are the social and moral props used to create the psychological conditions to wage new wars.

War memorials are quiet, still, reverential, and tasteful. And, like church, such sanctuaries are important, but they allow us to forget that these men and women were used and often betrayed by those who led the nation into war. The memorials do not tell us that some always grow rich from large-scale human suffering. They do not explain that politicians play the great games of world power and stoke fear for their own advancement. They forget that young men and women in uniform are pawns in the hands of cynics, something Pat Tillman's family sadly discovered. They do not expose the ignorance, raw ambition, and greed that are the engine of war.

There is a burning need, one seen in the collective memory that has grown up around World War II and the Holocaust, to turn the horror of mass murder into a tribute to the triumph of the human spirit. The reality is too unpalatable. The human need to make sense of slaughter, to give it a grandeur it does not possess, permits the guilty to go free. The war-makers—those who make the war but never pay the price of war—live among us. They are our elder statesmen, our war criminals. Any honest war memorial would have these statesmen hanging in effigy. Any honest democracy would place them behind bars.

Primo Levi, who survived Auschwitz, fought against the mendacity of collective memory until he took his own life. He railed against the human need to mask the truth of the Holocaust and war by giving it a false, moral narrative. He wrote that the contemporary history of the Third Reich could be "reread as a war against memory, an Orwellian falsification of memory, falsification of reality, negation of reality." He wondered if "we who have returned" have "been able to understand and make others understand our experience."

Levi wrote of the Jewish collaborator Chaim Rumkowski, who ran the Łódź ghetto on behalf of the Nazis, that "we are all mirrored in Rumkowski, his ambiguity is ours, it is our second nature, we hybrids molded from clay and spirit. His fever is ours, the fever of Western civilization that 'descends into hell with trumpets and drums.'" We, like Rumkowski, "come to terms with power, forgetting that we are all in the ghetto, that the ghetto is walled in, that outside the ghetto reign the lords of death, and that close by the train is waiting."[30] We are, Levi understood, perpetually imprisoned within the madness of self-destruction. The rage of Cindy Sheehan, who lost her son Casey in Iraq, is a rage Levi felt. But it is a rage most of us do not understand.

A war memorial that attempted to depict the reality of war would be too subversive. It would condemn us and our capacity for evil. It would show that the line between the victim and the victimizer is razor-thin, that human beings, when the restraints are cut, are intoxicated by mass killing, and that war, rather than being noble, heroic and glorious, obliterates all that is tender, decent, and kind. It would tell us that the celebration of national greatness is the celebration of our technological capacity to kill. It would warn us that war is always morally depraved, that even in "good" wars such as World War II, all can become war criminals. We dropped the atomic bomb on Hiroshima and Nagasaki. The Nazis ran the death camps. But this narrative of war is unsettling. It does not create a collective memory that serves the interests of those who wage war and permit us to wallow in self-exaltation.

There are times—World War II and the Serb assault on Bosnia would be examples—when a population is pushed into a war. But this violence always deforms and maims those who use it. My uncle, who drank himself to death in a trailer in Maine, fought for four years in the South Pacific during World War II. He and the soldiers in his unit never bothered taking Japanese prisoners.

The detritus of war, the old cannons and artillery pieces rolled out to stand near memorials, were curious and alluring objects in my childhood. But these displays angered my father, a Presbyterian minister who was in North Africa as an Army sergeant during World War II. The lifeless, clean, and neat displays of weapons and puppets in uniforms were being used, he said, to purge the reality of war. These memorials sanctified violence. They turned the instruments of violence—the tanks, machine guns, rifles, and airplanes—into an aesthetic of death.

These memorials, while they pay homage to those who made "the ultimate sacrifice," dignify slaughter. They perpetuate the old lie of honor and glory. They set the ground for the next inferno. The myth of war manufactures a collective memory that ennobles the next war. The intimate, personal experience of violence turns those who return from war into internal exiles. They cannot compete against the power of the myth. This collective memory saturates the culture, but it is "a tale told by an idiot, full of sound and fury, signifying nothing."[31]

Reality Check from
the Brink of Extinction

OCTOBER 19, 2009

We can join Bill McKibben on October 24 in nationwide protests over rising carbon emissions. We can cut our consumption of fossil fuels. We can use less water. We can banish plastic bags. We can install compact fluorescent light bulbs. We can compost in our backyard. But unless we dismantle the corporate state, all those actions will be just as ineffective as the Ghost Dance shirts donned by native American warriors to protect themselves from the bullets of white soldiers at Wounded Knee.

"If we all wait for the great, glorious revolution there won't be anything left," author and environmental activist Derrick Jensen told me when I interviewed him in a phone call to his home in California:

> If all we do is reform work, this culture will grind away. This work is necessary, but not sufficient. We need to use whatever means are necessary to stop this culture from killing the planet. We need to target and take down the industrial infrastructure that is systematically dismembering the planet. Industrial civilization is functionally incompatible with life on the planet, and is murdering the planet. We need to do whatever is necessary to stop this.

The oil and natural gas industry, the coal industry, arms and weapons manufacturers, industrial farms, deforestation industries, the automotive industry, and chemical plants will not willingly accept their own extinction. They are indifferent to the looming human catastrophe. We will not significantly reduce carbon emissions by drying our laundry in the backyard and naively trusting the power elite. The corporations will continue to cannibalize the planet for the sake of money. They must be halted by organized and militant forms of resistance. The crisis of global heating is a social problem. It requires a social response.

The United States, after rejecting the Kyoto Protocol, went on to increase its carbon emissions by twenty percent from 1990 levels. The European Union countries during the same period reduced their emissions by two percent. But the recent climate negotiations in Bangkok, designed to lead to a deal in Copenhagen in December, have scuttled even the tepid response of Kyoto. Kyoto is dead. The European Union, like the United States, will no longer abide by binding targets for emission reductions. Countries will unilaterally decide how much to cut. They will submit their plans to international monitoring. And while Kyoto put the burden of responsibility on the industrialized nations that created the climate crisis, the new plan treats all countries the same. It is a huge step backward.

"All of the so-called solutions to global warming take industrial capitalism as a given," said Jensen, who wrote *Endgame* and *The Culture of Make Believe*:

> The natural world is supposed to conform to industrial capitalism. This is insane. It is out of touch with physical reality. What's real is real. Any social system—it does not matter if we are talking about industrial capitalism or an indigenous Tolowa people—their way of life is dependent upon a real, physical world. Without a real, physical world you don't have anything. When you separate yourself from the real world you start to hallucinate. You believe the machines are more real than real life. How many machines are within ten feet of you and how many wild animals are within a hundred yards? How many machines do you have a daily relationship with? We have forgotten what is real.

The latest studies show polar ice caps are melting at a record rate and that within a decade the Arctic will be an open sea during summers. This does not give us much time. White ice and snow reflect eighty percent of sunlight back to space, while dark water reflects only twenty percent, absorbing a much larger heat load. Scientists warn that the loss of the ice will dramatically change winds and sea currents around the world. And the rapidly melting permafrost is unleashing methane chimneys from the ocean floor along the Russian coastline. Methane is a greenhouse gas twenty-five times more toxic than carbon dioxide, and some scientists have speculated that the release of huge quantities of methane into the atmosphere could asphyxiate the human species. The rising sea levels, which will swallow countries such as the Marshall Islands and turn cities like New Orleans into a new Atlantis, will combine with severe droughts, horrific storms, and flooding to eventually dislocate more than a billion people. The effects will be suffering, disease, and death on a scale unseen in human history.

We can save groves of trees, protect endangered species, and clean up rivers, all of which is good, but to leave the corporations unchallenged would mean our efforts would be wasted. These personal adjustments and environmental crusades can too easily become badges of moral purity, excuses for inaction. They can absolve us from the harder task of confronting the power of corporations.

The damage to the environment by human households is minuscule next to the damage done by corporations. Municipalities and individuals use ten percent of the nation's water, while the other ninety percent is consumed by agriculture and industry. Individual consumption of energy accounts for about a quarter of all energy consumption; the other seventy-five percent is consumed by corporations. Municipal waste accounts for only three percent of total waste production in the United States. We can, and should, live more simply, but it will not be enough if we do not radically transform the economic structure of the industrial world.

"If your food comes from the grocery store and your water from a tap, you will defend to the death the system that brings these to you because your life depends on it," said Jensen, who is holding workshops around the country called Deep Green Resistance to build a militant resistance movement:

> If your food comes from a land base and if your water comes from a river, you will defend to the death these systems. In any abusive

system, whether we are talking about an abusive man against his partner or the larger abusive system, you force your victims to become dependent upon you. We believe that industrial capitalism is more important than life.

Those who run our corporate state have fought environmental regulation as tenaciously as they have fought financial regulation. They are responsible for our personal impoverishment as well as the impoverishment of our ecosystem. We remain addicted, courtesy of the oil, gas, and automobile industries and a corporate-controlled government, to fossil fuels. Species are vanishing. Fish stocks are depleted. The great human migration from coastlines and deserts has begun. And as temperatures continue to rise, huge parts of the globe will become uninhabitable. NASA climate scientist James Hansen has demonstrated that any concentration of carbon dioxide greater than 350 parts per million in the atmosphere is not compatible with maintenance of the biosphere on the "planet on which civilization developed and to which life on earth is adapted." He has determined that the world must stop burning coal by 2030—and the industrialized world well before that—if we are to have any hope of ever getting the planet back down below that 350 number. Coal supplies half of our electricity in the United States.[32]

"We need to separate ourselves from the corporate government that is killing the planet," Jensen said:

> We need to get really serious. We are talking about life on the planet. We need to shut down the oil infrastructure. I don't care, and the trees don't care, if we do this through lawsuits, mass boycotts, or sabotage. I asked Dahr Jamail how long a bridge would last in Iraq that was not defended. He said probably six to twelve hours. We need to make the economic system, which is the engine for so much destruction, unmanageable. The Movement for the Emancipation of the Niger Delta has been able to reduce Nigerian oil output by twenty percent. We need to stop the oil economy.[33]

The reason the ecosystem is dying is not because we still have a dryer in our basement. It is because corporations look at everything, from human beings to the natural environment, as exploitable commodities. It is because consumption is the engine of corporate profits. We have allowed the corporate state to sell the environmental crisis as a matter of personal choice when actually there is a need for profound social and economic reform. We are left powerless.

Aleksander Herzen, speaking a century ago to a group of Russian anarchists working to topple the Czar, reminded his followers that they were not there to rescue the system.

"We think we are the doctors," Herzen said. "We are the disease."[34]

War Is a Hate Crime

OCTOBER 26, 2009

Violence against lesbian, gay, bisexual, and transgender people is wrong. So is violence against people in Afghanistan and Iraq. But in the bizarre culture of identity politics, there are no alliances among the oppressed. The Matthew Shepard and James Byrd Jr. Hate Crimes Prevention Act, the first major federal civil-rights law protecting lesbian, gay, bisexual, and transgender people, passed last week, was attached to a $680 billion measure outlining the Pentagon's budget, which includes $130 billion for ongoing military operations in Iraq and Afghanistan. The Democratic majority in Congress, under the cover of protecting some innocents, authorized massive acts of violence against other innocents.

It was a clever piece of marketing. It blunted debate about new funding for war. And behind the closed doors of the caucus rooms, the Democratic leadership told Blue Dog Democrats, who are squeamish about defending gays or lesbians from hate crimes, that they could justify the vote as support for the war. They told liberal Democrats, who are squeamish about unlimited funding for war, that they could defend the vote as a step forward in the battle for civil rights. Gender equality groups, by selfishly narrowing their concern to themselves, participated in the dirty game.

"Every thinking person wants to take a stand against hate crimes, but isn't war the most offensive of hate crimes?" asked U.S. Representative Dennis Kucinich, who did not vote for the bill, when I spoke to him by phone:

> To have people have to make a choice, or contemplate the hierarchy of hate crimes, is cynical. I don't vote to fund wars. If you are op-

posed to war, you don't vote to authorize or appropriate money. Congress, historically and constitutionally, has the power to fund or defund a war. The more Congress participates in authorizing spending for war, the more likely it is that we will be there for a long, long time. This reflects an even larger question. All the attention is paid to what President Obama is going to do right now with respect to Iraq and Afghanistan. The truth is the Democratic Congress could have ended the war when it took control just after 2006. We were given control of the Congress by the American people in November 2006 specifically to end the war. It did not happen. The funding continues. And while the attention is on the president, Congress clearly has the authority at any time to stop the funding. And yet it doesn't. Worse yet, it finds other ways to garner votes for bills that authorize funding for war. The spending juggernaut moves forward, a companion to the inconscient force of war itself.

The brutality of Matthew Shepard's killers, who beat him to death for being gay, is a product of a culture that glorifies violence and sadism. It is the product of a militarized culture. We have more police, prisons, inmates, spies, mercenaries, weapons, and troops than any other nation on Earth. Our military, which swallows half of the federal budget, is enormously popular—as if it is not part of government. The military values of hypermasculinity, blind obedience, and violence are an electric current running through reality television and trash-talk programs where contestants endure pain while they betray and manipulate those around them in a ruthless world of competition. Friendship and compassion are banished.

This hypermasculinity is at the core of pornography, with its fusion of violence and eroticism, as well as its physical and emotional degradation of women. It is an expression of the corporate state, where human beings are reduced to commodities and companies have become protofascist enclaves devoted to maximizing profit. Militarism crushes the capacity for moral autonomy and difference. It isolates us from each other. It has its logical fruition in Abu Ghraib, the wars in Iraq and Afghanistan, along with our lack of compassion for our homeless, our poor, our mentally ill, our unemployed, our sick, and, yes, our gay, lesbian, transgender and bisexual citizens.

In his study titled *Male Fantasies*, which draws on the bitter alienation of demobilized veterans in Germany following the end of World War One, Klaus Theweleit argues that a militarized culture attacks all that is culturally defined as the feminine, including love, gentleness, compassion, and acceptance of difference. It sees any sexual ambiguity as a threat to male "hardness" and the clearly defined roles required by the militarized state. The continued support for our permanent war economy, the continued elevation of military values as the highest good, sustains the perverted ethic, rigid social roles, and emotional numbness that Theweleit explored. It is a moral cancer that ensures there will be more Matthew Shepards.

Fascism, Theweleit argued, is not so much a form of government or a particular structuring of the economy or a system, but the creation of potent slogans and symbols that form a kind of psychic economy that places sexuality in the service of destruction. The "core of all fascist propaganda is a battle against everything that constitutes enjoyment and pleasure," Theweleit wrote.[35] And our culture, while it disdains the name of fascism, embraces its dark ethic.

New York Times columnist Thomas Friedman, on the May 30, 2003, edition of the PBS show *Charlie Rose*, spoke in this sexualized language of violence to justify the war in Iraq, a moment preserved on YouTube:

"What they needed to see was American boys and girls going house to house, from Basra to Baghdad, and basically saying, 'Which part of this sentence don't you understand?'" Friedman said. "'You don't think, you know, we care about our open society? You think this bubble fantasy, we're just gonna let it grow? Well, suck on this.' That, Charlie, was what this war was about. We could have hit Saudi Arabia, it was part of that bubble. Could have hit Pakistan. We hit Iraq because we could."[36]

This is the kind of twisted logic the killers of Matthew Shepard would understand.

The philosopher Theodor Adorno wrote, in words gay activists should have heeded, that exclusive preoccupation with personal concerns and indifference to the suffering of others beyond the self-identified group made fascism and the Holocaust possible.

"The inability to identify with others was unquestionably the most important psychological condition for the fact that something like Auschwitz could have occurred in the midst of more or less civilized and innocent people," Adorno wrote:

> What is called fellow traveling was primarily business interest: one pursues one's own advantage before all else, and simply not to endanger oneself, does not talk too much. That is a general law of the status quo. The silence under the terror was only its consequence. The coldness of the societal monad, the isolated competitor, was the precondition, as indifference to the fate of others, for the fact that only very few people reacted. The torturers know this, and they put it to test ever anew.[37]

The Pictures You Aren't
Supposed to See

War is brutal and impersonal. It mocks the fantasy of individual heroism and the absurdity of utopian goals like democracy. In an instant, industrial warfare can kill dozens, even hundreds of people, who never
see their attackers. The power of these industrial weapons is indiscriminate and staggering. They can take down apartment blocks in seconds,
burying and crushing everyone inside. They can demolish villages and
send tanks, planes, and ships up in fiery blasts. The wounds, for those
who survive, result in terrible burns, blindness, amputation, and lifelong pain and trauma. No one returns the same from such warfare. And
once these weapons are employed, all talk of human rights is a farce.

In Peter van Agtmael's *2nd Tour Hope I Don't Die* and Lori
Grinker's *Afterwar: Veterans from a World in Conflict*, two haunting
books of war photographs, we see pictures of war almost always hidden from public view. These pictures are shadows, for only those who
go to and suffer from war can fully confront the visceral horror of it,
but they are at least an attempt to unmask war's savagery.

Next to a photograph of the bloodied body of a soldier in an operating room, we read this description in Agtmael's book:

> Over ninety percent of this soldier's body was burned when a road-
> side bomb hit his vehicle, igniting the fuel tank and burning two
> other soldiers to death. His camouflage uniform dangled over the
> bed, ripped open by the medics who had treated him on the heli-
> copter. Clumps of his skin had peeled away, and what was left of it

was translucent. He was in and out of consciousness, his eyes stabbing open for a few seconds. As he was lifted from the stretcher to the ER bed, he screamed "Daddy, Daddy, Daddy, Daddy," then "Put me to sleep, please put me to sleep." There was another photographer in the ER, and he leaned his camera over the heads of the medical staff to get an overhead shot. The soldier yelled, "Get that fucking camera out of my face." Those were his last words.

"I visited his grave one winter afternoon six months later," Agtmael writes, "and the scene of his death is never far from my thoughts."[38]

"There were three of us inside, and the jeep caught fire," Israeli soldier Yossi Arditi, quoted in Grinker's book, says of the moment when a Molotov cocktail exploded in his vehicle. "The fuel tank was full and it was about to explode, my skin was hanging from my arms and face—but I didn't lose my head. I knew nobody could get inside to help me, that my only way out was through the fire to the doors. I wanted to take my gun, but I couldn't touch it because my hands were burning."

Arditi spent six months in the hospital. He had surgery every two or three months, about twenty operations, over the next three years.

"People who see me, see what war really does," he says.[39]

Filmic and most photographic images of war are shorn of the heart-pounding fear, awful stench, deafening noise, and exhaustion of the battlefield. Most such images turn confusion and chaos, the chief elements of combat, into an artful war narrative. They turn war into porn. Soldiers and Marines, especially those who have never seen war, buy cases of beer and watch movies like *Platoon*, movies meant to denounce war, and as they do they revel in the despicable power of the weapons shown. The reality of violence is different. Everything formed by violence is senseless and useless. It exists without a future. It leaves behind nothing but death, grief, and destruction.

Chronicles of war, such as these two books, that eschew images and scenes of combat, begin to capture war's reality. War's effects are what the state and the media, handmaiden of the war-makers, work hard to keep hidden. If we really saw war, what war does to young minds and bodies, it would be harder to embrace the myth of war. If we had to stand over the mangled corpses of the eight schoolchildren killed in Afghanistan a week ago and listen to the wails of their parents, we would not be able to repeat clichés about "liberating the women of Afghanistan" or "bringing freedom to the Afghan people." This is why war is carefully sanitized. This is why we are given war's perverse and dark thrill but are spared from seeing war's consequences. The mythic visions of war keep it heroic and entertaining. And the media are as guilty as Hollywood. During the start of the Iraq war, television reports gave us the visceral thrill of force and hid from us the effects of bullets, tank rounds, iron fragmentation bombs, and artillery rounds. We tasted a bit of war's exhilaration, but were protected from seeing what war actually does.

The wounded, the crippled, and the dead are, in this great charade, swiftly carted offstage. They are war's refuse. We do not see them. We do not hear them. They are doomed, like wandering spirits, to float around the edges of our consciousness, ignored, even reviled. The message they tell is too painful for us to hear. We prefer to celebrate ourselves and our nation by imbibing the myth of glory, honor, patriotism, and heroism, words that in combat become empty and meaningless. And those whom fate has decreed must face war's effects often turn and flee.

Saul Alfaro, who lost his legs in the war in El Salvador, speaks in Grinker's book about the first and final visit from his girlfriend as he lay in an army hospital bed.

"She had been my girlfriend in the military and we had planned to be married," he says. "But when she saw me in the hospital—I don't know exactly what happened, but later they told me when she saw me she began to cry. Afterwards, she ran away and never came back."[40]

The public manifestations of gratitude are reserved for veterans who dutifully read from the script handed to them by the state. The veterans trotted out for viewing are those who are compliant and palatable, those we can stand to look at without horror, those who are willing to go along with the lie that war is about patriotism and is the highest good. "Thank you for your service," we are supposed to say. They are used to perpetuate the myth. We are used to honor it.

Gary Zuspann, who lives in a special enclosed environment in his parent's home in Waco, Texas, suffering from Gulf War syndrome, speaks in Grinker's book of feeling like "a prisoner of war" even after the war had ended.

"Basically they put me on the curb and said, okay, fend for yourself," he says in the book. "I was living in a fantasy world where I thought our government cared about us and they take care of their own. I believed it was in my contract, that if you're maimed or wounded during your service in war, you should be taken care of. Now I'm angry."[41]

I went back to Sarajevo after covering the 1990s war for the *New York Times* and found hundreds of cripples trapped in rooms in apartment blocks with no elevators and no wheelchairs. Most were young men, many without limbs, being cared for by their elderly parents. Glorious war heroes left to rot.

Despair and suicide grip survivors. More Vietnam veterans committed suicide after the war than were killed during it. The inhuman qualities drilled into soldiers and Marines in wartime defeat them in peacetime. This is what Homer taught us in the *Iliad*, the great book on war, and the *Odyssey*, the great book on the long journey to recovery by professional killers. Many never readjust. They cannot connect again with wives, children, parents, or friends, retreating into personal hells of self-destructive anguish and rage.

"They program you to have no emotion—like if somebody sitting next to you gets killed you just have to carry on doing your job and shut up," Steve Annabell, a British veteran of the Falklands War, says to Grinker. "When you leave the service, when you come back from a situation like that, there's no button they can press to switch your emotions back on. So you walk around like a zombie. They don't deprogram you. If you become a problem they just sweep you under the carpet.

"To get you to join up they do all these advertisements—they show people skiing down mountains and doing great things—but they don't show you getting shot at and people with their legs blown off or burning to death," Annabell says. "They don't show you what really happens. It's just bullshit. And they never prepare you for it. They can give you all the training in the world, but it's never the same as the real thing."[42]

Those with whom veterans have most in common when the war is over are often those they fought.

"Nobody comes back from war the same," says Horacio Javier Benitez, who fought the British in the Falklands and is quoted in Grinker's book. "The person, Horacio, who was sent to war, doesn't exist anymore. It's hard to be enthusiastic about normal life; too much seems inconsequential. You contend with craziness and depression."

"Many who served in the Malvinas," he says, using the Argentine name of the islands, "committed suicide, many of my friends."[43]

"I miss my family," reads a wall graffito captured in one of Agtmael's photographs. "Please God forgive the lives I took and let my family be happy if I don't go home again."

Next to the plea, someone had drawn an arrow toward the words and written in thick, black marker, "Fag!!!"[44]

Look beyond the nationalist cant used to justify war. Look beyond the seduction of the weapons and the pornography of violence. Look beyond Barack Obama's ridiculous rhetoric about finishing the job or fighting terror. Focus on the evil of war. War begins by calling for the annihilation of the others but ends ultimately in self-annihilation. It corrupts souls and mutilates bodies. It destroys homes and villages and murders children on their way to school. It grinds into the dirt all that is tender and beautiful and sacred. It empowers human deformities—warlords, Shiite death squads, Sunni insurgents, the Taliban, al-Qaida, and our own killers—who can speak only in the despicable language of force. War is a scourge. It is a plague. It is industrial murder. And before you support war, especially the wars in Iraq and Afghanistan, look into the hollow eyes of the men, women, and children who know it.

The New Secessionists

APRIL 26, 2010

Acts of rebellion that promote moral and political change must be nonviolent. And one of the most potent nonviolent alternatives in the country, an alternative that defies the corporate state and calls for an end to imperial wars, is the secessionist movement bubbling up in some two dozen states including Vermont, Texas, Alaska, and Hawaii.

These movements do not always embrace liberal values. Most of the groups in the South champion a "neo-Confederacy" and are often exclusively male and white. Secessionists, who call for statewide referendums to secede, do not advocate the use of force. It is unclear, however, if some will turn to force if the federal structure ever denies them independence.

These groups at least grasp that the old divisions between liberals and conservatives are obsolete and meaningless. They understand that corporations have carried out a coup d'état. They recognize that our permanent war economy and costly and futile imperial wars are unsustainable, and they demand that we take popular action to prevent citizens from being further impoverished and robbed by Wall Street speculators and corporations.

"The defining characteristic of the Second Vermont Republic is that there are two enemies, the United States government and corporate America," Thomas Naylor, who founded Vermont's secessionist movement, told me when I reached him by phone at his home ten miles south of Burlington. "One owns the other one. We are not like the Tea Party. The underlying premise of the Tea Party movement is that the system is fixable."

As reported by Christopher Ketcham in a recent issue of *GOOD* magazine, Naylor points to the nation's decline. The secessionist leader notes, in Ketcham's words, "Of all the western democracies, the United States stands near dead last in voter turnout, last in health care, last in education, highest in homicide rates, mortality, STDs among juveniles, youth pregnancy, abortion, and divorce."[45]

The nation, he says grimly, has trillions in deficits it can never repay, is beset by staggering income disparities, has destroyed its manufacturing base, and is the planet's most egregious polluter and greediest consumer of fossil fuels. With some 40 million Americans living in poverty, tens of millions more in a category called "near-poverty" and a permanent underclass trapped by a real unemployment rate of seventeen percent, there is ample tinder for internal combustion. If we do not undertake a dramatic reversal soon, he asserts, the country and the global environment will implode with catastrophic consequences.

The secessionist movement is gaining ground in several states, especially Texas, where elected officials increasingly have to contend with secessionist sentiments.

"Our membership has grown tremendously since the bailouts, since the tail end of the Bush administration," said Daniel Miller, the leader of the Texas Nationalist Movement, when I spoke with him by telephone from his home in the small town of Nederland, Texas:

> There is a feeling in Texas that we are being spent into oblivion. We are operating as the cash cow for the states that cannot manage their budgets. With this Congress, Texas has been squarely in their crosshairs, from cap-and-trade to the alien transfer and exit program. So many legislative pieces coming down the pike are offensive to people here in Texas. The sentiment for independence here is very high. The sentiment inside the legislature and state capitol is one of guarded optimism. There are scores of folks within state government who are supportive of what we are doing, although there is a need to see the public support in a more tangible way. This is why we launched our Let Texas Decide petition drive. We intend to deliver over a million signatures on the opening day of the [state legislative] session on January 11, 2011.

Miller, like Naylor, expects many in the Tea Party to migrate to secessionist movements once they realize they cannot alter the structure or power of the corporate state through electoral politics. Polls in Texas show the secessionists have support from about thirty-five percent of the state's population, and Vermont is not far behind.

Naylor, who taught economics at Duke University for thirty years, is, along with Kirkpatrick Sale and Donald Livingston, one of the intellectual godfathers of the secessionist movement. His writing can be found on The Second Vermont Republic Web site (http://www.vermont republic.org), on the Web site Secession News (http://secessionnews .com), and in postings on the Middlebury Institute Web site (http://www .middleburyinstitute.org). Naylor first proposed secession in his 1997 book *Downsizing the U.S.A.* He comes out of the "small is beautiful" movement, as does Sale. Naylor lives with his wife in the Vermont village of Charlotte.

The Second Vermont Republic arose from the statewide antiwar protests in 2003. It embraces a left-wing populism that makes it unique among the national movements, which usually veer more toward Ron Paul libertarianism. The Vermont movement, like the Texas and Alaska movements, is well organized. It has a bimonthly newspaper called the *Vermont Commons*, which champions sustainable agriculture and energy supplies based on wind and water, and calls for locally owned banks that will open lines of credit to their communities. Dennis Steele, campaigning for governor as a secessionist, runs Radio Free Vermont, which gives a venue to Vermont musicians and groups as well as being a voice of the movement. Vermont, like Texas, was an independent republic, but on March 4, 1791, voted to enter the union. Supporters of the Second Vermont Republic commemorate the anniversary by holding a mock funeral procession through the state capital, Montpelier, with a casket marked "Vermont." Secessionist candidates in Vermont are currently running for governor, lieutenant governor, eight state Senate seats, and two House seats.

"The movement, at its core, is antiauthoritarian," said Sale, who works closely with Naylor and spoke with me from his home in Charleston, South Carolina. "It includes those who are libertarians and those who are on the anarchic community side. In traditional terms these people are left and right, but they have come very close together in their antiauthoritarianism. Left and right no longer have meaning."

The movement correctly views the corporate state as a force that has so corrupted the economy, as well as the electoral and judicial process, that it cannot be defeated through traditional routes. It also knows that the corporate state, which looks at the natural world and human beings as commodities to be exploited until exhaustion or collapse occurs, is rapidly cannibalizing the nation and pushing the planet toward irrevocable crisis. And it argues that the corporate state can be dismantled only through radical forms of nonviolent revolt and the dissolution of the United States. As an act of revolt it has many attributes.

"The only way we will ever stop these wars is when we stop paying for them," Naylor told me. "Vermont contributes about $1.5 billion to the Pentagon's budget. Do we want to keep supporting these wars? If not, let's pull out. We have two objectives. The first is returning Vermont to its status as an independent republic. The second is the peaceful dissolution of the empire. I see these as being mutually complementary.

"The U.S. government has lost its moral authority," he went on:

It is corrupt to the core. It is owned, operated, and controlled by Wall Street and corporate America. Its foreign policy is controlled by the Israeli lobby. It is unsustainable economically, socially, morally, militarily, and environmentally. It is ungovernable and therefore unfixable. The question is, do you go down with the Titanic or do you seek other options?

The leaders of the movement concede that sentiment still outstrips organization. There has not been a large proliferation of new groups, and a few old groups have folded because of a lack of leadership and support. But they insist that an increasing number of Americans are receptive to their ideas.

"The number of groups has not grown as I hoped it would when I started having congresses," said Sale, who addresses groups around the country. "But the number of people, of individuals, of Web sites, and the number of libertarians who have come around has grown leaps and bounds. Many of those who were disappointed by the treatment of Ron Paul have come to the conclusion that they cannot have a Libertarian Party or a libertarian Republican. They are beginning to talk about secession."

"Secessionists have to be very careful not to be militaristic," Sale warned:

> This cannot be won by the gun. You can be emphatic in your secessionism, but it won't happen by carrying guns. I don't know what the Tea Party people think they are going to accomplish with guns. I guess it is a statement against the federal government and the fear that Obama is about to have gun control. It appears to be an assertion of individual rights. But the Tea Party people have not yet understood how they are going to get their view across. They still believe they can elect people, either Republicans or declared conservatives, to office in Washington and have an effect, as if you can escape the culture of Washington and the characteristics of government that has only gotten bigger and will only continue to get bigger. Electing people to the House and Senate is not going to change the characteristics of the system.

The most pressing problem is that the movement harbors within its ranks Southern secessionists who wrap themselves in the Confederate flag, begin their meetings singing "Dixie," and celebrate the slave culture of the antebellum South. Secessionist groups such as the Southern National Congress and the more radical League of the South, which the Southern Poverty Law Center has labeled a "racist hate group," openly embrace a return to uncontested white, male power. And this aspect of the movement deeply disturbs leaders such as Naylor, Sale, and Miller.

What all these movements grasp, however, is that the American empire is over. It cannot be sustained. They understand that we must disengage peacefully, learn to speak with a new humility, and live with a new simplicity, or see an economic collapse that could trigger a perverted Christian fascism, a ruthless police state, and internecine violence.

"There are three or four possible scenarios that will bring down the empire," Naylor said:

One possibility is a war with Iran. Another will see the Chinese pull the plug on Treasury bills. Even if these do not happen, the infrastructure of the country is decaying. This is a slower process. And they do not have the economy fixed. It is smoke and mirrors. This is why the price of gold is so high. The economy and the inability to stop the wars will alone be enough to bring us down. There is no escape now from our imperial overstretch.

No One Cares

MAY 3, 2010

We are approaching a decade of war in Afghanistan, and the war in Iraq is in its eighth year. Hundreds of thousands of Iraqis and thousands more Afghani and Pakistani civilians have been killed. Millions have been driven into squalid displacement and refugee camps. Thousands of our own soldiers and Marines have died or been crippled physically and psychologically. We sustain these wars, which have no real popular support, by borrowing trillions of dollars that can never be repaid, even as we close schools, states go into bankruptcy, social services are cut, our infrastructure crumbles, tens of millions of Americans are reduced to poverty, and real unemployment (which considers the out-of-work, the underemployed, and those who have stopped looking for work) approaches seventeen percent. Collective, suicidal inertia rolls us forward toward national insolvency and the collapse of empire. And we do not protest. The peace movement, despite the heroic efforts of a handful of groups such as Iraq Veterans Against the War, the Green Party, and Code Pink, is dead. No one cares.

The roots of mass apathy are found in the profound divide between liberals, who are mostly white and well educated, and our disenfranchised working class, whose sons and daughters, because they cannot get decent jobs with benefits, have few options besides the military. Liberals, whose children are more often to be found in elite colleges than in the Marine Corps, did not fight NAFTA in 1994 and the dismantling of our manufacturing base. They did nothing when the Democrats gutted welfare two years later and stood by as our banks were turned over to Wall Street speculators. They signed on, by supporting the Clinton and Obama Democrats, for the corporate rape carried out in the name of globalization and endless war, and they ignored the plight of the poor. And for this reason the poor have little interest in the moral protestations of liberals. We have lost all credibility. We are justly hated for our tacit complicity in the corporate assault on workers and their families.

Our passivity has resulted, however, in much more than imperial adventurism and a permanent underclass. A slow-motion coup by a corporate state has cemented into place a neofeudalism in which there are only masters and serfs. And the process is one that cannot be reversed through the traditional mechanisms of electoral politics.

On April 29, 2010, I traveled to Washington to join U.S. Representative Dennis Kucinich for a public teach-in on the wars. Kucinich used the Capitol Hill event to denounce the new request by Barack Obama for an additional $33 billion for the war in Afghanistan. The Ohio Democrat has introduced House Concurrent Resolution 248, with sixteen cosponsors, which would require the House of Representatives to debate whether to continue the Afghanistan war. Kucinich, to his credit, is the only member of Congress to publicly condemn the Obama administration's authorization to assassinate Anwar al-Awlaki, a U.S. citizen and cleric living in Yemen, over alleged links to a failed Christmas airline bombing in Detroit. Kucinich also invited investigative journalist Jeremy Scahill, writer/activist David Swanson, retired Army Colonel Ann Wright, and Iraq war veteran Josh Stieber to the event.

The gathering, held in the Rayburn Building, was a sober reminder of our insignificance. There were no other Congress members present, and only a smattering of young staff members attended. Most of the audience of about seventy were peace activists who, as is usual at such events, were joined by a motley collection of conspiracy theorists who believe 9/11 was an inside job, or that Senator Paul Wellstone of Minnesota, who died in a 2002 plane crash, was assassinated. Scahill and Swanson provided a litany of disturbing statistics that illustrated how corporations control all systems of power. Corporations have effectively taken over our internal security and intelligence apparatus. They run our economy and manage our systems of communication. They own the two major political parties. They have built a private military. They loot the U.S. Treasury at will. And they have become unassailable. Those who decry the corporate coup are locked out of the national debate and become as marginalized as Kucinich.

"We don't have any sort of communications system in the country," said Swanson, who cofounded an antiwar coalition (AfterDowning Street.org) and led an unsuccessful campaign to impeach George W. Bush and Dick Cheney:

> We have a corporate media cartel that overlaps with the war industry. It has no interest in democracy. The Congress is bought and paid for. It is absolutely corrupted by money. We kick ourselves for not being active enough and imposing our demands, but the bar is set very high for us. We have to try very, very hard and make very, very big sacrifices if we are going to influence this Congress prior to getting the money out and getting a decent media system. Hypocritical Congress members talk about money all the time, how we have to be careful about money, except when it comes to war. It is hypocritical, but who is going to call them on that? Not their colleagues, not their funders, not the media, only us. We have to do that, but we don't, in large part because they switch parties every number of years and we are on one team or the other.

Scahill—who has done most of the groundbreaking investigative reporting on private contractors including the security firm Blackwater, renamed Xe Services LLC—laid out how the management of the wars in Iraq and Afghanistan is being steadily transferred by the Pentagon to unaccountable private contractors. He lamented the lack of support in Congress for a bill, put forward by U.S. Representative Jan Schakowsky of Illinois, known as the *Stop Outsourcing Security Act*, House Resolution 4102, which would "responsibly phase out the use of private security contractors for functions that should be reserved for U.S. military forces and government personnel."

"It is one of the sober realities of the time we are living in that you can put forward a bill that says something as simple as 'we should not outsource national security functions to private contractors,' and you only get twenty members of Congress to support the bill," Scahill said:

> The unfortunate reality is that Representative Schakowsky knows that the war industry is bipartisan. They give on both sides. For a while there it seemed *contractor* was the new *Israel*. You could not find a member of Congress to speak out against them because so many members of Congress are beholden to corporate funding to keep their House or Senate seats. I also think Obama's election has wiped that out, as it has with many things, because the White House will dispatch emissaries to read the riot act to members of Congress who don't toe the party line.

"The entire government is basically privatized," Scahill went on:

> In fact, 100 percent of people in this country that make $100,000 or less might as well remit everything they owe in taxes to contractors rather than paying the government. That is how privatized the society is, that is how much of government has been outsourced in this society. There are eighteen U.S. intelligence agencies on the military and civilian side, and seventy percent of their combined budget is outsourced to for-profit corporations who simultaneously work the United States government as well as multinational corporations and foreign governments. We have radically outsourced the intelligence operations in this country because we have radically outsourced everything. Sixty-nine percent of the Pentagon's entire workforce, and I am not talking only about the battlefield, is now privatized. In Afghanistan we have the most staggering statistics. The Obama administration is infinitely worse in Afghanistan in terms of its employment of mercenaries and other private contractors than the Bush administration. Right now in Afghanistan there are 104,000 Department of Defense contractors alongside 68,000 U.S. troops. There is almost a 2-to-1 ratio of private-sector for-profit forces that are on the U.S. government payroll versus the active-duty or actual military forces in the country. And that is not taking into account the fact that the State Department has 14,000 contractors in Afghanistan.

"Within a matter of months, and certainly within a year, the United States will have upwards of 220,000 to 250,000 U.S. government-funded personnel occupying Afghanistan, a far cry from the 70,000 U.S. soldiers that those Americans who pay attention understand the United States has in Afghanistan," Scahill said. "This is a country where the president's national security adviser, General James Jones, said there are less than one hundred al-Qaida operatives who have no ability to strike at the United States. That was the stated rationale and reasoning for being in Afghanistan. It was to hunt down those responsible for 9/11."

Josh Stieber spoke at the end of the event. Stieber was deployed with the Army to Iraq from February 2007 to April 2008. He was in Bravo Company, 2d Battalion, 16th Infantry, or Bravo 2-16, which was involved in the July 12, 2007, Apache helicopter attack on Iraqi civilians in Baghdad depicted in a video released by the Web site WikiLeaks. Stieber, who left the Army as a conscientious objector, has issued a public apology to the Iraqi people.

"This was not by any means the exception," he said of the video, which showed helicopter pilots nonchalantly gunning down civilians, including a Reuters photographer and children, in a Baghdad street:

It is inevitable given the situation we were going through. We were going through a lot of combat at the time. A roadside bomb would go off or a sniper would fire a shot, and you had no idea where it was coming from. There was a constant paranoia, a constant being on edge. If you put people in a situation like that where there are plenty of civilians, that kind of thing was going to happen and did happen and will continue to happen as long as our nation does not challenge these things. Now that this video has become public, it is our responsibility as a people and a country to recognize that this is what war looks like on a day-to-day basis.

I was depressed as I walked from the Rayburn Building to Union Station to take the train home. The voices of sanity, the voices of reason, those who have a moral core, those like Kucinich or Scahill or Wright or Swanson or Stieber, have little chance now to be heard. Liberals, who failed to grasp the dark intentions of the corporate state and its nefarious servants in the Democratic Party, bear some responsibility. But even an enlightened liberal class would have been hard-pressed to battle back against the tawdry emotional carnivals and the political theater that have thrust the nation into collective self-delusion. We were all seduced. And we, along with thousands of innocents in Iraq, Afghanistan, Pakistan, and beyond, will all be consumed.

They Kill Alex

Carlos Arredondo, a native Costa Rican, stands in a parking lot of a Holiday Inn in Portland, Maine, next to his green Nissan pickup truck. The truck, its tailgate folded down, carries a flag-draped coffin and is adorned with pictures of his son, Lance Corporal Alexander S. Arredondo, twenty, a Marine killed in Iraq in 2004. The truck and a trailer Carlos pulls with it have become a mobile shrine to his boy. He drives around the country, with the aid of donations, evoking a mixture of sympathy and hostility. There are white crosses with the names of other boys killed in the war. Combat boots are nailed to the side of the display. There is a wheelchair, covered in colored ribbons, fixed to the roof of the cab. There is Alex's military uniform and boots, poster-size pictures of the young Marine shown on the streets of Najaf, in his formal Marine portrait, and then lying, his hands folded in white gloves, in his coffin. A metal sign on the back of the truck bears a gold star and reads: "USMC L/CPL ALEXANDER S. ARREDONDO."

"This is what happens every week to some family in America," says Carlos. "This is what war does. And this is the grief and pain the government does not want people to see."

Alex, from a working-class immigrant family, was lured into the military a month before September 11, 2001. The Marine recruiters made the usual appeals to patriotism, promised that he would be trained for a career, go to college, and become a man. They included a $10,000 sign-on bonus. Alex was in the Marine units that invaded Iraq. His father, chained to the news reports, listening to the radio and two televisions at the same time, was increasingly distraught. "I hear nothing about my son for days and days," he says. "It was too much, too much, too much for parents."

In August 2004, Alex was back in Iraq for a second tour. In one of his last phone calls, Alex told Carlos: "Dad, I call you because, to say, you know, we've been fighting for many, many days already, and I want to tell you that I love you and I don't want you to forget me." His father answered: "Of course I love you, and I don't want—I never forget you." The last message the family received was an e-mail around that time which read: "Watch the news online. Check the news, and tell everyone that I love them."

Twenty days later, on August 25, a U.S. government van pulled up in front of Carlos' home in Hollywood, Florida. It was Carlos's 44th birthday, and he was expecting a birthday call from Alex. "I saw the van and thought maybe Alex had come home to surprise me for my birthday or maybe they were coming to recruit my other son, Brian," he says. Three Marine officers climbed out of the van. One asked, "Are you Carlos Arredondo?" He answered, "Yes."

"I'm sorry, we're here to notify you about the death of Lance Corporal Arredondo," one of the officers told him. Alex was the 968th soldier or Marine to be killed in the Iraq war.

"I tried to process this in my head," Carlos says. "I never hear that. I remember how my body felt. I got a rush of blood to my body. I felt like it's the worst thing in my life. It is my worst fear. I could not believe what they were telling me."

Carlos turned and ran into the house to find his mother, who was in the kitchen making him a birthday cake. "I cried, 'Mama! Mama! They are telling me Alex got killed! Alex got killed! They kill Alex! They kill Alex! They kill Alex!'" His mother crumbled in grief. Carlos went to the large picture of his son in the living room and held it. Carlos asked the Marines to leave several times over the next twenty minutes, but the Marines refused, saying they had to wait for his wife. "I did this because I was in denial. I think if they leave none of this will happen." Crazed and distraught with grief, the father went into his garage and took out five gallons of gasoline and a propane torch. He walked past the three Marines in their dress blues and began to smash the windows of the government van with a hammer.

"I went into the van," he says:

I poured gasoline on the seats. I pour gasoline on the floor and in the gas tank. I was, like, looking for my son. I was screaming and yelling for him. I remember that one day he left in a van and now he's not there. I destroy everything. The pain I feel is the pain of what I learned from war. I was wearing only socks and no shoes. I was wearing shorts. The fumes were powerful and I could not breathe no more, even though I broke the windows.

As Carlos stepped out of the van, he ignited the propane torch inside the vehicle. It started a fire that "threw me from the driver's seat backwards onto the ground." His clothes caught fire. It felt "like thousands of needles stabbing into my body." He ran across the street and fell onto the grass. His mother followed him and pulled off his shirt and socks, which were on fire, as he screamed, "Mama! Mama! My feet are burning! My feet are burning!" The Marines dragged him away, and he remembers one of them saying, "The van is going to blow! The van is going to blow!" The van erupted in a fireball, and the rush of hot air, he says, swept over him. The Marines called a fire truck and an ambulance. Carlos sustained second- and third-degree burns over twenty-six percent of his body. As I talk to him in the Portland parking lot, he shows me the burn scars on his legs. The government chose not to prosecute him.

"I wake up in the hospital two days later and I was tied with tubes in my mouth," he says. "When they take the tubes out, I say, 'I want to be with my son. I want to be with my son.' Somebody was telling me my son had died. I get very emotional. I kept saying, 'I want to be with my son' and they think I want to commit suicide."

He had no health insurance. His medical bills soon climbed to $55,000. On September 2, 2004, Carlos, transported in a stretcher, attended his son's wake at the Rodgers Funeral Home in Jamaica Plain, Massachusetts. He lifted himself, with the help of those around him, from his stretcher, and when he reached his son's open casket he kissed his child. "I held his head and when I put my hands in the back of his head I felt the huge hole where the sniper bullet had come out," he says.

"I climbed into the casket. I lay on top of my son. I apologized to him because I did not do enough to avoid this."

Arredondo began to collect items that memorialized his son's life. He tacked them to his truck. A funeral home in Boston donated a casket to the display. He began to attend antiwar events, at times flying the American flag upside down to signal distress. He has taken his shrine to the Mall in Washington, D.C., and to Times Square in New York City. He has traveled throughout the country presenting to the public a visual expression of death and grief. He has placed some of his son's favorite childhood toys and belongings in the coffin, including a soccer ball, a pair of shoes, a baseball, and a Winnie the Pooh. The power of his images, which force onlookers to confront the fact that the essence of war is death, has angered some who prefer to keep war sanitized and wrapped in the patriotic slogans of glory, honor, and heroism. Three years ago vandals defaced his son's gravestone.

"I don't speak," he says. "I show people war. I show them the caskets they are not allowed to see. If people don't see what war does, they don't feel it. If they don't feel it they don't care."

Military recruiters, who often have offices in high schools, prey on young men like Alex, who was first approached when he was sixteen. They cater to their insecurities, their dreams, and their economic deprivation. They promise them what the larger society denies them. Those of Latino descent and from divorced families, as Alex was, are especially vulnerable. Alex's brother Brian was approached by the military, which suggested that if he enlisted he could receive $60,000 in signing bonuses and more than $27,000 in payments for higher education. The proposed *Development, Relief and Education for Alien Minors Act*, or *DREAM*, is designed to give undocumented young people a chance at citizenship provided they attend college—not usually an option for poor, often poorly educated and undocumented Latino youths who are prohibited from receiving Pell Grants—for at least two years, or enlist and serve in the military. The military helped author the pending act and is lobbying for it. Twelve percent of Army enlistees are Hispanic, and this percentage is expected to double by 2020 if the current rate of recruitment continues. And once they are recruited, these young men and women are trained to be killers, sent to wars that should never be fought, and returned back to their families often traumatized and broken and sometimes dead.

Alex told Carlos in their last conversation there was heavy fighting in Najaf. Alex usually asked his father not to "forget" him, but now, increasingly in the final days of his life, another word was taking the place of *forget*. It was *forgive*. He felt his father should not forgive him for what he was doing in Iraq. He told his father, "Dad, I hope you are proud of what I'm doing. Don't forgive me, Dad." The sentence bewildered his father. "Oh my God, how can I forgive you? . . . I love you, you're my son, very proud, you're my son."

"I thought, when he died, 'My God, he has killed somebody,'" Carlos says quietly as he readied for an antiwar march organized by Veterans for Peace. "He feels guilty. If he returned home his mind would be destroyed. His heart would be torn apart. It is not normal to kill. How can they do this? How can they take our children?"

Notes

INTRODUCTION

1. George Orwell, "Why I Write," in *George Orwell: An Age Like This, 1920–1940*, ed. Sonia Orwell and Ian Angus (Boston: David R. Godine, 2000), 6.

2. George Orwell, "Wells Hitler and the World State," in *All Art is Propaganda: Critical Essays* (New York: Mariner Books, 2009), 150.

POLITICS

1. Sheldon J. Wolin, *Democracy Incorporated: Managed Democracy and the Specter of Inverted Totalitarianism* (Princeton, N.J.: Princeton University Press, 2010), 58.

2. Kieslowski. See www.facets.org/decalogue/synopsis.html.

3. Ludwig Wittgenstein, *Philosophical Grammar, Part I: The Proposition, and Its Sense* (Berkeley: University of California Press, 1974), 370.

4. Naomi Klein, *No Space, No Choice, No Jobs, No Logo* (New York: Macmillan, 2002), 124.

5. Benjamin DeMott, "Junk Politics: A Voter's Guide to the Post-literate Election," *Harper's Magazine* (November 2003), 36.

6. Walter Lippmann, *Public Opinion* (New York: Harcourt, Brace and Company, 1922), ix.

7. Warren I. Susman, "'Personality' and the Making of Twentieth-Century Culture," in *New Directions in American Intellectual History*, ed. John Higham and Paul K. Conkin (Baltimore: John Hopkins University Press, 1979), 220.

8. Howard Schneider, "Obama to Speak at Campus Where Political Freedoms Are Few," *Washington Post*, June 3, 2009, www.washingtonpost.com/wpdyn/content/article/2009/06/02/AR2009060203697.html.

9. Luke Mitchell, "We Still Torture: The New Evidence from Guantánamo," *Harper's*, July 2009, www.harpers.org/archive/2009/07/0082566.

10. Walter Lippmann, *The Phantom Public: A Sequel to Public Opinion* (New York: Harcourt Brace, 1925), 37–38.

11. Komunyakaa, conversation with author. (See *The Death of the Liberal Class*.)

12. Houston A. Baker, *Betrayal: How Black Intellectuals Have Abandoned the Ideals of the Civil Rights Era* (New York: Columbia University Press, 2008), 72.

13. Martin Luther King, Jr., *Testament of Hope: The Essential Writings of Martin Luther King, Jr.* (New York: HarperCollins, 1990), 562.

14. Ralph Nader, interview, by phone from Connecticut, August 8, 2009.

15. Allen Dobson, et al. "How a New 'Public Plan' Could Affect Hospitals' Finances and Private Insurance Premiums," *Health Affairs* 28.6 (November 2009): 1013–1024.

16. Paul Kane, "Lawmakers Reveal Health-Care Investment," *Washington Post*, June 13, 2009, www.washingtonpost.com/wpdyn/content/article/2009/06/12/AR2009061204075.html.

17. Erich Fromm, *Psychoanalysis and Religion* (New Haven: Yale University Press, 1959), 84.

18. Frederick Douglass, *Frederick Douglass on Slavery and the Civil War: Selections from His Writings*, ed. Philip Sheldon Foner (New York: Dover, 2003), 42.

19. John Ralston Saul, *Voltaire's Bastards: The Dictatorship of Reason in the West* (New York: Vintage, 1993), 30–31.

20. See Christian J. Peters, et al. "Testing a complete-diet model for estimating the land resource requirements of food consumption and agricultural carrying capacity: The New York state example," *Renewable Agriculture and Food Systems* 22:2 (2007): 145–153; Christian J. Peters, et al. "Mapping potential foodsheds in New York State: A spatial model for evaluating the capacity to localize food production," *Renewable Agriculture and Food Systems* 24.1 (2009): 72–84.

21. Wendell Berry, *The Unsettling of America: Culture & Agriculture* (San Francisco: Sierra Club, 1996), 108.

22. Ibid., 74.

23. Ibid., 6.

24. Quoted in Jeff Cohen and Norman Solomon, *Adventures in Medialand: Behind the News, Beyond the Pundits* (Monroe: Common Courage, 1993), xii.

25. Ibid.

26. James Carey, *Communication as Culture: Essays on Media and Society* (New York: Routledge, 2008), 114.

27. Robert Fisk, *The Age of the Warrior: Selected Essays* (New York: Nation, 2008), xiv.

28. Ibid.

29. Quoted in Molly Ivins, *Molly Ivins Can't Say That, Can She?* (New York: Random House, 1992), 231.

30. David Cay Johnston, interview, by phone from Rochester, New York, March 7, 2010.

31. Ibid.

32. W.B. Yeats, "The Second Coming."

33. David Cay Johnston, interview, by phone from Rochester, New York, March 7, 2010.

34. Albert Camus, *The Myth of Sisyphus and Other Essays* (New York: Vintage, 1991), 212.

35. Albert Camus, *The Rebel: An Essay on Man in Revolt* (New York: Vintage, 1984), 306.

36. Václav Havel, *The Power of the Powerless: Citizens Against the State in Eastern Europe*, ed. John Keane (Armonk: M.E. Sharpe, 1985), 63.

37. Albert Camus, *Essays Lyrical and Critical* (London: H. Hamilton, 1967), 132.

38. Mario Savio, speech on the steps of Sproul Hall, University of California, Berkeley, Calif., Free Speech Movement Sit-in, December 2, 1964, www.americanrhetoric.com/speeches/mariosaviosproulhallsitin.htm.

39. Pindar, "Pythian Ode 3," used by Camus for the epigraph to "Myth of Sisyphus."

40. Albert Camus, *The Myth of Sisyphus and Other Essays* (New York: Vintage Books, 1991).

41. Lewis F. Powell, "Attack on the American Free Enterprise System," U.S. Chamber of Commerce, August 23, 1971, www.reclaimdemocracy.org/corporate_accountability/Powell_memo_lewis.html.

42. Norman Finkelstein, interview, New York, March 14, 2010.

43. Ibid.

44. Ibid.

45. Hannah Arendt, *Eichmann in Jerusalem: A Report on the Banality of Evil* (New York: Viking, 1963), 49.

46. John Ralston Saul, *Voltaire's Bastards: The Dictatorship of Reason in the West* (New York: Vintage Books, 1993), 110.

47. Ian Urbina, "U.S. Said to Allow Drilling Without Needed Permits," *New York Times*, May 13, 2010, www.nytimes.com/2010/05/14/US/14agency.html.

48. Karl Polanyi, *The Great Transformation: The Political and Economic Origins of Our Time* (New York: Beacon, 2001), 76–77.

49. Joseph A. Tainter, *The Collapse of Complex Societies* (Cambridge: Cambridge University Press, 1990), 214.

50. Ronald Wright, *A Short History of Progress* (New York: Carroll & Graf, 2005), 117.

51. Irving Howe, "This Age of Conformity," in *The Partisan Review Anthology*, eds. Philip Rahv and Williams Phillips (New York: Holt, Rinehart and Winston, 1962), 151.

52. Ibid., 31.

53. Wendell Berry, *The Long-Legged House* (Berkeley: Counterpoint, 2003), 46.

54. "The Peace of Wild Things," copyright © 1998 by Wendell Berry from *The Selected Poems of Wendell Berry*, reprinted by permission of Counterpoint.

55. Tim Flannery, *The Future Eaters* (New York: Grove Press, 2002).

56. Ronald Wright, "Fools' Paradise," in *A Passion for This Earth,* eds. Michelle Benjamin, Bill McKibben, and the David Suzuki Foundation (Berkeley: Greystone, 2008), 159.

57. Zwally and Hanson quoted in Seth Borenstein, "'The Arctic is screaming': summer sea ice could be gone in five years," *Seattle Times*, December 11, 2007, http://seattletimes.nwsource.com/html/nationworld/2004065889_webarctic 11.html

58. Ibid.

59. Clive Hamilton, *Requiem for a Species: Why We Resist the Truth About Climate Change* (London and Washington, D.C.: Earthscan, 2010), 27.

60. Ibid., 22.

61. Ibid., 31.

62. Ching Kwan Lee, *Against the Law: Labor Protests in China's Rustbelt and Sunbelt* (Berkeley: University of California Press, 2007), 164.

ISRAEL AND PALESTINE

1. Norman G. Finkelstein, *The Holocaust Industry* (New York: Verso, 2003), 47.

2. Christopher R. Browning, *Ordinary Men: Reserve Police Battalion 101 and Final Solution in Poland* (New York: HarperCollins, 1993).

3. Roth, quoted on the "Let Israelis Show You Israel," www.israelfree.com/quickreferral_letter.html.

4. *King Lear*, 3.4.34–36

5. UPI Match 10, 2010

6. "Revenge," translated by Peter Cole, Yahya Hijazi, and Gabriel Levin, translation copyright © 2006 Peter Cole, reprinted by permission of the translator. Muhammad Ali's own remarkable story is told in *So What: New and Selected Poems* (Copper Canyon, 2006), by the same translators, and in a biography of him, *My Happiness Bears No Relation to Happiness: A Poet's Life in the Palestinian Century,* Adina Hoffman (Yale University Press, 2009).

7. Jeremiah Wright, sermon, September 16, 2001, Trinity United Church of Christ, Chicago, Ill., quoted in Brian Ross and Rehab El-Buri, "Obama's Pastor: God Damn America, U.S. to Blame for 9/11," ABCNews.com. Accessed November 21, 2010, http://abcnews.go.com/Blotter/DemocraticDebate/story ?id=4443788&page=1

8. Edward Said, "Gods That Always Fail," in *Representations of the Intellectual: The 1993 Reith Lectures* (New York: Vintage, 1994), 74.

9. Rachel Corrie, "Dispatch from Rafah, Occupied Palestine," in *We Are the People: Voices from the Other Side of American History*, eds. Nathaniel May, Clint Willis, and James W. Loewen (Cambridge: Da Capo, 2003), 153.

10. "Rypin," in *War & Love, Love & War: New and Selected Poems*, Aharon Shabtai, translated by Peter Cole (New York: New Directions 2010), pp. 3–4. Translation copyright © 2010 Peter Cole. Reprinted by permission of New Directions Publishing Corp.

THE MIDDLE EAST

1. Reinhold Niebuhr, *Moral Man and Immoral Society* (New York: Scribner's, 1934), 95.

2. Obama's speech at Cairo University on June 4, 2009.

3. Costa quoted in Michelle Nichols, "Afghan opium feeding Europe, Russia, Iran addicts," *Reuters,* October 21, 2009, www.reuters.com/article/id USN20440001.

4. Matthew Hoh's resignation letter, www.washingtonpost.com/wp-srv/hp/ssi/wpc/ResignationLetter.pdf.

THE DECAY OF EMPIRE

1. Interview with Kelly Nickell in *The Complete Handbook of Novel Writing,* 2 ed. (Cincinnati: Writer's Digest Books, 2010), 436.

2. *Hamlet*, 5.1.46–47

3. Marcel Proust, "Days of Reading (I)," in *Against Sainte-Beauve and Other Essays,* trans. John Sturrock (Harmondsworth: Penguin, 1994), 210.

4. *Henry IV, Part 1*, 4.2.64–66

5. Stratis Myrivilis, *Life in the Tomb* (River Vale, New Jersey: Cosmos, 2003), 146.

6. *MacBeth*, 4.2.73–79

7. Virgil, *The Eclogues,* trans. Guy Lee (New York: Penguin, 1984), 97.

8. Charles Maier, *Among Empires: American Ascendancy and Its Predecessors* (Cambridge: Harvard University Press, 2006), 239.

9. Andrew Bacevich, *The Limits of Power: The End of American Exceptionalism* (New York: Macmillan, 2009), 172.

10. See Scott McDonnell's interview with Robert Pape, "The Logic of Suicide Terrorism," *The American Conservative*, July 18, 2005, www.amconmag.com/2005_07_18/article.html.

11. Immanual Kant, "Religion Within the Bounds of Mere Reason," in *Religion and Rational Theology* (Cambridge: Cambridge University Press, 2001), 69.

12. Joseph Conrad, "An Outpost of Progress," in *The Nigger of the Narcissus and Other Stories*, Digireads.com, 2009, 49.

13. Ibid., 62.

14. Joseph Conrad, "Letter to R.B. Cunninghame Graham, 8 February 1899," in *Joseph Conrad Life and Letters*, ed. Jean Aubrey (London: William Heinemann, 1927), 1: 269.

15. Joseph Conrad, "Anatole France" (1904), in *Notes on Life and Letters*, ed. J. H. Stape (Cambridge: Cambridge University Press, 2003), 30.

16. Joseph Conrad. "Letter to R.B. Cunninghame Graham (July 28, 1900)" in *The Collected Letters of Joseph Conrad, Vol. 2* (Cambridge: Cambridge University Press, 1986), 157–158.

17. Quoted in Edward Said, *Joseph Conrad and the Fiction of Autobiography* (New York: Columbia University Press, 2007), 201.

18. *Collected Letters of Joseph Conrad, 1920–1922*, eds. Frederick Robert Karl, Laurence Davies, and J. H. Stape (Cambridge: Cambridge University Press, 2005), 543.

19. Joseph Conrad, *Heart of Darkness and The Secret Sharer* (New York: Penguin, 2008), 117.

20. Edward O. Wilson, *Consilience: The Unity of Knowledge* (New York: Vintage Books, 1999), 315.

21. William P. Mahedy, *Out of the Night: The Spiritual Journey of Vietnam Vets* (New York: Ballantine, 1988), 6.

22. Ibid., 97.

23. Michael Hudson, *Global Research*, June 13, 2009.

24. John Lanchester, "It's Finished," *London Review of Books*, May 28, 2009 (31:10), 3–13, www.lrb.co.uk/v31/n10/john-lanchester/its-finished.

25. Benedicto Martinez Orozco, interview, Pittsburgh, September 20, 2009.

26. Larry Holmes, interview, Pittsburgh, September 20, 2009.

27. Chirac's speech at Group of Seven summit in Halifax, Canada, on June 16, 1995.

28. John Ralston Saul, *The Collapse of Globalism* (Toronto: Penguin, 2009), 291–292.

29. Larry Holmes, interview, Pittsburgh, September 20, 2009.

30. Primo Levi, *The Drowned and the Saved* (New York: Vintage International, 1989), 69.

31. *MacBeth*, 5.5.27–29

32. James Hanson, et al. "Target Atmospheric CO2: Where Should Humanity Aim?" *Open Atmospheric Science Journal*, vol. 2 (October 15, 2008): 217.

33. Ibid.

34. Cited in John Ralston Saul, *The Collapse of Globalism: And the Reinvention of the World* (New York: Overlook Press, 2005), 104.

35. Klaus Theweleit, *Male Fantasies, Vol. 2* (Minneapolis: University of Minnesota Press, 1989), 7.

36. Tom Friedman, interview on *Charlie Rose*, Public Broadcasting System, May 30, 2003, http://video.google.com/videoplay?docid=3800770925110269 212#.

37. Theodor Adorno, "Toward a New Categorical Imperative," in *Can One Live After Auschwitz?*, ed. Rolf Tiedemann (Stanford: Stanford University Press, 2003), 30.

38. Peter van Agtmael, *2nd Tour, Hope I Don't Die* (Portland, Ore.: Photolucida, 2009), 88.

39. Lori Grinker, *Afterwar: Veterans from a World in Conflict* (Milford, N.Y.: de.MO, 2005), 58–59.

40. Ibid., 63.

41. Ibid., 96–107.

42. Ibid., 120–121.

43. Ibid., 124–125.

44. Peter van Agtmael, *2nd Tour, Hope I Don't Die*, 64–65.

45. Christopher Ketcham, "Most Likely to Secede," *GOOD*, issue 008 (January, 10, 2008), www.good.is/post/most-likely-to-secede/.

Bibliography

Adorno, Theodor. "Toward a New Categorical Imperative." In *Can One Live After Auschwitz?* Edited by Rolf Tiedemann. Stanford, Calif.: Stanford University Press, 2003.

Arendt, Hannah. *Eichmann in Jerusalem: A Report on the Banality of Evil.* New York: Viking, 1963.

Bacevich, Andrew. *The Limits of Power: The End of American Exceptionalism.* New York: Macmillan, 2009.

Baker, Houston. *Betrayal: How Black Intellectuals Have Abandoned the Ideals of the Civil Rights Era.* New York: Columbia University Press, 2008.

Berry, Wendell. *The Long-Legged House.* Berkeley, Calif.: Counterpoint, 2003.

———. *The Unsettling of America: Culture & Agriculture.* San Francisco, Calif.: Sierra Club, 1996.

———. *The Selected Poems of Wendell Berry.* Berkeley: Counterpoint Press, 1993.

Browning, Christopher R. *Ordinary Men: Reserve Police Battalion 101 and Final Solution in Poland.* New York: HarperCollins, 1993.

Camus, Albert. *The Myth of Sisyphus and Other Essays.* New York: Vintage, 1991.

———. *The Rebel: An Essay on Man in Revolt.* New York: Vintage, 1984.

———. *Essays Lyrical and Critical.* London, U.K.: H. Hamilton, 1967.

Carey, James. *Communication as Culture:Essays on Media and Society.* New York: Routledge, 2008.

Ching Kwan Lee. *Against the Law: Labor Protests in China's Rustbelt and Sunbelt.* Berkeley, Calif.: University of California Press, 2007.

Cohen, Jeff, and Norman Solomon. *Adventures in Medialand: Behind the News, Beyond the Pundits.* Monroe, Maine: Common Courage, 1993.

Conrad, Joseph. *The Nigger of the Narcissus and Other Stories.* Digireads .com, 2009.

———. *Heart of Darkness and The Secret Sharer.* New York: Penguin, 2008.

———. *Collected Letters of Joseph Conrad, 1920–1922.* Edited by Frederick Robert Karl, Laurence Davies, and J. H. Stape. Cambridge, Mass.: University Press, 2005.

————. *Joseph Conrad Life and Letters*. Edited by Jean Aubrey. London: William Heinemann, 1927.

Corrie, Rachel. "Dispatch from Rafah, Occupied Palestine." In *We Are the People: Voices from the Other Side of American History*. Edited by Nathaniel May, Clint Willis, and James W. Loewen. Cambridge, Mass.: Da Capo, 2003.

DeMott, Benjamin. "Junk Politics: A Voter's Guide to the Post-literate Election." Harper's Magazine, November 2003.

Dobson, Allen et al. "How a New 'Public Plan' Could Affect Hospitals' Finances and Private Insurance Premiums." *Health Affairs* 28.6 (November 2009): 1013–1024.

Douglass, Frederick. *Frederick Douglass on Slavery and the Civil War: Selections from His Writings*. Edited by Philip Sheldon Foner. New York: Dover, 2003.

Finkelstein, Norman G. *The Holocaust Industry*. New York: Verso, 2003.

Fisk, Robert Fisk. *The Age of the Warrior: Selected Essays*. New York: Nation, 2008.

Flannery, Tim. *The Future Eaters*. New York: Grove Press, 2002.

Erich Fromm. *Psychoanalysis and Religion*. New Haven, Conn.: Yale University Press, 1959.

Grinker, Lori. *Afterwar: Veterans from a World in Conflict*. Milford, N.Y.: de.MO, 2005.

Hamilton, Clive. *Requiem for a Species: Why We Resist the Truth About Climate Change*. London and Washington, D.C.: Earthscan, 2010.

Hanson, James et al. "Target Atmospheric CO2: Where Should Humanity Aim?" *Open Atmospheric Science Journal*, vol. 2 (October 15, 2008): 217.

Havel, Václav. *The Power of the Powerless: Citizens Against the State in Eastern Europe*. Edited by John Keane. Armonk, N.Y.: M.E. Sharpe, 1985.

Howe, Irving. "This Age of Conformity." In *The Partisan ReviewAnthology*. Edited by Philip Rahv and Williams Phillips. New York: Holt, Rinehart, and Winston, 1962, 145–164.

Ivins, Molly. *Molly Ivins Can't Say That, Can She?* New York: Random House, 1992.

Kane, Paul. "Lawmakers Reveal Health-Care Investment." *Washington Post*, June 13, 2009. www.washingtonpost.com/wp-dyn/content/article/2009/06/12/AR2009061204075.html.

Kant, Immanual. "Religion Within the Bounds of Mere Reason." In Religion and Rational Theology. New York: Cambridge University Press, 2001.

Ketcham, Christopher. "Most Likely to Secede." GOOD Magazine, January, 10, 2008. www.good.is/post/most-likely-to-secede.

King, Martin Luther, Jr. *Testament of Hope: The Essential Writings of Martin Luther King, Jr.* New York: HarperCollins, 1990.

Klein, Naomi. *No Space, No Choice, No Jobs, No Logo.* New York: Macmillan, 2002.

Lanchester, John. "It's Finished." *London Review of Books* May 28, 2009 (31:10), 3–13.

Levi, Primo. *The Drowned and the Saved.* New York: Vintage International, 1989.

Lippmann, Walter. *The Phantom Public: A Sequel to Public Opinion.* New York: Harcourt Brace, 1925.

————. *Public Opinion.* New York: Harcourt, Brace and Company, 1922.

Mahedy, William P. *Out of the Night: The Spiritual Journey of Vietnam Vets.* New York: Ballatine, 1988.

Maier, Charles. *Among Empires: American Ascendancy and Its Predecessors.* Cambridge, Mass.: Harvard University Press, 2006.

Mitchell, Luke. "We Still Torture: The New Evidence from Guantánamo." *Harper's,* July 2009. www.harpers.org/archive/2009/07/0082566.

Myrivilis, Stratis. *Life in the Tomb.* London, U.K.: Quartet, 1987.

Niebuhr, Reinhold. *Moral Man and Immoral Society.* New York: Scribner's, 1934.

Peters, Christian J. et al. "Mapping Potential Foodsheds in New York State: A Spatial Model for Evaluating the Capacity to Localize Food Production." *Renewable Agriculture and Food Systems* 24.1 (2009): 72–84.

————, et al. "Testing a Complete-Diet Model for Estimating the Land Resource Requirements of Food Consumption and Agricultural Carrying Capacity: The New York State Example." *Renewable Agriculture and Food Systems* 22:2 (2007): 145–153.

Polanyi, Karl. *The Great Transformation: The Political and Economic Origins of Our Time.* New York: Beacon, 2001.

Powell, Lewis F. "Attack on the American Free Enterprise System." U.S. Chamber of Commerce: August 23, 1971. www.reclaimdemocracy.org/corporate_accountability/Powell_memo_lewis.html.

Proust, Marcel. "Days of Reading (I)." In *Against Sainte-Beauve and Other Essays.* Translated by John Sturrock. Harmondsworth: Penguin, 1994.

Said, Edward. *Joseph Conrad and the Fiction of Autobiography.* New York: Columbia University Press, 2007.

————. "Gods That Always Fail." In *Representations of the Intellectual: The 1993 Reith Lectures.* New York: Vintage, 1994.

Saul, John Ralston. *The Collapse of Globalism.* Toronto: Penguin, 2009.

————. *Voltaire's Bastards: The Dictatorship of Reason in the West.* New York: Vintage, 1993.

Savio, Mario. Speech on the steps of Sproul Hall. University of California, Berkeley, California.Free Speech Movement Sit-in, December 2, 1964. www.americanrhetoric.com/speeches/mariosaviosproulhallsitin.htm.

Howard Schneider. "Obama to Speak at Campus Where Political Freedoms Are Few." *Washington Post*, June 3, 2009. www.washingtonpost.com/wp-dyn/content/article/2009/06/02/AR2009060203697.html.

Shabtai, Aharon. *War & Love, Love & War.* New York: New Directions, 2010.

Susman, Warren I. "'Personality' and the Making of Twentieth-Century Culture." *New Directions in American Intellectual History*. Edited by John Higham and Paul K. Conkin. Baltimore, Md.: John Hopkins University Press, 1979.

Tainter, Joseph A. *The Collapse of Complex Societies*. Cambridge, Mass.: Cambridge University Press, 1990.

Theweleit, Klaus. *Male Fantasies*, Vol. 2. Minneapolis, Minn.: University of Minnesota Press, 1989.

Urbina, Ian. "U.S. Said to Allow Drilling Without Needed Permits." *New York Times*, May 13, 2010. www.nytimes.com/2010/05/14/US/14agency.html.

van Agtmael, Peter. *2nd Tour, Hope I Don't Die*. Portland, Ore.: Photolucide, 2009.

Virgil. *The Eclogues*. Translated by Guy Lee. New York: Penguin, 1984.

Wilson, Edward O. *Consilience: The Unity of Knowledge*. New York: Vintage Books, 1999.

Wittgenstein, Ludwig. *Philosophical Grammar, Part I: The Proposition, and Its Sense*. Berkeley, Calif.: University of California Press, 1974.

Wolin, Sheldon J. *Democracy Incorporated: Managed Democracy and the Specter of Inverted Totalitarianism*. Princeton, N.J.: Princeton University Press, 2010.

Wright, Ronald. "Fools' Paradise." In *A Passion for This Earth*. Edited by Michelle Benjamin, Bill McKibben, and the David Suzuki Foundation. Berkeley, Calif.: Greystone, 2008, 159–167.

———. *A Short History of Progress*. New York: Carroll & Graf, 2005.

Index

truthdig ▼
www.truthdig.com

Truthdig (www.truthdig.com) is a progressive online news site founded in 2005 that provides in-depth coverage of current affairs and thoughtful, provocative content from a variety of sources, including original commentary from around the world. Updated throughout the day, Truthdig "drills beneath the headlines" with "digs," columns, reports, reviews, interviews, podcasts, videos, and political cartoons by some of the most influential writers and contributors of our time. Truthdig has won many prestigious awards, including three Webbys for the world's Best Political Blog and multiple honors from the Los Angeles Press Club and the Society of Professional Journalists.
